the new forensics

the new forensics

Investigating Corporate Fraud and the Theft of Intellectual Property

Joe Anastasi

WILEY

JOHN WILEY & SONS, INC.

Published by John Wiley & Sons, Inc., Hoboken, New Jersey.
Published simultaneously in Canada.

For general information on our other products and services please contact our Customer Care Department within the United States at (800) 762-2974, outside the United States at (317) 572-3993 or fax (317) 572-4002.

Wiley also publishes its books in a variety of electronic formats. Some content that appears in print may not be available in electronic books. For more information about Wiley products, visit our Web site at www.wiley.com.

Library of Congress Cataloging-in-Publication Data:

Anastasi, Joe, 1953–
   The new forensics : investigating corporate fraud and the theft of intellectual property / Joe Anastasi.
      p. cm.
Includes bibliographical references and index.
   ISBN 0-471-26994-8 (cloth : alk. paper)
   1. White collar crime investigation—Data processing—Case studies.
2. Fraud investigation—Data processing—Case studies.   3. Forensic accounting—Case studies.   4. Computer security—Case studies.   I. Title.
   HV8079.W47A5 2003
   363.25'968—dc21

                                                                        2003001697

Printed in the United States of America.

10 9 8 7 6 5 4 3 2 1

FOREWORD

Joe Anastasi's *The New Forensics* is a timely book that addresses some of today's crucial issues.

He describes in fascinating detail how our national security is dependent, in part, by computers analyzing raw data collected by communication satellites. The story is told how forensic accountants using computers were able to achieve some sense of justice by locating and identifying "dormant accounts" in Swiss banks that belonged to victims of Nazi persecution. There is also a chilling story of the cyber theft of credit cards by persons operating solely within Russia.

But the main thrust of the book is the story of how forensic investigators using computers today can detect fraud and other corporate criminal activities. The facts of Enron, WorldCom, and the other major scams are carefully laid out as is the arrogance of the major actors. Any questions one may have as to how they were carried out and how they were solved are answered.

The technology is explained in simple, understandable terms. Today's Sergeant Joe Friday does not write in a small notebook in the course of solving crimes, he now reconstructs the data from imaging hard drives.

The real value of the book, however, is not in the explanations given, but rather in the moral issues it raises. It is a tale of contrasts the stunning achievement of science in uncovering vast webs of criminal activities and the shocking revelation of human greed and corruption at the highest corporate levels. Their frauds were known or at least suspected by a number of people within and working with those companies.

Why were there not more whistle blowers? Where were all the other (possible) Sherron Watkins, Cynthia Coopers, and Gene Morses? More alarming yet, where were the investment bankers, the accountants, the lawyers and the bankers who help set up these schemes?

This is the question posed by the book. It is one that each of us in one of these professions must answer. If we ignore it or fail to deal with it, we will have lost the opportunity to restore public confidence in corporate America. The choice is ours.

HON. CHARLES RENFREW
Former U.S. Deputy Attorney General
(Carter Administration),
and Former U.S. Federal District Judge,
Northern District of California

PREFACE

The initial motivation to write this book was to explain the use of computer forensics and other technologies in investigations. As must happen with most literary efforts–though of this, I can only surmise–the darn book took on a life of its own. Even before the year 2002 unfolded, the hunt for al Qaeda terrorists brought to the attention of many, the notion of computer forensics. Many clues were being unearthed as a result of the forensic examination of computer laptops recovered by law enforcement authorities across the world. Then the Enron scandal imploded.

Early in 2002, things started to get very strange. The deletion of documents and e-mails in the corporate world interested almost everyone in this country. Suddenly what I do for a living became of interest to people who were not even members of my immediate family. And as the WorldCom fraud unfolded, it became hard for anyone to escape the daily news accounts of one aspect or another of the corporate fraud that seemed to have become endemic during the days of the Internet Bubble. As the year progressed, I continued with my daily business, and the writing of this book.

I have been scrupulous in attempting to avoid the breaching of any attorney-client or work-product privilege regarding the particulars of any of the cases that I have analyzed in the book. I selected cases for examination that possessed a peculiar and perverse elegance. They were cases in which people had either (1) already been sentenced to prison, (2) had pled guilty and were cooperating with the authorities, (3) were currently under indictment, or (4) were in a situation where information about their shenanigans had somehow been tossed on the garbage heap of our new age—the public record. In several of these cases, the attorney-client privilege and any work-product privilege had already been waived, or documents were already residing in the public domain, as the corporations themselves had decided to cooperate with law enforcement and investigative agencies. In the numerous interviews conducted during the research related to this book, I have never had a document proffered to me by an interviewee, nor have I asked to see a document. This book is significantly oriented toward the nature of the various human interactions and behaviors leading to fraud, and the use of technology to uncover fraud.

I chose to fictionalize certain aspects of several of the cases examined. I did this even though the perpetrators of the corporate frauds were cooling their heels in prison. For reasons I prefer not to go into, I felt it to be somewhat more circumspect to fictionalize a name here or there—or two, or three. Then, because I was now on a roll, I continued with the subterfuge. Dates fell by the wayside; then entire cities and geographies—even the size of the corporations involved. Sometimes in my rush to achieve the desired aspect of anonymity, even the industry in which the specific corporation competed was disguised. One day, I awoke and thought to change some of the products and brands that had been involved in the scandal. Another day, I resolved to change the amount of money involved in the fraud, though I allowed it to remain dollar-denominated. In a later pang affecting my conscience, I even changed other details—sometimes it had to do with the weather, other times it regarded the height, weight, and age of a particular perpetrator—the color of their hair, even.

In my writing of this work, I took not an inconsiderable amount of comfort and solace from the very existence of Lord Moran and a book he had written, published in 1966. It was a book detailing his daily relationship with Prime Minister Winston Churchill. This 859-page memoir was published shortly after the great man's death, to the astonished gasp of the medical establishment. This was because Moran had served as Churchill's personal physician during the last 25 years of the Prime Minister's life. "What about the doctor-patient relationship?" asked members of the profession. The "shrill voice of professional piety" raised its hue and cry—but was not sustained. Why? Because as Alistair Cooke has written, ". . . a large reading population, half the medical profession, and posterity itself had confirmed the unique value . . ." of Moran's memoir.

*   *   *

As the year 2002 rolled by, one sector after another of our global economy bubbled to the surface as having been affected by the phenomenon of the Internet Bubble. It had not, after all, simply been an Internet Bubble. The label originally affixed to the malaise of this particular bubble implied that only investors in Internet stocks would feel its effect. This, though, is simply not true. Its symptoms were becoming manifest in many seemingly

unrelated industries. Its aftermath rippled out in an ever-broadening circle: the technology sector bubbled up first; then the telecom and energy
sectors; a little later, the consumer products industry; and then after that,
even the healthcare industry. As I wrote on, completing chapter after
chapter, I started noticing parallels in the outside world unspooling in
real time. The parallels were to the particular cases I was examining in
this book—Morgan Fay, for example.

And so I went back to the beginning, rethreading the narrative
through the needle, as I now more clearly perceived it.

There appeared to me now, a commonality—in the human behaviors
that seemed to have been occurring during these past 10 years or so; and
a commonality in practices, expectations or reward systems that had been
put in place during that last decade or two that seemed to be driving some
of these untoward behaviors. Behaviors that led to calamity, and for more
than just a few. I identify these observations as a particular brand of corporate culture. I believe it is important for all of us to recognize the elements of this phenomenon, and when we see aspects of it again, in the
real world and in the future, to recognize it for what it is. And not suc-
cumb to it. The confidence we all wish to be able to place in our financial systems, for all of our mutual future benefit, will not be misplaced if
the lessons we learn today are remembered, and appropriately acted
upon, in the tomorrow. But these are individual decisions. They are made
daily. And they are made on a case-by-case basis. By people everywhere,
as they go about their daily business affairs.

*   *   *

For 28 years—all of my professional career, really—I have worked for two
very large firms. The first 23 years were with Price Waterhouse. The years
since 1997, Deloitte. The opinions and conclusions put forward in this
work are mine and mine alone, and do not represent the opinions of any
other representative of either of these two fine firms. Any mistakes, or
mistaken conclusions, in this work also remain mine alone.

ACKNOWLEDGMENTS

During the many long weekends, late evenings, missed vacation days, and holiday time absorbed by the writing of this book, my wife, Patti, was unbelievably patient and supportive. Beyond this, she also served as part-time transcriptionist, initial reader, and editor, and to cap it all, she read the complete manuscript several times. All of this was done cheerfully and with love and understanding, and for this I will be forever grateful.

Two individuals urged the undertaking of this book: Andrée Abecassis, my literary agent, and Samira Baroody, my muse. To them, my many thanks. Throughout the process of writing and researching, Lisa Lomba provided terrific editorial support and served as a valuable transcriptionist, as did at times my son, Keith. Weekends at my house sometimes were very busy; often there were three or four computers, as well as two printers, going at the same time on various elements of this book.

David Cooke of the firm of Allen, Matkins, Leck, Gamble & Mallory provided me with invaluable advice and editorial assistance of which I am very grateful: Thank you, David. My production managers, Nancy Land and Brenda Hunter at Publications Development Company, were a pleasure to work with. I could not have had a better working relationship than I experienced with Matt Holt, my editor at John Wiley & Sons.

The following individuals provided technical support and assistance along the way and I thank them and acknowledge their contributions: Gene Morse, Jonathon Vanderveen, Mike Murphy, Kris Haworth, Lee Teitsworth, John Suit, Tony Rosen, Jaco Sadie, Alex Jarvis, Jeff Waxman, Laurel Sutcliffe, Matt Larson, Manish Khera, Tomas Castrejon, Frank Quijada, Tom Arnold, John O'Connor, Julia Umnov, Lisa Liao, Leland Altschuler, Emmett Bergman, Ken Avery, Mark Nigrini, Jim Littley, Fred Roffman, Frank Piantidosi, Mary Jane Schirber, Frank Hydoski, Judge Charles Renfrew, George Vinson, Mark Radke, Laura Unger, Tom

Aleman, Jen Engler, Aubrei Stimphig, Shelly Connor, Lisa Dane, Kerry Francis, Dave Gully, Stephen Hibbard, Lou Pichini, Bill Leimbach, David Sikorski, Kevin Redinger, Jim Wilson, Dan Wetzel, Barbara Monteiro, Barbara Lombardo-Reynolds, Robin Reynolds (no relation to Barbara), Alan Ripp, and Duane Coda. Thank you all, and see you next time around.

J. A.

CONTENTS

CHAPTER ONE

"Just Move Away from Your Computer Please"

"I need you to step away from your computer please," Lee Altschuler said.

Morgan Fay's chief financial officer glanced up from her computer screen. She regarded the man standing at her office doorway for a moment. "Excuse me?" Cindy Shalott asked.

"We'd like you to please conclude your business for the day," Lee Altschuler said. "I'd appreciate it if you could complete whatever you're doing as quickly as you can. Please leave your computer in the way that it is now. Don't turn it off."

The chief financial officer swung her desk chair around.

"Just move away from your computer please," Altschuler repeated.

"Who are you?" Cindy Shalott asked.

The middle-aged man in the brown suit stood respectfully, just inside the door to her office. He had his beat-up leather carrybag stuffed under his left armpit. He was holding his rumpled brown raincoat in his other hand. "I'm with Deloitte," Lee Altschuler said. "Would you just please just finish the sentence you're on. Or whatever it is you're doing with your computer. You can save it if you'd like. But I need for you to move away from your computer."

The staff sitting outside Cindy Shalott's office had popped their heads above their cubicles to see the fireworks. Cindy was known to ignite without even a match having been lit. And the clerical staff outside

1

her office had just seen the company's CEO, Robin Malory, do something almost unbelievable.

The burly 250-pound Robin Malory had walked out the company's front door in a big huff.

*   *   *

Lee Altschuler's eyes were closed. He was standing at his desk in the office with the telephone to his ear, trying to make sense of things. Mike Murphy, one of the firm's lead forensic and investigative services partners, was on the other end of the line.

"You need to get over there now," Murphy was saying. "Make sure you take some people with you."

Mike was calling from somewhere in Minneapolis or Omaha—Altschuler hadn't yet been able to put all the pieces of the puzzle together. Lee Altschuler put his free hand to his forehead to concentrate as he listened to Mike Murphy's instructions.

As Murphy spoke, Altschuler bent a little to scribble the address and the name of the company on a piece of paper. "Morgan Fay," he wrote down.

Mike Murphy told Altschuler that things with Morgan Fay were urgent. The Securities and Exchange Commission (SEC) had just been informed that an investigation was commencing.

"I've got the computer forensics people coming in from Dallas," came Murphy's voice over the line, "They'll hit the ground in a couple of hours."

"Who?" Altschuler asked.

"Kris Haworth and Eric Schwarz," Murphy responded.

*   *   *

Lee Altschuler had absolutely no idea what Morgan Fay's office space looked like. "What does a publicly traded headquarters space look like, anyhow?" he'd asked himself as he prepared to head over with the two tech-support staffers in tow he'd managed to round-up on such short notice. "Do they have a thousand people? Two thousand?"

He'd not seen any floor plans before going over. And he had no idea where people sat. Where was he to find what Mike Murphy wanted him to get?

Altschuler was a bit thrown when he got off the elevator because the sign outside the door read *Avalon Partners*. Then he recalled that Avalon was one of the corporate names that Mike Murphy had mentioned during their brief telephone discussion.

Upon meeting Robin Malory, the chief executive officer, Altschuler explained that he had no sense of the floor layout. Altschuler was interested in who worked where and he requested a quick tour of the premises.

As Malory conducted the tour, Altschuler noted the floor's set up. The central part of the floor space consisted of administrative support areas. There were maybe 40 different work areas on the entire floor. Not so big a deal after all.

Everywhere they went, Altschuler noted Morgan Fay marketing materials lying around. There were a lot of boxes of *Lady of the Lake* products sitting on top of some desks. Posters of the various and sundry *Mount Baden Bread* products lined the walls. Over in one corner there were empty boxes of *Excalibur* biscuits—the brand featuring the sword being removed from a golden bar of butter. More marketing collateral could be seen in the lunchroom.

After providing Altschuler with the tour he'd requested, Robin Malory deposited Lee Altschuler and his two minions in the computer room where the corporation's servers were housed. Robin Malory was clearly miffed.

The two technical support staffers Altschuler had brought with him described to Malory what they needed to do with the computer servers. "No," they told him, they couldn't say how long they would be. Robin Malory couldn't get any more out of Altschuler's team than he'd had been able to get out of Morgan Fay's outside counsel, Caxton & Williams.

As Altschuler followed Robin Malory from one space to another, he noted the looks his team was getting from the administrative staff they passed. Altschuler got the distinct impression that he and his companions were unwelcome. Robin Malory's attitude wasn't helping things.

Robin Malory had taken the conference call from the corporation's outside counsel only 20 minutes before Altschuler and his two goons had shown up. As far as Malory was concerned, Altschuler's visit was an imposition and he let Altschuler know it.

Robin Malory turned around to look at the three men following him. The two younger men accompanying Lee Altschuler were wearing black slacks, black turtleneck tee shirts, and black leather jackets. Robin Malory shook his head. What the hell kind of a professional services firm would send out people looking like that? Sending them to the headquarters of a publicly traded $4 billion corporation? It was outrageous. And with no appointment. It was unforgivable, and Robin Malory told Altschuler this in the reception area.

No, the chairman and chief executive officer of Morgan Fay wasn't having any of it. Not one bit. It was "highly irregular," he'd shouted at the Caxton & Williams attorneys on the conference call he'd taken earlier. It

had been seven in the evening back in New York. Didn't they have families to go home to? They ought to get a life.

Malory immediately placed a call to the chairman of the corporation's audit committee. He reached the Morgan Fay board member at
home. "The whole thing is bullshit," Malory argued over the telephone.
"It's improper."

Robin Malory received the same refrain from the audit committee
chair that he got from Altschuler; the same line the New York-based attorneys had given him: "The board has a requirement to exercise their
fiduciary obligation. The board needs to look out for the interests of the
shareholders." In addition, the audit committee chair informed Malory
that the board had instructed the attorneys to "take whatever steps were
necessary."

Robin Malory was 72 years old. Prior to forming Morgan Fay, he had
risen to the very pinnacle of a Fortune 100 corporation. Having invested
28 years there, he had every reason to expect that he would close out his
career by serving as the company's Chairman and CEO. Robin Malory
would retire as chairman of a company that marketed one of the best-
known brands in the world.

But it hadn't happened that way. There went 28 years of investment
down the drain; 28 years of sacrifice, of climbing over other executives,
climbing to the very summit, to the number 2 spot, and receiving
promises that he would be the next CEO and chairman. He had been next
in line. And then to be passed over by the board of directors in favor of
an outsider. It was outrageous.

Then he was out, having to start over.

Now at Morgan Fay he was pushing worn-out brands. Products that
had seen their best days long ago. But Robin Malory had never quit on
himself, ever. He had risen to the top and he could do it again. He had
a plan; one that was sure to bring his ship in and to bring it in on his
terms. He didn't need some jack-assed board of directors appointing him
to the top position. He couldn't spend 28 years climbing and pushing
his way past others to get to the top again. If he couldn't be appointed
chairman and chief executive officer of a Fortune 100 company, he'd
start his own company. He no longer had the luxury of time. He'd do it
the smart way. His way.

He'd bought the rights to a whole bunch of worn-out brands—the
cast-offs of other brand companies, like Nabisco or General Foods. He
scrounged the seed money from here and there; he had a hell of a resume.
He was bankable, goddammit.

The brands he'd acquired were no longer attractive to their former
owners. But Robin Malory had a plan—he knew how to rejuvenate brands.
Each and every one of the brands he'd snapped-up were household names.

They were products you would find in almost any kitchen in America; and most of these products had been in existence for going on 50 years now. So the brands were tired. So what?

They just needed a little more oomph. They needed marketing dollars to rebuild market awareness. And Robin Malory and his company Morgan Fay had been able to accumulate the #1 and #2 brands in each of the product categories in which he had decided they would compete. The company didn't need to be in a whole lot of categories. That was the beauty of the plan.

Morgan Fay could never compete across the board with General Mills or Nabisco. But so what? That was never part of Malory's plan. You needed to have a plan to succeed. And then you needed to stick with the damn thing. You needed to see it through. Robin Malory was seeing this one through. Morgan Fay had been able to corner the market in those product categories the giants had forgotten to pay attention to.

Now Morgan Fay had scale. At the moment, they had manufacturing and distribution centers in Omaha and Minneapolis, with plans to open another manufacturing operation in San Leandro, California. And Robin Malory had brought together all of these waifs and strays, all of these neglected brands, to be manufactured in these two centers. With these centers, Morgan Fay would achieve distribution synergies that the giants could never achieve; and marketing synergies, as well. This is because Robin Malory had a plan.

The plan had four phases. First, you acquired brands that others had taken for granted. And because they'd been taken for granted, these castoffs hadn't been receiving the nurturing they deserved. Naturally they would have been under-performing. That brought you to the second element of the plan. Since the brands had been underperforming, you could buy them out for pennies on the dollar.

Plan element #3: You reinvigorate the products, with marketing and brand development and investment dollars. Then the cash would start coming in the door—because the brands he'd been hunting for his portfolio were terrific. They truly were. How else could each of these products have been a basic part of Americana for the past 50 years? After the "reinvigoration," and resulting enhanced cash flow, you would be ready to execute the final phase of the plan.

You take the damn thing public and watch the marketplace establish the proper value for these things that you've invigorated.

The four years prior to starting Morgan Fay, Robin Malory had a hell of a stormy stint as the chief executive officer of another, smaller company. After tangling with the board of directors on how best to expand the company, he'd been forced to leave. And before that, he'd had a two-year spell in England, with a company that ended up in bankruptcy and litigation.

But now, three years had passed since Robin Malory first formulated this plan. And now all four of his plan's objectives had been met. The initial public offering had occurred just last year.

Bam! Just like that, the stock had taken off like a bottle rocket. And now the officer and director's stock "lock-up" period was fast running its course. He and the other founding executives had received stock options as part of taking Morgan Fay public. One of the legal requirements of the Initial Public Offering (IPO) had been that no senior executive could sell any of their shares for a period of two years following the IPO. This kind of lock-up period was designed to protect the little shareholders. A lock-up period would protect the little shareholders from possible predatory practices of dishonest stock promoters.

Prior to the Depression, after raising money through an IPO, unscrupulous promoters would turn around and immediately dump their own shareholdings on the market. So the various states had passed Blue Sky laws to protect the investing public. In addition, Congress had established the Securities and Exchange Commission (SEC), which placed all kinds of restrictions and reporting requirements on publicly traded companies.

The notion of a lock-up was one of these protections. A lock-up required management to hang in there with all of these other new shareholders. That way, everyone would be motivated to build the company into something that would be self-sustaining over the long haul.

The expiration of Robin Malory's stock lock-up period, though, was now only seven months in the future. Robin only had to put one last fiscal year-end "close" behind him, plus two more quarters. Then he would be out from under the lock-up. Then, this time, he could retire for real.

He'd retire on top of the pack, "in the money," and with the respect he had been due all along. In seven months, they all could begin unloading their stock. They could all cash out.

*   *   *

"Why don't you save whatever it is you're working on?" Lee Altschuler said to Robin Malory. Altschuler was standing just inside the threshold of Malory's office. Altschuler had just finished posing the same suggestion to one of the executive vice presidents, who had readily complied with the request.

"After you hit save," Altschuler continued, "you can just leave your computer the way it is now."

Robin Malory did not respond to this, and Lee Altschuler could see the blood rushing to the big man's face; the veins were bulging in the man's neck. They were easy enough to see, the way they were standing out against the collar of the chairman's white shirt.

Robin Malory shook his head slowly.

"Tuh," he said in disgust as he pushed away from his desk. Altschuler observed silently as the chairman of Morgan Fay put on his raincoat.

Lee Altschuler, a former prosecutor in the U.S. Attorney's office in San Jose, considered what he would do if the burly chief executive attempted to close his laptop and stuff it in his briefcase.

Robin Malory replaced the small laptop on his desk. He snapped closed his briefcase and shouldered past as Altschuler stood off to the side.

Altschuler eyed the Morgan Fay chairman as he moved down the long hallway. Malory's topcoat was flying away to either side as he stalked off toward the reception area.

$$*\qquad*\qquad*$$

"Who the hell do you think you are?" Cindy Shalott barked back. "Do you have any idea who you are talking to?"

"I know that you're the chief financial officer here," Altschuler responded.

She went back to working on her computer. She was simply ignoring Altschuler and this caught him off guard; he'd never experience that kind of attitude before. She continued pecking away at her computer. "You have no business being here," she said.

"I've already explained to you why we're here. We're here at the direction of outside counsel."

She continued working as if Altschuler wasn't standing there. "I've got things to do," she said. "You don't just come in to some corporation like this, with no notice being given. Who the hell do you think you are?"

"I've already explained that," Altschuler said.

"You expect everybody to drop everything for you," she hissed at him, and she fixed Altschuler with her eyes. "I don't even know who you people are," she finally spit out.

"I've already told you who we are," Altschuler said. He fished out a business card and extended it to her.

She made no effort to accept the card. "You have no business being here," she said.

Lee Altschuler moved a step further into the office. "We've been instructed by your outside counsel to take control of your computer."

She pushed her chair from her desk. "You have that in writing?"

"No. I don't have it in writing," Altschuler said. "But Robin has already been informed by the attorneys. And he's complied."

"Well, I'm not Robin," she said. She pointed with her index finger. "And I don't see why I have to give you access to my computer," she said. "It's my computer."

"It's the company's computer," Altschuler gently reminded her. He put down his briefcase.

"I don't need you telling me whose computer it is. I have work to do and this is a major interruption."

She went back to work on her computer, and Altschuler just stood there, observing her.

Cindy Shalott finally broke the impasse. "What is it that you want to do with my computer?" she asked.

"I can't really say," Lee Altschuler replied. "But when you come in tomorrow morning, everything on your computer will be exactly the way you left it."

She folded her arms. "Why can't you describe exactly what it is you're going to do?"

"We just need access to it," Altschuler said. "And we're going to need the run of the place tonight."

"Well, then," she said. "I can't help you if you won't tell me what it is you're going to do. I've got work to do now. And you are bothering me."

"I'm sorry, but I'm not leaving," Altschuler said. He took off his suit-coat and laid it on top of the raincoat he'd lain over the back of the chair in front of her desk.

She exercised her index finger again, pointing it directly at him. "I want you to leave my office," she said. She was glaring at him now.

They remained locked like this—eyeball to eyeball—for a full minute. Again, she was the one to finally break the silence. "Why is it that you have to be here now? Why does it have to be right now? Why can't you come back tomorrow?"

"Because those aren't my instructions."

"I don't care about your instructions. I have things to do. And I don't have time for you now."

She moved her chair in closer to her desk. "Why are you standing there?" She pointed to a chair in front of her desk. "Why don't you sit down?"

Altschuler moved a step closer to the chair, but only rested his brief-case against it. "I really need for you to move away from your computer please," he finally said.

The chief financial officer sat there, glowering at him. It was all she could do to maintain her composure.

She sat as far forward in her seat as she could, lifted her right hand again and pointed her index finger directly at Altschuler's face; they were only a couple feet apart now. "You better reflect on what it is you're doing here."

"I know exactly what I'm doing," he responded.

"You are going way beyond the scope of your instructions. You people are totally out of control."

"I don't agree," he responded.

"You are totally out of control," she insisted as she pointed at him.

"I'm not out of control."

She shook her head.

Altschuler took in her aspect as she sat there pecking away at her keyboard. She was ignoring him again. She looked to be 40 to 45 years old, and not very well preserved by his reckoning, though he knew that by now his point of view was becoming pretty biased. Her hair was blond, though with brown showing at the roots. She wasn't a slender woman; as far as he was concerned, she was headed toward that middle-age richness that comes with too many desserts. A little too much makeup, too, at least for his taste; pancake makeup he called it. She was well dressed though.

She finally looked away from her computer. "I hope the people who are giving you direction know exactly what it is you're doing."

"They do," Altschuler replied.

"Bullshit," she barked right back. "They can't have any idea how it is that you are conducting yourself. You have no right to be coming in here like this. And demanding things the way you are. You are totally out of control. The way you are demanding things is outrageous."

"I don't think it's so outrageous."

She got up from her chair and began pacing back and forth behind her desk. Altschuler estimated her height at 5′3″. And now she was really working up a head of steam. "Demanding to take someone's computer?" she fired at him. "That's not outrageous?"

"I'm not demanding it," Altschuler said. "I am authorized by counsel to request that you surrender it for the evening."

"Bullshit! You're demanding it! 'Stop what you're doing,' you instructed me. You commanded me to step away from my computer. And that's not outrageous? Who the hell do you think you are?"

She continued pacing as she talked, but then she stopped and stood behind her chair as she faced Altschuler. "It's unheard of," she said. "It's the most outrageous thing I've ever heard of. Never in my life have I heard of anything so outrageous. Who the hell do you think you are? Coming in here like this."

Lee Altschuler looked at his watch. The confrontation had already taken up 25 minutes. "Look," he said. "Everybody else is with the program. Robin's already left. He's letting us do our work. Why don't you check with him?"

Cindy Shalott's eyes lit on Altschuler. She glared at him for what seemed like forever to Altschuler. And then she gave up. She moved passed him, and went out of the office.

CHAPTER TWO

"It's Gonna Be a Raid"

Down in Dallas, Kris Haworth rummaged through the computer forensics lab, looking for anything that might prove useful. She was responsible for operating the computer forensics lab in the firm's San Francisco office, and she had ten or so direct-reports; all computer forensics and data mining specialists. The lab had a bunch of dedicated servers and was located in a specially configured space, and required its own air conditioning unit because the racks of servers threw off tons of heat. The servers had over 5 terabytes of combined storage capacity. With that amount of data storage capacity, there was hardly any computer forensics or data mining problem that couldn't be tackled. Now she was rummaging through the firm's Dallas lab, and she wasn't sure where everything was stored.

Up until yesterday, she'd been working in Pennsylvania, on a very high-profile corporate investigation that was in all the newspapers. She had taken a flight into Dallas earlier this morning, however. The plan had been for her team to regroup in the Dallas lab, where there were servers that could handle the volume of information collected during her Pennsylvania site visit.

But Mike Murphy's telephone call had been kind of a shock to her. Now she was packing everything to fly back home to San Francisco. Murphy was asking her to undertake what she referred to as "a raid."

In Kris Haworth's world, "a gig" was a run-of-the-mill project—arrange to image a couple of PCs, perform an analysis of the contents of the hard drives, and provide the investigators or attorneys with whatever it was that they had been wanting to see.

A raid, though, meant dropping everything to get ready to parachute-drop into some company in order to seize control of their computer operations or a whole bunch of PCs, and image them before anybody had a chance to destroy evidence.

A raid meant things would be hot. And if this one was going to be a raid, the team would get only one shot at the computers they were targeting. That's why she needed to make sure she had plenty of everything.

Mike Murphy was already involved in another part of the investigation. He had called from Minneapolis, from one of the operating divisions under investigation. Murphy explained the situation to her over the phone. "You need to get in there and get all the electronic information," he said.

She was to go to a management company called Avalon Partners, located in downtown San Francisco. Murphy explained that Avalon Partners was a management company for a publicly traded company named Morgan Fay.

She'd never heard of Morgan Fay before Mike Murphy's call. None of what he described about the two companies made much sense to Kris, but she got it all down on paper anyway. That the corporate structure thing was kind of dense and murky to her didn't bother her too much. It wasn't her job to make sense of complicated corporate structures. Her job was to get in, image the computers she found, and get out.

"Take the next flight out," Murphy told her.

"And bring some help," he added. He then told her to call Lee Altschuler with any instructions she might have. Altschuler was on the ground in San Francisco and would handle things for her there until she arrived. Then, "click," Murphy got off the line. Kris Haworth knew to pay attention to what he was saying, because he'd be gone quickly, and you wouldn't know when you were going to hear from him again until he showed up in your doorway.

Her partner in the raid, Eric Schwartz, was handling the logistics for transportation; they would need to get all of this equipment to the airport. The flight they'd be taking out of Dallas would get them into San Francisco around five o'clock that evening. Once there, they'd work through the night.

Doing a raid always meant an all-nighter.

Kris Haworth looked around the lab one last time and found a zip drive. They'd need that if they ran into a zipped cartridge. She packed an IOMEGA drive; and then as many different kinds of drives as she could find in the lab. The team would need to be ready for any kind of loose media they might run into—Zip cartridges, Jaz cartridges, everything.

She was packing the equipment in a large black case specifically designed for shipping computer equipment. The two portable imaging units were already packed in foam; the portable unit she'd brought along from Pennsylvania, and the other one that had been in the Dallas lab.

Kris had no idea what kind of computers she would find when the team hit the ground at Avalon Partners in San Francisco. The team would need the flexibility the imaging units provided. The imaging units were plug and play; any variety of multiple hard drives could easily be added or removed. The imaging units could deal with tiny laptop hard drives, removable drives, or any kind of hard drive the team might come across.

She gathered up her loose materials and began stuffing them into the rolling cart. She owned 12 different kinds of screwdrivers and she found a place for them in the rolling cart. She then put in her flashlights, her rolls of electric tape, the twist-ties she kept in a baggie, the box of screws, and finally the jumpers—everything she'd ever needed over the years on one assignment or another.

She had long ago given up on trying to board an airplane with these things as carry-ons because of heightened security measures.

*   *   *

Kris Haworth surveyed Lee Altschuler's face in wonderment. Eric Schwarz stood next to her. The three of them were standing in the lobby of Avalon Partners in downtown San Francisco. It was late, and she didn't need this. She unslung her computer bag from her shoulder and lowered it to the parquet floor.

She, Eric, and one of his staff had just spent the last couple of hours trying to retrieve all their stuff from baggage claim at SFO. There'd been a hangup there; one of the portable imaging units hadn't shown up on the baggage carousel and it had taken another hour with the baggage claim people to finally locate it. Even though it was nearing midnight, however, the small team had taken a taxi and hustled directly to the Avalon Partners' offices to meet up with Lee Altschuler and his team.

Rob Heller stood behind Kris and Eric. Rob had the black shipping case containing their equipment. The three computer forensic specialists had just arrived and had stopped in their tracks as a result of Altschuler's announcement that Cindy Shalott, Morgan Fay's CFO, had been deleting files like crazy from her machine.

Kris Haworth's antennae immediately had gone up. "How would you know that?" she had asked Altschuler.

Lee Altschuler was a former white-collar crime prosecutor. He'd been an A.U.S.A., law enforcement lingo for an Assistant U.S. Attorney, and Kris Haworth knew Altschuler didn't know the first thing about deleted files. He could write a letter using WordPerfect. Probably. That was about the extent of his computer skills.

Altschuler pointed to the guy in a black tee shirt with the goatee sitting in an office behind them. Kris recognized the guy as Andy; one-half of the Andy-and-Alan team. The men in black. She could never remember either of their last names, nor could she remember which was Andy and which was Alan. When describing them to others, she simply referred to the two of them as "the sneaker guys"—the hacker guys from the third floor at the office—the operational part of the cyber-intrusion detection team. She knew what she needed to know—these guys were the "good" hackers.

"Where's Alan?" she asked Andy, guessing right this time, which was which.

"In the computer room," the little guy with the black hair sitting at Cindy Shalott's computer said.

"Where the servers are," Andy added.

Eric Schwarz looked around the office space behind them. "I'll take care of the servers," Eric said. He headed off toward the computer room.

Kris nodded and returned her attention to Andy. He was staring at the computer screen as his fingers raced over the keyboard.

The sneaker guys attempted to break into corporate computer systems. They worked in a special lab, set up just for them. These two guys in black sat all day long, pinging away at some corporation's network, trying to hack their way in. The weirdest thing about it, though, was they had the corporation's permission to hack away. And the firm was paid for it.

Both Alan and Andy were in their thirties. Their joy in life was trying to crack systems. And when they got bored with the computer hacking thing, the other thing they did was attempt to break through a company's physical security.

Really.

The two of them would go into some corporation dressed up like maintenance workers. And when they found themselves alone, they'd boost one up to crawl through a ceiling, or whatever it took to get past security.

One of them would call up some corporate department head and announce that it was network IT support calling. They'd say they had been told to fix something. Then one of them would ask the department head what his password was. Some people would call this kind of thing identity theft; they called it social engineering.

Then they'd use all the technology and tools in their possession to break in, to see if the corporation's firewall was secure. Kris could remember working down on the third floor in their lab one day when they had cracked into some corporation's system. Joy! High-fives all around.

Now Andy had managed to compromise her work plan. When she'd called Lee Altschuler from the Dallas airport, she'd specifically instructed him to "make sure nobody touches anything."

"Just secure the computers," she had said. "Don't turn them on. Don't turn them off. Just leave them as they are until we get there."

But here she was, looking at Andy the Sneaker, who had already gone into this machine and was poking around in the damn thing. There was no sense in getting all worked up about it though. Frankly, it happened a lot. And more often than not, it would be someone in law enforcement who did something like this, poking around in a computer, leaving some trace of his or her activity.

The effect of Andy's poking around was that he had effectively modified the computer record to some limited extent. If Kris ended up in court someday on this matter, testifying about this job, the judge might have to stop the proceedings to scold her. "I thought you testified that nobody was around these computers," the judge would say. "Why is it that on this specific day I see all this activity?" You didn't want that kind of question coming up. Especially in front of a jury.

In anticipation of this, she would have to write a memo, indicating that Andy's activities were limited to this one hour of time. He didn't delete anything. He didn't add anything. He was just looking around.

The memo would be part of her record of *chain of custody,* a documented record of who had access, and when, to the computer records. Her assignment was to image the computers, which meant she was to obtain a perfect image of the hard drives, of every byte on each of the computers. Any analysis Kris would undertake would be on this perfect image of the hard drive. The chain-of-custody record would document that she was working with uncontaminated evidence—that no one had been given an opportunity to change the record prior to, or subsequent to, her analysis. If need be, she could prepare an affidavit to that effect.

She shot a glance at Altschuler.

"What?" Altschuler asked in response to her sidelong glance. "Murphy told me there was no way this was going criminal."

*   *   *

Kris Haworth continued unscrewing the back of the PC that was sitting in front of her. She recalled Mike Murphy's admonition during his telephone conversation with her.

"This is big," he had said, and he had wanted her to be careful. She was to make sure she got everything she needed. And she remembered how he had told her the controller in Omaha said there was probably over $220 million in fraudulent entries. "For the Omaha division alone," Murphy had said. And he'd gone on to say, "The controller in Minneapolis was cooperating, too."

Murphy had indicated that he believed there was another $200 million in adjustments for the Minneapolis division.

It was now approaching midnight, West Coast time, and her day had started at five that morning. In Pennsylvania. She had taken the first flight out of Philadelphia to Dallas. And because of the jet lag, she hadn't been able to sleep well the couple of nights she'd been in Pennsylvania. All she could remember was that Mike Murphy believed there was "Maybe a couple hundred million dollars in question." Seemed like big numbers to her.

The investigation in Pennsylvania had been huge. Front page stuff. But that wasn't her investigation; she'd just been assisting on that one. This one would be hers. And even though this one wouldn't be anywhere as big as the investigation in Pennsylvania, as far as she was concerned this one was big enough; a $400 million fraud would be the biggest investigation she'd ever run. After getting off the phone with Mike Murphy, the adrenaline began running.

Calls like the one from Mike Murphy always came in at the last minute. That was because somebody had come to the conclusion that something so bad had happened that they needed to act immediately. It could never wait until the next morning. That was because either the attorneys or the company didn't want the employees to know that Kris and her forensics team were coming in.

So it was always "It's five o'clock; you gotta drop everything; get out there; image as many computers as you possibly can; and get out again." These people must all read the same kind of crime novels.

For Kris, though, the excitement of the whole thing was that she would never know, in advance, what it was she would be up against. When she asked, nobody ever knew. "It wasn't their thing," they always responded. Yet, the clock would be ticking. The computer forensics team always "had" to get done before the next morning's start of business. And she could be encountering any kind of technology, and any set of circumstances. And that was what made it fun, the need to pull it all together.

The adrenaline didn't stop the whole way to San Francisco.

*   *   *

Once onsite, Kris Haworth developed a plan of attack. One of her immediate challenges was that all of the Avalon employees had gone home. There was nobody there who could definitively answer any of her questions. She could physically see all of the computers, but identifying who belonged to which computer was the challenge. To begin with, she needed to document the layout of the floor.

The idea was to image as many of the computers as possible that night. But as a backup plan, she had a "Top Ten List." Mike Murphy had provided her with a list of the really important employees. Midway through the evening, she hooked up with Eric Schwarz in the computer room. He pointed out a server to her that seemed to have been completely cannibalized.

The computer room was not very big at all, maybe 12 feet by 10 feet. And the cannibalized machine was sitting on a countertop, pretty much completely pulled apart—an empty shell, with the tape drives pulled out.

Kris also noted that over in the corner there was what was called a *cube-server,* an e-mail server. Kris wasn't familiar with that technology, so she left it to Eric Schwarz to work that end of things. There was another PC in the IT manager's office. This machine also appeared to have been functioning at one time as a server. It too was just an empty shell, with all its drives missing.

Lee Altschuler had come into the room and was taking pictures of the scene with his digital camera.

Alan, one of the two sneaker guys, was also in the small room. With the four of them in there and the server running, the room was pretty warm.

Eric glanced up from what he was doing. "Can't find the drives to either of them," he said. "Both machines were on the network at one time. I can't tell when they were taken off."

Kris nodded.

Existing within the network, each machine had a unique identification or Internet Protocol (IP) address. Because the two cannibalized servers possessed an identification that was recognized by the network, their IP addresses informed Eric that these servers had once existed on the network. They weren't just some random machines that had been placed to one side.

*   *   *

Both imaging units were up and running. It would take two-to-three hours per computer to obtain perfect images of their hard drives.

The imaging units would read a hard drive bit by bit. There was a big difference between what she was doing and what a Help Desk might do for your machine at the office. When the Help Desk copied your hard drive, they would be copying specific files only. But Kris was interested in every bit of data that resided on the hard drive. That's what ate up the time.

Connecting a hard drive to a portable imaging unit was the fastest way to transfer data. That way the hard drive was communicating directly with the imaging unit's motherboard.

In some cases, when Kris was really in a pinch and did not have permission to "crack the case" (i.e., open the machine), the only option was to go through the machine's parallel port. But that was immensely slower. Doing it that way could take 24 hours because the parallel port limited the transfer rate.

*   *   *

There were a couple hundred floppy disks lying around the Avalon office. Kris knew there was no way they would be able to image all of them before simply running out of time. She made the executive decision to gather the rest of them up. They would take them along back to the lab at 50 Fremont Street. She could image them later. Lee Altschuler could figure out how to return them.

She'd also found some Travan backup tapes in Avalon's computer room, together with some DAT, a smaller version of the same thing. Kris had directed the backup tapes to be taken, too. Two of the file servers had been cannibalized. She knew that some of the data that once had resided on both of the cannibalized servers could possibly be reconstructed from some of these backup tapes. In any event, the best course of action was to take away any data they'd found. She'd take the stuff into custody and then seal it off. From what she had heard from Altschuler about the reception he had initially received, she assumed getting a second bite of this apple wasn't going to happen.

*   *   *

Kris Haworth worked on imaging hard drive after hard drive. By her calculations, with the two portable imaging units they had with them, and considering all the machines they had to image, they'd have to work all night. If they were lucky, they'd finish by five in the morning.

As they worked, she would find herself checking her watch periodically. Whenever they finished with the imaging of a hard drive, Kris would remove it from the portable imaging unit. She'd hand the drive to either Andy or Alan, who would then reinstall it in the personal computer from which it had been taken.

Throughout the all-nighter, Kris would go to her black rolling case, store the hard drive that had been "used-up" by the imaging process and take a fresh hard drive. After inserting the fresh drive into the portable imaging unit, they moved on to the next office to image a new machine, and she'd cross off another office on her hand drawn floor plan.

She had enough hard drives. They all were either brand-new or had been "wiped down" by Kris personally. She always wiped the hard drives clean seven times. Force of habit; four times would have been enough as far as she knew. But with seven wipes, she knew that her procedures would more than comply with Department of Defense (DOD) standards.

Peter Gutmann, regarded as the grandfather of the computer hard drive elimination methodology, has described the process of computer wiping as something more akin to "overwriting with indelible ink" rather than as a wiping of its surface. By this, he means that wiping down a hard drive involves laying random characters over its entire surface.

Gutmann knew that simply reformatting a drive would not be a secure method of eliminating data. This is because the reformatting process simply provides for the removal of the *File Allocation Table* (to those in the know, it's *FAT*). Without the computer's FAT index, the computer's operating system is no longer aware that data (which once related to the index) is stored on the drive. Put another way, the operating system will simply act as if the data is not there. And without the FAT index, the user's standard computer software applications will not be able to recover the data.

The problem with all of this is, that in a forensic world, the data still survives on the hard drive. Kris Haworth had run into this on a recent case. A computer user had hurriedly reformatted the computer before Kris arrived on the scene. Reformatting the hard drive wiped out the computer's FAT table. However, the user's underlying data still resided on the hard drive and Kris had been able to retrieve it.

The DOD's concerns run far deeper than this though. The DOD is concerned that when data is overwritten, only some portion of the data may be overwritten. This sounds nonsensical, but visualize this with the following example. Think of a teenager mowing your lawn. Now suppose for a minute that this teenager is not very concientious; he is not paying close attention to what he's doing (hard as this may be for you to envision). As a result, every once in a while the wheels of the mower do not track exactly with the previous swath. Our teenager is not too bothered with this. The mower just didn't cover well. So it missed an inch or so. No big deal. We'll get it next week. It's impossible to see it from the curb anyway. The important thing for our example, though, is this one thing—the wheels of the mower didn't always overlap completely with the last swath of grass cut, leaving some shadows of taller grass.

The same thing happens when data is overwritten in a computer. The disk drive mechanism includes an arm that tracks on a computer's hard disk when it is writing information to the drive. The arm may not always perfectly trace over the data that had been written there earlier, leaving shadow data behind.

An imaged hard drive can be forensically examined for remnants of shadow data. This examination is performed in a lab using advanced equipment such as scanning probe microscopes or magnetic force microscopes.

With these tools, any recovered fragments can be pieced together to reconstruct the original document. This is why the DOD insists on multiple wipings of a hard drive to be certain that it has truly been wiped clean—that all shadow data is removed.

Many private sector forensic specialists appear to operate under the mistaken belief that seven wipes constitute the DOD's standard. However, the DOD's national security standard 5220.22 requires only three separate overwrites. The first of the three prescribed wipings consists of depositing a series of zeroes over the entire surface of the hard drive; the second wipe deposits a series of ones; and the final wipe deposits any randomly generated character between two and nine.

With Kris doing her seven wipes before beginning any forensic analysis, she is able to assure any court that the data she analyzes is a perfect replica of the hard drive of the machine under investigation, and that her analysis had not been corrupted with extraneous data somehow left over from her last investigation.

*   *   *

Many times a computer user will try to hide his tracks if what he is engaged in is improper. But the techniques used by the typical computer user will often be obvious to a forensic specialist like Kris Haworth. Sometimes a computer user will have advance knowledge that Kris, or other members of the forensics team, are on their way, and the user tries to cover his tracks by attempting to wipe his hard drive clean.

This is always one of the first things that someone like Kris looks for. She would be able to see whether someone had used a true wipe to eliminate data. A complete wipe would stick out like a Mini-Cooper in downtown Modesto in 1959—most hard drives just aren't going to have random data written on *every space* of the drive. Nor would one ever expect that certain areas of the hard drive would be completely empty. There are always clues to that kind of thing.

For regular computer users interested in achieving this overwriting of data, there are two different types of products available on the market today. One category, called wipers, provides for "basic computer hygiene." They do this for you by only selectively overwriting the spaces on the hard drive containing the extraneous file remnants residing in the *slack space,* or *swap files, temporary file spaces,* and *file caches,* as well as in *unallocated space.* Everything else on the hard drive remains untouched and intact.

The second category, called scrubbers, comprises some heavy-duty applications. Scrubbers overwrite every single byte of space existing on the hard drive, including every application system and the operating system itself. After using a scrubber, none of the data that had once resided on the hard drive will remain. The only thing on the hard drive will be the random characters deposited on the surface of the hard drive's by the scrubber itself. The very randomness of these bits of data, though, will provide a forensic specialist with a clue that a scrubber has, in fact, been used.

Here comes a forensic tidbit: The formatting of a hard drive involves the partitioning of its surface into what are referred to as *tracks* and *sectors*. A combination of two or more sectors on a single track is called a *cluster,* the basic storage unit of a hard drive.

When a file is saved to a hard drive, it may not fully occupy *all* of the space available in a particular cluster. The extra space in a cluster is called *slack space*. The very presence of this slack space can provide an investigator with important clues.

A hypothetical drawn from a recent murder trial illustrates how an important piece of forensic evidence can be found in this kind of slack space. Newspapers throughout the United States referred to this case as the "Dog Mauling Trial."

The story elements are bizarre, almost unbelievable. Sadly though, the story is true.

CHAPTER THREE

"A Dog's Just Run Past"

Diane Whipple headed toward the intersection of Pacific Avenue and Fillmore Street. The 33-year-old women's lacrosse coach at Saint Mary's College of California had just finished her grocery shopping. As she entered the lobby of her building, it was just a little past four o'clock on a Friday afternoon, January 26, 2001.

The elevator door opened on her floor. Grocery bags in hand, Whipple headed down the hallway toward her apartment. What happened next on the sixth floor of the Pacific Heights apartment building is best described by the grand jury testimony of Esther Birkmaier, who lived directly across the hallway from Diane Whipple's apartment. Esther Birkmaier had lived in the Pacific Heights apartment building for almost 28 years.

"The barking started," the 76-year-old Ms. Birkmaier testified. "And it just got progressively louder, to the point where it piqued my interest."

Esther recalled thinking, "'What is going on with these dogs?'"

James Hammer looked up from the manila folder he held in front of him. "As it got louder, what did you do?" the San Francisco Assistant District Attorney asked.

"As it got louder," Esther responded, "I didn't really get up from the table where I was sitting until I heard someone cry, 'Help me. Help me.'"

Later in the grand jury proceedings, David Keuenzi, a New Yorker visiting a friend in the building, described what he heard that afternoon with a little more edge to the detail. "She was screaming in a major way," he testified. "I personally thought she was being mugged or raped."

In her grand jury testimony, Esther Birkmaier described getting up from where she had been sitting at her dining room table, just off the kitchen area. From what she was hearing, the dogs were right outside her front door, and by now, they were "very loud."

She moved toward the front door to her apartment. Looking through the peephole, she could see a body lying on the floor; a woman's body; the woman was lying face down.

Esther testified that a dark object was on top of the body and that the door to Diane Whipple's apartment directly opposite was partially open. She recalled that she could see the top of the woman's head, where it lay across the doorsill.

Still with her eye to the peephole, Esther Birkmaier could see the woman's light-colored clothes, and her blond hair.

"But then the dark object covered her," she testified.

The dark object covering the middle of the body of Diane Whipple was a dog. A 122-pound Presa Canario attack dog. The dog's name was Bane, and at this moment, it was vigorously attacking the neck of the young woman.

In fact, just outside Esther Birkmaier's locked door were two Presa Canarios, with a combined weight of 233 pounds. The breed originated in the Canary Islands but was found to be so vicious that they were ultimately outlawed there. Presa Canarios are believed by many to be the most vicious breed of dog anywhere in the world.

Esther Birkmaier found herself in a panic. She stepped away from the peephole and tried to compose herself for a moment. What to do? She rushed into her kitchen, picked up the receiver, and dialed 911.

When she returned to the peephole in her front door, the banging of the dog bodies against her door was very loud. She described what she heard. "It was very loud. In fact, it was crashing. It was so loud that instinctively, I put on the chain [on the door], thinking, if this door breaks down, at least the chain will hold the door for another split second while I can escape or lock myself in the bedroom."

The banging was constant, coming fast. As she put her eye back to the peephole, Esther was, in her own words, "just panic stricken."

By now, all that could be seen were groceries everywhere. Esther had her eye to the peephole again. She blinked once to clear her field of vision. The groceries Diane Whipple had been carrying were in view; they were scattered all over the floor. But the woman who had been laying at the open doorway, and the dark object that had loomed above her—neither could now be seen. Esther's field of vision was limited to just a few feet to either side of her doorway, and it was hard to see the hallway floor.

Jim Hammer, the San Francisco prosecutor, asked whether at some point Esther had heard anyone else yell during the whole incident.

Esther nodded. "I heard the words, 'Get off. Get off. Stop. Stop.' And, 'No. No,'" she responded. "And I knew it was Marjorie's voice," she said.

Marjorie Knoller's voice had been loud and shrill when she had been shouting these commands at the two Presa Canarios. There is no doubt that both dogs had been mauling Diane Whipple. According to Esther's grand jury testimony, the two Presa Canarios were "growling, snarling, or barking the entire time. There was no silence."

Esther Birkmaier could easily recognize Marjorie Knoller's voice. Marjorie and her husband Robert Noel had lived in the apartment down the hall for 11 years. Esther was very clear in her testimony that the commands issued to the two Presa Canarios only came after Esther had gone to the peephole at her front door for the second time—after having gone back to the kitchen to dial 911, and after she had spoken to the 911 operator. The commands sounded to Esther Birkmaier as if Marjorie Knoller was standing somewhat "further away from the door."

San Francisco Police Officer Leslie Forrestal arrived on the scene within minutes. The radio dispatcher had reported two dogs running out of control on a hallway on the sixth floor at 2398 Pacific Avenue. Just outside the apartment building, a man was waving down Forrestal's patrol car. Forrestal rolled down her car window as her partner stopped the patrol car. The man reported that he had called 911. He pointed toward the top floor of 2398 Pacific. "There's a woman screaming and dogs barking on one of the floors up there." Forrestal acknowledged the information. She asked the gentleman to step aside so that her partner, Officer Sidney Laws, could pull the patrol car to the curb.

Inside in the lobby, a maintenance worker met the two female police officers. He also reported a woman screaming and dogs barking on one of the levels above. The two police officers decided to split up; Laws would take the stairs, and Forrestal the elevator.

Laws reported her progress on her hand-held radio as she made her way up the stairwell. Inside the elevator, Forrestal could visualize her partner's progress as Laws reported hitting each landing. The old elevator was rising at about the same rate Laws climbed the stairwell. As the tiny elevator rose past the fifth floor, Forrestal could hear Laws coming over the radio, "A dog's just run past. On the landing above."

The elevator door locked onto the sixth floor and Forrestal swung open the elevator door. On the floor to the right of the elevator door, a woman lay naked—but for one sock and shoe. Forrestal stood stunned, surveying the horrific scene.

She could see that a large puddle of very thick blood had pooled below the victim's neck. Bloodstained clothing was strewn all over the hallway. Forrestal could also see groceries scattered everywhere. The whole corridor reflected chaos.

Officer Forrestal pulled out her baton. She moved down the hallway toward where Diane Whipple lay. Diane Whipple's head was lying closest to the elevator, face down. A path of blood stained the carpet, marking Whipple's attempt to reach her door; she was now clearly in shock, and was too weak to lift herself enough to even crawl.

Officer Forrestal knelt by the young woman. She tried to comfort her. "Lie still," Forrestal said. "You need to lie still. An ambulance is on the way."

Bloody handprints covered the walls on either side of the doorway, and a blood-soaked nylon leash lay a few feet away.

After the dog-mauling death of Diane Whipple, the San Francisco newspapers had a field day. The story wouldn't die; in fact, it expanded daily, each revelation more outrageous than the previous.

Authorities discovered that almost one year earlier, two Aryan Brotherhood gang members, Paul "Cornfed" Schneider and Dale Bretches, had been found guilty of operating an attack-dog breeding scheme from within their Pelican Bay maximum security prison cell. The target market of their business operation: Southern California drug dealers and gang members. Noel and Knoller now served as "Cornfed" Schneider's attorneys.

The two cellmates were serving life sentences without parole; Bretches for a 1979 murder in San Diego; Schneider for multiple attacks, including the attempted murder of another inmate. The two prisoners utilized third parties and attorneys to run the dog breeding operation on the outside.

Janet Coumbs, a resident of Trinity County, one of the most rural counties in Northern California, apparently had no idea of the vortex the two prisoners would suck her into. "It turned into a nightmare," she said. The kennel owner quickly found the seven dogs she boarded for the two prisoners to be completely uncontrollable. "No matter what I did," she would later say, "they killed. They ate all my sheep, all my chickens, and my house cat." Coumbs found herself having to install a steel reinforced door to keep the Presa Canarios from continuing to smash down the doors to her home.

The revelations continued daily in the San Francisco newspapers. Within days of the fatal mauling, Robert Noel, 59, and Marjorie Knoller, 45, were granted an adoption decree by a San Francisco family court, making them the parents of the 38-year-old inmate, Paul "Cornfed" Schneider. The adoption had apparently been in the works for months, but the timing nonetheless shocked the community. To the pressing media, a spokesperson for the California Department of Corrections could only respond, "We're a little puzzled about this. That is pretty much our reaction."

In response, Robert Noel accused the law enforcement community of breaching the confidentiality of his client, Paul "Cornfed" Schneider, by disclosing to the press that Noel and Marjorie Knoller had adopted the 38-year-old prisoner as their son.

Noel expressed outrage at the fact that the adoption was made public. "The disclosure of that information by representatives of the State of California was a violation of Fourth Amendment privacy rights, and the provisions of the California Code of Regulations Title 15," he stated.

As for the dog breeding operation, Noel answered a reporter's question as follows, "The dogs have a trust account—anything that came in for them has a paper [trail]. The dogs have lawyers, and we are their lawyers."

In an 18-page missive he fired off to San Francisco District Attorney Terrence Hallinan, Noel implied that Whipple caused her own death by repeatedly entering the hallway, instead of staying inside her apartment after Knoller allegedly had gotten control of the two Presa Canarios. Noel even suggested that Diane Whipple, a lacrosse coach, may have been taking steroids, or wearing a pheromone-based fragrance, which may have provoked aggressive behavior from the animals. Noel wrote, "We have previously requested that you insure the preservation of all cosmetics and dietary supplements in Ms. Whipple's apartment and workplace for forensic examination."

After this, Noel and Knoller conducted a 40-minute press conference outside the gates to the Pelican Bay State Prison. In response to a question posed by a reporter, Noel repeated his assertions about the folly of Whipple's actions: "I would not think a reasonable person, under those circumstances, would crawl back into the hall and face the dog—or to come back out (from) a position of safety."

Noel then lit into San Francisco District Attorney Terry Hallinan for considering, even for a moment, investigating either Noel or Knoller's conduct. "Mr. Hallinan has proven he is not a reasonable prosecutor and is a disgrace to the office."

Within a week though, X-rated photos featuring none other than "Cornfed" Schneider's newly adopted "mother," Marjorie Knoller, would be found by law enforcement authorities as a result of a court authorized search of Schneider's Pelican Bay cell. Noel's response to the discovery of the X-rated photos was, "I'm not going to confirm it, or deny it." Noel then went on to assert that if the Department of Corrections had disclosed any confidential attorney-client protected writings, "then it will be added to the $100 million claim that we're going to file for breach of the confidentiality of our adoption."

Noel then directed a salvo at the San Francisco Police Department. The police had obtained a court order for the search of the Noel and Knoller apartment. The couple was out of town though, and when the police forced the door, it splintered. Noel accused the police of "Gestapo Tactics."

Thirteen days after the death of Diane Whipple, Knoller appeared on ABC's *Good Morning America*. Whatever she and Noel had hoped to achieve with this TV appearance was completely blown when Knoller showed absolutely no remorse about Whipple's death. Knoller argued that Whipple could have avoided any harm by simply entering her apartment and closing the door behind her. Knoller stated that she tried to force Whipple into Whipple's apartment, but that the younger woman resisted vehemently, incensing the dogs to maul her.

As the grand jury began its deliberations, Noel and Knoller left San Francisco by car, with San Francisco undercover police following their movements. Within three hours, and as the grand jury continued deliberations, Noel was stopped by the California Highway Patrol for speeding in excess of 90 mph. Afterward, as Noel continued driving north that evening—drawn inexplicably back toward "family," in Pelican Bay state prison—the grand jury's indictment of the two was handed down.

Noel and Knoller surrendered where they stopped at a ranch in Corning, California. Both Knoller and Noel were charged with manslaughter; in addition, Knoller was charged with second-degree murder.

Before this case would ever get to a jury, things would become more surreal. Authorities learned of a contract put out by the Aryan Brotherhood on the high-profile assistant-prosecutor, Kimberly Guilfoyle. From that point forward until the completion of the trial, Guilfoyle would be placed under 24-hour protective surveillance. As the case moved toward a trial date, the press reported that bestiality would be an issue in the case. The trial judge, Superior Court Judge James Warren, would subsequently rule that any such allegation would not be admissible at trial.

*   *   *

During the grand jury proceedings, the prosecutors informed the press that an expert was in the process of reviewing the hard drive "for any alterations or other deletions," implying that the two attorneys may have deleted documents from their computer.

The original documents found in Schneider's cell would be used by the prosecutors in court to demonstrate Noel and Knoller's knowledge of the dangerous nature of the two Presa Canarios; this was vital for the prosecutor's second degree murder charge to stand. One of the more damning documents in the record of grand jury proceedings was a letter written by Noel to Schneider.

In the letter, Noel described Whipple's first encounter with the two Presa Canarios. Noel referred to his neighbor as "a timorous little mousy blonde," who "almost (had) a coronary" after suddenly coming upon the two massive animals. In contrast, Noel referred to the two Presa Canarios as "the dynamic duo."

During the grand jury proceedings, Prosecutor James Hammer confronted Noel. "Are you concerned that she almost had a coronary at the time?" Hammer asked.

"Not particularly, no," Noel responded.

One of the more significant issues in the case would turn on whether Noel and Knoller were aware of the danger to society the two Presa Canarios posed. Trial testimony from a veterinarian who had given the young dogs their shots at the kennel where they had been kept was telling on this subject. The vet testified that the head and jaws of the Presas were simply massive. He recalled that upon first being confronted with the animals, he had feared for his life for the first time in his long career. He went on to testify that he would agree to give the dogs their shots only if the most aggressive of the dogs was confined behind a fence.

The veterinarian also testified at the trial that he had been so affected by the experience that he wrote a letter to Noel and Knoller. In this letter, he warned the couple that it was his professional opinion that the dogs were unfit as human companions and were a danger to society.

Noel and Knoller ignored the concerns of the kennel owner, as well as the veterinarian, and returned with the two huge dogs to their apartment in Pacific Heights in San Francisco. Notwithstanding all of the evidence mounting against them, both Noel and Knoller were steadfast in their assertion that the two dogs were gentle, loving animals.

*   *   *

Judge Warren had sentenced Marjorie Knoller and Robert Noel to prison on manslaughter charges a couple of months earlier. On this sunny day, though, Lee Teitsworth and I were ambling our way up Market Street on our way to lunch in downtown San Francisco, and every once in a while, trolley cars would rumble past in either direction on the brick and concrete of the broad tree-lined avenue. Teitsworth had retired from the FBI a couple of years earlier, after closing out his career as Special Agent-in-Charge (SAC) of the FBI's Portland, Oregon, office. These days he was now working with us on complex white-collar crime investigations in the private sector.

Teitsworth is an unabridged car nut. Unabashed might be another descriptor. In any event, he definitely has the affliction. This day, he was educating me on the advantages of a 1960 Austin Healey 3000 MkI open two-seat roadster. His descriptions weren't rooting very deeply, however, as I generally find it difficult to discern the difference between a torque wrench and a crescent wrench. The nuances of this particular conversation were pretty much escaping my grasp. After a couple of blocks of car talk, our discussion turned to the use of computer forensics in investigations, and how important this specialty was turning out to be. Especially in the last year or so. The forensic examination of computer hard drives had become a critical aspect of the investigations now underway in different parts of the world. A few examples follow.

The FBI's Minneapolis office was vociferous in their desire to obtain a court order to examine the computer belonging to the so-called "20th hijacker," arrested the month preceding the events of September 11. Why? They wanted to perform a forensic examination of the hard drive in the laptop. What was one outcome of the Israelis invasion of the West Bank in the spring of 2002? Upon their withdrawal from the West Bank, they took with them many confiscated computer hard drives for forensic analysis. How are our intelligence agencies piecing together al Qaeda's worldwide network, including "sleeper cells?" The forensic examination of computer hard drives that have been confiscated from European-based al Qaeda cells has provided investigators rich insights into al Qaeda's worldwide tentacles.

To understand the value of these types of forensic examinations, though, it is necessary to have a sense of the anatomy of a computer hard drive.

Think of a hard drive as a bunch of spinning platters. Imagine three or four of these platters, stacked on top of one another, like pancakes, but only millimeters apart. These platters are all spinning in unison at 5,000 to 10,000 times a minute. When you save a file, your data is written magnetically in concentric circles on the platters as they spin, by a tiny arm resembling a record player arm. Today, an advanced drive can store the equivalent of 75 novels within the space of a second.

When a file is saved, the computer's operating system arranges for the data to be written to a specific cluster. When that specific cluster fills, a second cluster is sought. This process continues until the file being saved is completely stored. The clusters where a file is stored can be all over the place on the hard drive; they don't have to be contiguous.

To keep everything straight, the operating system maintains an index of where things have been stored. This index is referred to as the *File Allocation Table* (FAT), which I mentioned in Chapter 2. When you're ready to retrieve a file, the FAT brings everything back together for you.

An intriguing possibility is introduced by all of the foregoing—when you save a file, if the final cluster being written to is not completely filled, the remaining space is made available to the operating system for other purposes. This leftover space is referred to as *slack space*.

Think of a maître d' at a restaurant as being analogous to the operating system's file allocation table. When you place a dinner reservation for three, the maître d' will reserve for you the restaurant's basic unit of cluster, a table seating four. When you arrive for dinner, the fourth seat at your table will go unused. This unused seat is analogous to the slack space in an occupied cluster—space at the table unneeded for the current seating.

The difference between this restaurant metaphor and the slack space within a cluster is very stark though. In every restaurant, after a group of diners depart, the table is completely cleared and a new tablecloth and settings are placed. Within the world of hard drives though, this does not happen; new data is simply overlaid over old. The operating system's FAT keeps track of exactly where the new data in your file resides. The FAT, by default, has simply ignored the slack space.

Unlike the restaurant world though, the slack space in a hard drive will always contain data from prior sessions in which it has been accessed, even though the file itself has been deleted from the FAT. Your computer is also continuously archiving files that you have in use. It does this without you being aware. Every time you close a file, your computer clears its memory; it does this by dumping the file contents to existing slack space on your hard drive. The operating system also clears your keyboard buffer (specific memory space containing a record of your recent keystrokes). The operating system does this by dumping your latest keystrokes into the slack space on your hard drive. And the very next time you fire up your computer, the operating system will again repeat the same process when you've finished working on a file. If it runs out of slack space to dump to, it will simply overwrite on existing slack space. Now comes the significant part.

At the instant the hard drive is being forensically imaged by somebody like Kris Haworth, all kinds of things can be residing in the hard drive's slack space. Using special tools to access the slack space, an investigator sometimes finds interesting information

Lee Teitsworth and I compared the investigative methodology of a couple of years ago to that which might face an investigator today. Teitsworth recalled a case he had investigated when he had been with the FBI a couple of years earlier. In this case, a criminal defendant had managed to falsify an alibi through the fabrication of a letter. The letter demonstrated that the defendant had been in a different city, some 1,400 miles away on "Date A," the day on which the crime had been committed. The defendant had thought of everything, save for the possibility that Teitsworth might visit the recipient of the letter, and that the recipient might inexplicably retain the envelope in which the letter had been mailed. Teitsworth's examination of the postmark on the envelope revealed a much later date, which for purposes of this discussion we can refer to as "Date B," and with that, the perpetrator's so-called alibi was blown.

The context of the discussion Lee Teitsworth and I had on our walk on this sunny afternoon, however, had more to do with the notion of file slack on a computer hard drive, and situations in which the same type of physical impossibility of evidence can be manifested. To explore this type of scenario, the creation of a simple hypothetical example is helpful. To do this, we can turn back to the Dog Mauling Trial.

Let's create the hypothetical. Assume "someone" foolishly believed it to be a good idea to create evidence supporting Marjorie Knoller's assertion that she had attempted to physically push Diane Whipple toward her apartment door to get her out of harm's way. But that Diane Whipple had, inexplicably, violently resisted these efforts—and that it was this "violent resistance" that was the precipitating cause of the fatal dog attack. Now assume that a letter evidencing this "version" of the fatal encounter is discovered on the Noel and Knoller computer. In this letter, written to a hypothetical sister, a reference is made to an earlier letter—one ostensibly written several months earlier.

This "earlier letter," which we can now refer to as "Letter A," is then also discovered on the computer hard drive (as the writer knew it would). In this earlier "Letter A" to the sister, our hypothetical writer asserts (several months before the attack) that during several encounters in the apartment hallway, Diane Whipple had been consistently antagonistic to Knoller, almost to the point of physically threatening Knoller in each of these encounters—while Knoller had the dogs with her, on leash. Assume that "Letter A" also states that the dogs sensed this antagonism. The letter even describes how the one dog, Bane, in each of these encounters, sensed a threat and acted protective of Knoller.

Let's also add to this hypothetical that, as in Lee Teitsworth's example, these letters were in fact fabricated to establish a helpful, but untrue fact pattern. How then could an examination of the slack space of the computer hard drive inform an investigator, one way or another?

Let's find out.

Let us assume that a certain "Letter B," is also found to be residing in the *very same cluster* of slack space of the writer's hard drive. This "Letter B," had been written to someone in Pennsylvania and turns out to be a transmittal letter. It is forwarding a personal check in the amount of $35.00. This check represents payment for a "set of twelve, long-handled silver spoons," which (in the writer's mind) would be "perfect" for use when serving tall glasses of iced tea. Now, again, this is a hypothetical that I have spun from whole cloth and has nothing to do with the actual purchase of an identical set of spoons, through eBay, by some unnamed individual, in my own household.

Really.

In analyzing the hypothetical situation in front of us, the very existence and definition of slack space comes into play. Though the dates of the letters clearly indicated that Letter A was written a month before Letter B, curiously, the physical layout of the data (where these two letters physically resided on the hard drive) indicated the contrary. In the slack space for the *specific* cluster in which both letters had been deposited, Letter A, ostensibly written a month before Letter B, was found to have been deposited *on top of* some of the contents of Letter B. I use the word "deposited" purposely here, because that is exactly what happens when a file is saved. The data comprising the file is *deposited* on the hard drive in the sector or cluster reserved for that file.

As we have seen earlier, each time you ask the operating system to close a file, the operating system *clears* its memory by writing to slack space whatever it was you had been working on. This is important for forensic analysis.

To illustrate the types of things that a forensic specialist could discover in a computer's slack space, consider the following. Suppose that you have just encrypted a sensitive document, and that you have used the most state-of-the-art encryption methodology. A computer forensics specialist still might be able to recover the original (unencrypted) document from the computer's slack space. This is because when you had physically completed the encryption process, the operating system *cleared* its memory—and it did this by dumping its contents (in this case, the original unencrypted file) into file slack.

Everything that is typed on a computer's keyboard ends up on the disk somewhere. Even passwords and user IDs can sometimes be discovered residing in file slack. It's happened. However, according to a recent study, a system's file slack will typically contain data from only the most recent session.

Don't count on it though.

In our hypothetical, we discovered that the "second" letter (Letter B) had been deposited *first*. And the "first" letter (Letter A), although purportedly written before Letter B, had been deposited (in places) *on top of* the contents of Letter B. This though, seemed a physical impossibility unless Letter B had been written first.

Lee Teitsworth had been able to demonstrate to the court that the alleged perpetrator had mailed the letter to himself to establish an alibi. And the alleged alibi was proven to be an impossibility when you considered the physical postmark on the outside of the envelope. The perpetrator hadn't thoroughly thought through that part of his ruse. Teitsworth had described a situation where the investigator was following a paper trail. Today, we are able to follow a digital trail.

CHAPTER FOUR

She'd Deleted a Helluva Lot of E-Mail

Kris Haworth led the small group out of the Avalon Partners' offices into the elevator lobby. It was five o'clock in the morning now. The computer forensics specialists had just finished everything they could do on-site at Avalon. Their equipment waited behind them in the darkened lobby, all packed up in the black rolling carts. She punched the down button.

As the team took the elevator down, nobody had anything to say; they were all pretty worn out from the all-nighter and the cross-country flights they had taken the day before. The elevator door opened and Haworth could see the security guard at the other end of the lobby. She worried about whether the guard would let them out of the building with their equipment. Surprisingly, the guard just waved at the five of them as the team moved to the front doors of the downtown office building. Saturday morning at 5 A.M.—no big deal, apparently.

Outside, the rain had stopped. There was no traffic at all on the street. Kris Haworth called for a taxi. The sun hadn't fully risen yet, though the sky above the high-rises was beginning to lighten to a dark blue with the morning light. The rain-slicked street reflected the red traffic light at the corner.

Before the taxi could arrive, the team decided to split up; the two computer forensics specialists from the Dallas office decided to walk the three blocks to the Mandarin Oriental Hotel. Kris Haworth and the two men-in-black would take the taxi when it came. Kris planned to grab a shower at home and head back to the office afterward.

Haworth wanted to backup everything that the team had spent the whole night imaging. From her experience, she knew that it was pretty rare to get a second bite of the apple. If something were to happen to one of the drives, she wanted to make sure she had a backup.

After that, she'd begin the forensic search. Mike Murphy, the lead investigator on the engagement, was flying pretty blind now because they were at the early stages of the investigation. Anything she could get to him at this point would be helpful. She would begin with the e-mail deletions. The team already knew that there had been a fair amount of that going on over the last day or so.

Haworth was able to get back to her office before 10 that Saturday morning. She got the backups going, then began developing the listing of deleted files; including the file name, when it was last accessed, when it was last modified, and when the file had originally been created. That way, she would know exactly what it was that the Avalon employees had been deleting from their computers immediately before Haworth had been able to arrive on the scene.

She liked the convenience of this approach; invariably, the people under investigation would delete whatever it was the investigators would typically like to see.

When a file is "deleted," the reference to that file is simply eliminated. However, the data comprising the so-called deleted file has not been deleted from the disk; it still resides there. The important change though, is that *all* of the space in the cluster, even that containing the original data from the deleted file, will now be made available for the storage of newly created files. With the passage of time and further computer use, a deleted file may subsequently become fully overwritten.

After recovering the files that had been deleted, Haworth retrieved all of the e-mail of the individuals under investigation. She began with Cindy Shalott's hard drive.

Haworth arranged to open Shalott's e-mails, and then she exported them to another file so that the staff consultants she and Mike Murphy had enlisted for the investigation could sift through them later for relevance.

Kris also undertook to do an automated search of Shalott's hard drive to recover any e-mail that had been deleted, or that was sitting in other temporary storage areas of the hard drive. She would undertake this type of search based on the metadata, essentially the header information, which would appear in the front-end of any incoming or outgoing e-mail. This way, Kris would be assured of finding pieces of e-mails and other files such as Word files, all over the place in Shalott's hard drive. Kris would find these file fragments in the file slack, in any remaining free space resident in the computer's hard drive, and in the swap files.

The computer's operating system makes use of a swap file to temporarily store information not currently in use. These files are maintained by the operating system at a binary level and are not accessible by the user through the use of the typical applications, but can be discovered using specific utilities or forensics tools.

Often you use your computer to multitask. When you are doing this, your computer's operating system will use swap files for temporary memory. Let's say you begin to create an e-mail, but decide to create a Word document and then an Excel file midstream. After this, you go back to the e-mail you were working on, and you attach these files to it. You have the impression that your operating system is allowing you to work on several things simultaneously. In truth, your operating system, at lightning speed, will have been going back and forth and storing your files in swap space as it needed to free up memory. Your operating system was temporarily storing that which you were not actively working on. Only a stub portion of the inactive file was being maintained in active memory, holding down a place, until you needed to access that program once again.

Think of the swap file as a scratch pad and you'll have the notion pretty well in mind. When the operating system doesn't have enough memory for swapping, it will begin swapping to the hard drive itself. There are two types of swap files: temporary and permanent. Temporary swap files collapse when we close the operating system. Permanent swap files continue to exist even after we shut down the operating system. This is what is important to the forensic examiner, because it represents a potential gold mine of otherwise hidden information.

*   *   *

There are other spaces on the hard drive referred to as *caches* that Kris Haworth knew to look for because they typically contain information of interest to a forensic specialist. She knew, for example, that to improve performance, Netscape's Web browser, Netscape Navigator, (as well as Microsoft's Internet Explorer), creates a cache file to retain information accessed whenever a user surfs the Internet.

Haworth knew to retrieve the information in the user's cache files when investigating improper access to the Internet. She had done this in investigations of unauthorized transmission of trade secrets, in which a company's intellectual property was being misappropriated. She has also had occasion to review cache files for investigations in which employees had downloaded child pornography. In other investigations, in which computer hacking had been evidenced, cache files revealed user visits to hacking sites, evidencing how the users had obtained their hacking tools. Cache files were always of interest; they provided a road map to where the user had traveled on the Internet.

If an individual had deleted their entire Microsoft e-mail file, Kris Haworth would see a series of .pst files residing in one folder, indicating to her that the entire e-mail file had been deleted en masse.

On the other hand, if Cindy Shalott had gone through her e-mails and deleted them one at a time, Kris Haworth would be able to see that by searching on Shalott's user name, which would be contained in header information on files Shalott had created.

She'd deleted a helluva lot of e-mail during the couple of hours prior to Haworth's arrival, but Avalon was using Microsoft Outlook, and all Kris Haworth had to do to find what Cindy Shalott had deleted was to open up Cindy Shalott's e-mail account, and look in her Deleted Files folder. Cindy Shalott hadn't even thought to empty her Deleted Files folder. Even if she had, though, Kris Haworth would still have the ability to reconstruct whatever it was that had been deleted from there. Kris would merely utilize certain specific forensic utilities that would allow her to identify the file names and their locations, and then reconstruct the files.

According to International Data Corporation, 10 billion electronic messages are transmitted on a daily basis. The growth in e-mail users, too, has been enormous. In 1990, there were only ten thousand or so users, primarily in the United States. In 2000, there were almost one billion electronic mailboxes, worldwide, with approximately half of those located in the United States.

When the computer is forensically imaged, it is as if a snapshot of the hard drive was taken at that very instant; everything in the computer's hard drive is frozen in place, available for recovery by a forensic specialist. According to Haworth, "A computer hard drive is sort of the psyche of the person who uses it. It captures everything that they ever did on it. We call it the electronic truth serum. People say astounding things in e-mail at the drop of the hat, and they'll think they deleted it. They don't understand that not only does the message still exist on their hard drive, but it is spread throughout the system."

Kris Haworth did a similar search for Excel, PowerPoint, Word, and other files Shalott had created. She performed the same data collection effort on every other computer that the team had imaged. Kris also made a list of any files Cindy Shalott had created that were password protected; Haworth would deal with those files later. She then performed a test to determine whether the file signatures matched the file headers.

A file signature is the suffix heading appended to a file, which tells the operating system what the nature of the file is. For example, .xls tells your machine that the file is an Excel file. Kris Haworth knew that people sometimes changed these suffix headings—by changing the suffix appended to the file so that it read as .exe, for example. That way, the computer, and anybody else looking through the user's hard drive would think that the file listing they were looking at was a program file, an execution file, and therefore not worth looking into. Cindy Shalott had not been that crafty.

CHAPTER FIVE

"You Need to Get Over There"

The telephone rang as Lee Altschuler worked at his desk. He picked up and cradled the phone to his ear. "Altschuler."

"We need all the Morgan Fay business records," came Mike Murphy's voice over the line. "You need to get over there."

Altschuler checked his watch. It was not quite 3 o'clock on Friday afternoon, and he had just been considering heading home early in order to beat the rush hour traffic to the South Bay. Altschuler ruefully let that notion go; Murphy sounded dead serious. This time Murphy was talking about the need to collect paper records over at the Avalon Partners' offices. Altschuler reflected on the nature of the request and Murphy's sense of urgency. Those were Morgan Fay's original business documents that were stored at Avalon Partners—anything and everything one might expect to be generated by the executives of a headquarters operation of a publicly traded company.

Altschuler had no notion of the volume of records that needed to be collected. The executives working in the Avalon Partners office space, essentially the entire workings of Morgan Fay's headquarters, encompassed an operation covering an entire floor in a downtown San Francisco high-rise. He found himself inwardly cursing. Anybody with half a mind could see this was coming. Why didn't we plan this out? Altschuler began roaming the two floors at 50 Fremont Street, looking for the biggest guys he could find in the forensics and investigative services group.

The only person available on such short notice (as in, "No, I need you right now.") was Emmett Bergman. At least Bergman was over six feet tall.

Altschuler headed down the hallway and poked his head into Shelly Connor's office. "I need you to get some banker's boxes."

"How many?" she asked.

Altschuler thought on this for a moment. "Why don't you get a hundred," he said.

* * *

Lee Altschuler and Emmett Bergman, the two-person Praetorian Guard of the board of directors of Morgan Fay, rumbled on over to the Avalon Partners' offices on foot. They had the one hand truck between them, and it squeaked incongruously with its light load of the 50 flats of banker's boxes Shelly Connor had been able to locate for them.

Outside, it had begun raining and both men had umbrellas up. Altschuler and Bergman waited for the light at Market Street to change. A turn-of-the-century trolley car rumbled past, painted green and silver, the colors of the Philadelphia streetcar line from which this particular car had been resurrected.

Robin Malory met Altschuler and Bergman in the reception area. Altschuler could see that the man was trembling with rage. Malory must have just been informed of the purpose of Altschuler's visit. "How kind of you to come by," Malory said, the sarcasm filling the small reception area.

The receptionist looked up from what she had been doing.

Malory's neck was bulging red above his white shirt collar. The deposed chairman of Morgan Fay glared at the two men in suits standing in front of him. He looked from one to the other: *Don Quixote*—Altschuler; with his sidekick, *Sancho Panza*—Bergman. The two visitors were dripping water onto the reception area from their drenched raingear and umbrellas. The deposed chairman did not disguise the contempt he held for the two men standing in front of him. Malory waved his arms. "Go ahead," he boomed. "Have at it." He jerked his thumb toward the office space behind the reception area. "Take whatever belongs to them."

Altschuler began to move, but he stopped upon hearing the next words from Malory.

"But I'm warning you right now," Malory intoned. "Don't you *dare* remove anything not belonging to Morgan Fay. And don't you dare examine any confidential records that do not belong to Morgan Fay."

Malory stood glaring as both men removed their wet raincoats. "Do you understand my meaning?" he asked.

Altschuler nodded.

"This is most unforgivable," Malory said imperiously. "This is a completely unbusinesslike way to go forward. You people should have made an appointment. I've never heard of someone making this kind of demand without having made prearrangements."

"I'm sorry," Altschuler responded. "I only just learned of it myself."

Malory measured the two men in suits standing in front of him, as he rocked back and forth on his heels, cogitating. "I don't know whether we have any facilities that are available that would accommodate what you need," he finally said to Altschuler.

Altschuler made no reply.

"How many people are you going to have here?" Malory demanded.

"A couple more," Altschuler responded.

Malory looked at the hand truck behind Emmett Bergman and shook his head.

As Altschuler and Bergman boxed documents, more forensics and investigative staff began arriving. Within a half-hour, there were eight people.

Altschuler assigned people to specific areas on the floor. He directed them to go through the file drawers and cabinets and shelves. They were to identify the corporate documents and then box and index them.

Something about the office space felt different to Altschuler as he moved through it. The floor seemed somehow more orderly than he recalled from his previous visit. He surveyed the space again—perimeter executive offices, cubicles just outside, the investor relations department. It seemed cleaner somehow.

Then it came to him.

Before, there had been boxes of product everywhere. There had been marketing collateral laying around in most of the cubicles. He remembered the boxes of *Excalibur* biscuits that had been in some of the cubes. And the boxes of *Lady of the Lake* products sitting on top of the desks. Now they were nowhere in sight. He looked around the floor. The wall decorations were also gone. The landscape scenes featuring Mount Baden were gone. It was as if Malory had swept from view any reminder of Morgan Fay.

Altschuler looked for the exemplar stock certificate that had been hanging on a wall, matted and framed under glass—a memento of the company's IPO. It too had disappeared.

Intrigued, Altschuler headed back toward the lobby. The gold-leaf words *Morgan Fay* that previously graced the front glass of the reception area had been scraped off. Morgan Fay no longer existed. The Avalon Partners' management team had psychologically expunged Morgan Fay from their memory.

Altschuler headed to Cindy Shalott's office. Since she was the chief financial officer, the corporate books of account would be in there. From just outside her doorway, Altschuler told Shalott that he would like to remove the financial records from her office.

"Stay there," she said. "I'll bring the documents to you." She got up from her desk.

Altschuler was building an even greater dislike toward the diminutive chief financial officer than he'd had on the first visit—this woman, who was telling him what he could, and could not do.

"See," she said to him from inside her office. "I'm opening this drawer," she said. She lifted an armful of files from the credenza and moved to where Altschuler stood at the door to her office. She dropped the armful of documents at Altschuler's feet. The papers went everywhere as they hit the carpet. Apparently, his sentiments were reciprocated.

The 5'3" former chief financial officer of Morgan Fay headed back to her desk. She returned to the doorway with another 18 inches of manila folders. WHAM! The papers hit the carpeting and spread. She turned on her heels and headed toward her credenza, saying over her shoulder, "This is what you get for coming without an appointment." Outside her doorway, heads were turning.

Shalott was standing now at her credenza. "See," she said. "I'm opening another drawer. No one's going to accuse me of being dishonest." She pulled out another armful of documents. "See," she said. "I'm giving you all the records."

She marched to the door. "You can take these records and do whatever the hell you want with them. I never want to hear of Morgan Fay again." She dropped the pile of documents to the carpet.

WHAM!

The documents were piling higher even as they spread across the carpet. Altschuler couldn't think of how to respond. The embarrassment of being treated like this, with everybody in the office watching what was going on, was overwhelming.

"You're a guest in our office space," Shalott called back over her shoulder to Altschuler. She was behind her desk again. "You should conduct yourself like a gentleman."

She walked toward the door and WHAM! Another set of papers hit the floor.

Altschuler knew that the clock was ticking. He didn't have many options. Everybody else on his team had his or her own assignment. He'd chosen Shalott's office for himself.

He stood there immobile, watching Shalott, and thinking to himself, "You can take your records, Cindy, and just shove 'em." He held his tongue.

He looked to the box behind him on the ground and bent down to put the files in the box the best he could. The team could sort the documents out later.

Shalott came again to the doorway. WHAM!

The embarrassment registered on Altschuler's face and neck as he worked in a crouch in the doorway, chasing the papers that were mounding and sliding there. "Keep emptying it, Cindy," he found himself saying to himself. "There will be a judgment day. On another day."

He was boxing as fast as he could now, but it was impossible to make boxes as quickly as she was emptying the drawers.

The papers continued to hit. And spread.

Finally, Shalott exited her office by stepping over the mounded pile of papers. "There. You got your documents," she said. "Good luck dealing with them," she added as she walked off, leaving Altschuler to wonder what she meant by that comment.

*   *   *

The forensics and investigative services team had been there about an hour by now. Altschuler had finished with the mess of documents outside Cindy Shalott's office. He surveyed the work that was going on around him. People were assembling banker's boxes, stuffing the three-ring binders into them, then filling out brief inventory sheets that identified the contents of the box. The inventory sheets were placed on top of the documents that went into the boxes before they were sealed. They had almost a hundred boxes filled already.

Shelly Connor had arrived 15 minutes earlier, bringing another 50 to 75 boxes with her. As Altschuler observed the work going on around him, a light began to go on, dimly at first—they were going to run out of boxes.

*   *   *

Robin Malory stood there observing the loading of the documents into the empty banker's boxes. He turned to Altschuler. "You people are being too disruptive to our operations," Malory said.

Altschuler straightened. "We'll get done and out of here and out of your way."

"I want you out now," Malory said. Cindy Shalott had come up and was now standing next to Malory.

"The less time we spend arguing," Altschuler responded softly, "the faster we'll be out of here."

"You're disrupting our business," Shalott said.

Altschuler shook his head slowly. She was chipping in like some yammering poodle.

"We want you out of here," Malory repeated.

Bergman stopped working.

"What we're doing is authorized by the board of directors," Altschuler responded.

"I want you people to leave," Malory said. "I want you all out of here. I don't want you on the premises any longer."

The word *premises* rattled around in Altschuler's mind as he stood there facing Malory. Altschuler knew that the leaseholder of the space was Avalon Partners, and not Morgan Fay. Avalon Partners was a separate and distinct management company, which had been formed by Robin Malory.

As a result, Malory and his management cronies were technically the masters here. They were the masters of these premises, this space specifically. The board of directors of Morgan Fay technically had no right to direct any operation within this space.

It was a technical point, really. Malory's management company, Avalon Partners, was charging Morgan Fay for management services. Altschuler knew, however, that if Malory wanted to push the technicality, he could have Altschuler and his whole team removed from the premises. Forcefully, if required.

"You move into the hallway." Cindy Shalott said. "We'll bring the documents to you there."

Emmett Bergman straightened. Altschuler had no desire to further provoke the controversy. It seemed like forever to Bergman before Altschuler came up with his response. "Fine," Altschuler finally said.

This new impediment cooked up by Malory and Shalott was brilliant. And to the forensics and investigative services staff, it would soon become surreal; for Cindy Shalott and Robin Malory were far from finished with Lee Altschuler for the day.

CHAPTER SIX

"You're Nothing but a Goon in a Suit"

Lee Altschuler's team now found themselves working in the elevator foyer just outside the door to Avalon Partners. Oil paintings graced one of the walls. On the other side of the elevator lobby were the entrances to the restrooms. Three Oriental carpets were laid side by side on the floor, covering most of the wood parquet floor of the elevator lobby. The whole setup reminded Altschuler of an elegant private club. The recessed lights in the lobby illuminated the approximately 120 boxes stacked against the far wall. Nobody talked as they worked.

Eight forensics and investigative services staff were involved in the document collection effort. The elevator bank lobby in which they were filling their boxes had three elevator doors, which opened on the long wall opposite the glass entranceway to Morgan Fay's corporate headquarters.

Each person on the team would build a box; take six to seven binders of documents, or an equivalent amount of paper, perhaps up to a couple thousand documents, they'd stuff all of this in a box, close up the box, and stack it with the others.

Robin Malory loomed large in the doorway again. Each encounter with Malory had been unpleasant. The hulking man would raise his voice and remonstrate with his arms as he railed about how the small team was going about what they were doing. Ever since Altschuler had arrived,

Malory had been barraging Altschuler with questions about his instructions. Malory expressed his anger with the team's every move.

Upon each exchange with Malory, Altschuler found himself responding to the deposed chairman in an ever quieter and smaller voice. Robin Malory's eyes fixed on Altschuler. "You're nothing but a goon in a suit," Malory said.

Everyone working in the lobby heard the insult. One or two paused for a moment in their work; others continued to work vigorously, unsure how to react. Long after the words themselves died away, what Malory had said would pound away at Lee Altschuler's memory.

Altschuler swallowed. "I'm just doing my job," he said quietly. "We can try and do this like gentlemen. And we'll be out of here."

"You'll be out of here by 5:00," Malory said. "We're closing our offices at five."

Cindy Shalott arrived at the elevator lobby entrance. She had an armful of documents in hand and she dropped them unceremoniously on the elevator lobby floor.

Altschuler, Bergman, and the other staff stopped what they were doing and watched as Shalott turned on her heels and headed back into the office area. Shortly after that, a series of people carrying files began arriving from inside the Avalon Partners' office space. Each stopped in the lobby entranceway and unloaded whatever documents they were carrying; there is a bit of controversy surrounding the unloading.

According to Altschuler, the Avalon employees weren't heaving the documents to the floor in anger. Nor, according to him, were they deliberately turning the hanging file-folders upside down to create further chaos. Altschuler believes the Avalon people had been instructed to simply drop the Morgan Fay documents at the entrance to the elevator lobby. Altschuler said that as the hanging file folders were dropped to the lobby floor, the papers and documents inside the folders slid out as the mountain of documents grew.

Emmett Bergman recalls things very differently. "The notebooks were flying into the elevator lobby," he told me during our interview.

My eyes went a little wide at this. "Through the air?" I asked.

He nodded.

I thought this assertion deserved a little clarification. "Like how far were they flying through the air?" I asked.

Emmett glanced around the small conference room in which we were sitting. "The length of this room," he responded.

"The length of this room?" I asked, a little incredulous.

Emmett nodded.

I asked him to reevaluate his response one more time. I asked him to take into account the dimensions of the room in which we were sitting. I pointed to the doorway. "It's 10 feet from the door there to the wall," I said to Emmett.

"Then it was 15 feet," Emmett said, matter of factly.

My eyebrows were arched in amazement. "They were tossing the documents and the notebooks 15 feet?" I asked.

Emmett nodded.

"From inside the reception area, into the lobby?"

Emmett nodded again.

Robin Malory took a step inside the dimly lit lobby. "You people have been rude and inconsiderate."

Altschuler and his team couldn't box up the documents as fast as they were being delivered. The pile of documents on the parquet floor of the lobby area began to mound.

Cindy Shalott stood with her arms folded just inside the open doorway of the Morgan Fay reception area. As the pile of documents got taller, the papers slid on the slick floor, until they were stopped by the edge of the oriental carpet.

"At five o'clock you have to leave," Shalott reiterated.

Bergman and Altschuler both straightened.

Robin Malory had now come up and was standing behind his chief financial officer.

"Our staff will not be remaining to help you with your document extraction," Malory said.

Altschuler bent down to resume boxing documents, trying to set an example for the rest of his staff. Emmett Bergman glanced at his watch; it was 20 minutes until 5. "Just box," Altschuler said quietly.

*   *   *

Altschuler headed down to the lobby with the hand truck in tow. Shelly Connor's cab pulled up in front of 555 California Street, and Altschuler wheeled the hand truck outside to the sidewalk. The late afternoon light was beginning to fade. He loaded the flats on the hand truck. "We need more," he said to her.

He considered whether there was enough time for her to take the cab back the 10 blocks to 50 Fremont Street, go upstairs, get more boxes, call another cab, and get back in enough time so that the team could load more Morgan Fay documents.

Altschuler turned to the cab driver. "Here's 50 bucks. Whatever this lady asks you to do, please do."

*   *   *

When Altschuler returned upstairs with the box flats, Robin Malory was standing there.

"The doors are going to be closing," the deposed chairman of Morgan Fay said.

Altschuler halted and tipped the hand truck, so that its load rested on the floor. "You can't do that. We insist on having these records."

"These records don't belong to you," Malory responded. "If we have to call the police, we'll call the police."

Altschuler felt helplessly boxed in.

Technically speaking, the management company Robin Malory had established, Avalon Partners, was the lessee of this space, not Morgan Fay itself. Malory would technically be within his rights to have Altschuler and his team ejected from the office space. And if Malory decided to play this card, there would be absolutely nothing that Altschuler could do about it.

*   *   *

Shelly Connor's taxi stopped in front of 50 Fremont Street. It had taken a full 15 minutes to cover the 10 blocks and cross Market Street because of rush hour traffic. When the cab finally pulled up in front of 50 Fremont Street, Shelly asked the cabby to wait. The fire drill was set to begin.

Shelly had called ahead and arranged for some of the other forensics and investigative services staff back at the office to scrounge up more boxes. Since the people in central records were unable to get their hands on more boxes, the forensics staff ran around the office, begging individuals to part with their secret stashes of stockpiled boxes.

As Shelly entered 50 Fremont, people were bringing flats to the lobby.

Some carried only 10 flats or so, some more. They were coming down into the lobby from all three elevator banks. Two of the more enterprising staff came into the lobby from outside the building; one enterprising staffer had hustled over to the law firm located in the building next door at 425 Market Street to borrow boxes, and another was able to hustle some boxes from the copy service on the corner.

Shelly Connor threw the shrink-wrapped packages of box flats in the trunk of the cab. What she couldn't get into the trunk, she threw into the back seat. She got in the front and told the cabbie to haul it back to California Street.

*   *   *

"We're going to have to close the offices," Robin Malory announced. "What you have now," he added, "you may take. But we're not going to keep our offices open later than this."

Shelly Connor looked dumbfounded on hearing this. She had just arrived with the additional box flats. Bergman had come down to meet her in the front lobby. He'd brought the hand truck down to help her. She looked at Altschuler. He shrugged. She began pitching in immediately by setting up the box flats she had hauled.

Altschuler went back to work. He was concerned that if they didn't get the documents that very afternoon Cindy Shalott and her staff would be shredding documents all through the weekend. Altschuler thought that if he were forced to leave without all of the Morgan Fay records, his mission would be a failure. He regarded what he and his team had already accomplished. They now had 180 boxes.

He considered the remaining pile of documents mounded in a heap in the elevator lobby. "There can't possibly be that much more inside," he thought. They had to have the lion's share of the documents in hand.

*   *   *

Tony Rosen put away what he was working on. It was Friday afternoon and Mike Murphy had just swung by. Murphy had wanted Tony to get the 10-Qs and 10-Ks for a company called Morgan Fay. Tony had done this numerous times for Murphy. And usually Murphy's request for something like this would come in late on a Friday afternoon; meaning they'd be working again this weekend. Murphy had a hard time distinguishing between a weekday and a weekend day. Tony believed it to be some kind of congenital thing.

A company's "Q," its quarterly SEC filing, was always the first thing Murphy asked for when he wanted to research what was going on with a company. He'd ask for the 10-K, a company's annual SEC filing, most times too, but sometimes the 10-K would be less helpful because it wouldn't be recent enough to disclose the company-specific financial information Murphy was usually looking for. "Get any articles on them, too," Murphy had said.

Tony Rosen used online databases for these research projects. He did these for the managers and partners all the time. For the news articles, he'd do a Lexis/Nexis search on the company. Murphy hadn't said what was going on. He never did. Tony did the news articles search first, to satisfy his own curiosity. He found a bunch of articles talking about the company. But nothing recent, so he still couldn't figure out what was up.

Tony logged on to the SEC's Web site; he got Morgan Fay's most recent SEC filings off of the SEC's electronic filing database. "EDGAR," the SEC called it. Who knew why? It was a stupid name as far as Tony was concerned. After that, Tony reviewed Bloomberg to see what else he could find. That pretty much blew the rest of his Friday night plans.

Murphy would need this stuff in a hurry. He always did. So you dropped whatever you were doing, or you risked getting your ass chewed out when Murphy returned and saw you were working on someone else's project.

Murphy had instructed Tony to print out and spiral-bind two copies of whatever he dug up.

"Why two sets?" Tony had asked.

Murphy responded that he would be providing one set for the Caxton & Williams attorneys who were flying in from New York to meet with him on Saturday.

But that was last Friday, and here it was late on a Friday afternoon again and Rosen's phone had just rung.

"How would you like to jump on a plane right now?" Altschuler's voice came from the other end of the line.

The question caught Tony Rosen off guard. It was three o'clock on a Friday afternoon and he was getting ready to wind down and go home to start the weekend. "To where?" Tony asked.

"Minneapolis," came Altschuler's voice. He then went on to say that he couldn't really fill Tony in on everything, but that Tony was to "Drop everything."

It was Friday afternoon. Nobody was telling him what was going on, but he was to drop everything, of course. And this time, he was to book the next flight out.

"If you don't have time to go home," came Altschuler's voice, "just get on the plane. You can buy clothes there." Altschuler added that Murphy was already in Minneapolis. Murphy would provide Tony with the details when he got there.

Tony hung up. "Whoa," he said to himself. Pretty amazing. His first "out-of-town" assignment. And he needed to get going right away.

He got on the phone with the travel people. The next flight connecting with Minneapolis left in 45 minutes. He'd never make that. He'd have to take the red-eye. At least that way he could go home and pack.

The phone rang. Why did it always ring like this on Friday afternoons?

It was Altschuler again, calling from Avalon Partners, or something like that. Downtown somewhere, in the Financial District. On California Street. "We need you over here," came Altschuler's voice. "And bring boxes. We don't have any boxes."

Tony's mind raced. "I have to go home and pack," he said.

When Altschuler found out that Tony was taking was the red-eye, he said, "Come over here first. And bring boxes. We don't have any boxes. You'll have plenty of time to go home and pack. Just bring as many boxes as you can carry."

Tony Rosen hung up the telephone. He had to go to central records for boxes and he had no idea where that was.

*   *   *

The light outside was beginning to fade and the streets were still rain-slicked. Tony Rosen had about 20 box flats in his arms. The boxes weren't very carrier friendly and they were heavy. He'd tried to get a cab but it was Friday afternoon, and everyone who lived in the city was going home. It would only be a 15-minute walk to Avalon Partners. Tony shifted the box flats around in his arms. They were really unwieldy. Actually, they were a pain. And everyone else on the sidewalk was heading home from work for the weekend.

"And here I am in the Financial District," Rosen said to himself. "Carrying these boxes. Going to this place I have no idea where. And I have to get on a plane in like five hours."

*   *   *

The elevator door opened onto the lobby and Tony Rosen stepped out. He stood there transfixed with the scene in front of him. The elevator lobby in front of the Avalon offices was a complete mess. There were maybe eight or nine forensics and investigative staffers there. Shelly Connor was sitting on the floor loading documents into a box, as were Emmett Bergman and Lee Altschuler.

The glass entry doors to the Avalon offices at the far end of the lobby were closed, and the dim lighting in the lobby area made the whole scene a little surreal. Tony Rosen looked around in confusion at the other forensic and investigative staffers sitting on the floor loading boxes—Jennifer Benicke, Lisa Liao. There were papers and notebooks strewn all over.

To Tony's eyes, the material spread around the lobby floor did not look like it had been placed there neatly. The forensics people were working feverishly to box up the mess of three-ring binders and the other loose materials. There were green binders lying on top of red-rope envelopes, tossed in little piles on the oriental carpets covering the wood floor. Tony scanned the multihued piles. Manila file folders lay strewn everywhere.

Interspersed with the file folders were a variety of other notebooks; some were blue, a bunch of red notebooks could be seen in one corner, and white notebooks were interposed throughout the pile.

Tony set down the box flats he had brought. He helped set some of them up, though no one had asked or bothered to explain what was going on. It was almost six o'clock on a Friday evening and it was obvious that everybody was working under some kind of time constraint. Even though they didn't really have time to stop and tell him the story, he asked; nobody had any real good explanation. It didn't matter. Tony was focused on one thing now—getting home to pack so that he could make his red-eye.

*   *   *

The guard station had a bank of closed-circuit TV monitors, including one focused on the loading dock area. The loading dock gate was locked and the mover's panel truck and half-ton pickup truck were in the camera's view at the loading dock. Emmett Bergman moved into the camera's view, standing in front of the 200 or so boxes of documents. The movers were there, too, waiting impatiently.

Lee Altschuler's patience had run out. It was now nine o'clock at night. He was standing in the lobby of this downtown San Francisco building and he was at an impasse with a very nice, elderly security guard. The guard would not allow the team to remove the documents from the building.

The guard pulled a memo from a notebook. "I'm not supposed to show this to anyone," the guard said.

Altschuler examined the document. It was a one-page typewritten memo on Morgan Fay letterhead. Altschuler could see that the memo had been signed by Cindy Shalott in blue ink and was addressed to the building manager. He realized that Shalott had written the memo that very afternoon. The memo read, "Be sure that no one leaves our space with property without a property pass."

"I don't fucking believe it," Altschuler said to the security guard.

Altschuler reflected on the position in which he found himself. He was a former assistant U.S. attorney, and a respected leader in the forensics practice of a leading professional services firm. And here he was arguing with a security guard at nine o'clock at night. Not for the first time this day, he found himself wishing for the good old days when the FBI would execute his search warrants. If someone had tried to pull a tenth of what these people were attempting to pull, they'd be wearing handcuffs.

"I'd like a copy of this," Altschuler said.

"I can't do that," the security guard replied.

*   *   *

Altschuler was standing in a small office with the building manager. "We are representatives of Morgan Fay," Altschuler said. "These are Morgan Fay records. You can examine them if you like."

The building manager wasn't buying any of Altschuler's story. Besides, Altschuler couldn't furnish authorization from anyone, at either Morgan Fay or Avalon Partners. The only thing he could show the building manager was his Deloitte identification, and that didn't get him anywhere with the man.

Altschuler talked his way into possession of a desk, telephone, and a set of Yellow Pages. He had already been able to reach Mike Murphy, who was in Philadelphia with the Caxton & Williams attorneys. "Here's Cindy's home phone number," Murphy had said. "And her cell phone number," he added. He provided Altschuler with the telephone number for Shalott's mother. "You call Cindy, and tell her this is bullshit!" Murphy said. "And if you can't get a hold of her, hire a private security firm."

"To do what?" Altschuler asked.

"To guard the records over the weekend," Murphy responded.

"Where?" Altschuler asked.

"At the loading dock," Murphy said. "Where else?"

Altschuler paged through the thumbed over San Francisco Yellow Pages, looking for rent-a-cops, or private security guard firms. He wondered whether it was even possible to find someone at 10 o'clock on a Friday night who could send someone immediately to run 24-hour shifts. Altschuler dialed and got through to one of the firms.

The man on the other end of the line sounded like he'd been a cigarette smoker since the age of five. "Where are you calling from?" the man asked.

"A loading dock in the financial district," Altschuler said into the receiver.

"And you want us for how long?" came the gravelly voice.

"From tonight through Sunday night."

"What's in the boxes?" the dispatcher asked.

"Documents," Altschuler replied. "Financial documents."

"Like stocks? Or bonds?"

"Just financial documents. No stocks. No bonds."

"I don't know," came the voice. "I have a guy down in San Mateo. And he may be getting off work in a few hours."

*   *   *

Altschuler's cellphone rang. Mike Murphy was on the other end. "Have you called that number?" came Murphy's voice.

"I've called them all," Altschuler responded. "Her mother doesn't know where she is." In addition to placing those calls, he'd been on the phone pretty much nonstop for the better part of the last hour, trying to locate a security firm to watch over the documents over the weekend.

"Have you left her a voicemail?" Murphy asked.

"I've left them at the office, on her cellphone, and at home."

"Keep calling," Murphy said.

It seemed to Altschuler now that Murphy was calling him every five minutes. Altschuler reflected on his situation; he was sitting at a little desk in the building manager's office, calling rent-a-cops at 10 o'clock on a Friday night; leaving messages all over town for Shalott, and with each call, thinking to himself that her voicemail boxes were going to fill up any minute. He was certain that Shalott was sitting at home with a glass of Chardonnay, listening to his messages as they came in. Not answering the phone and laughing her ass off.

The movers began making noises that they were going to have to charge double-time rates because they'd been told they would be done by now. Bergman went out to get them something to eat, while in the upstairs lobby, staffers were still loading boxes.

*   *   *

They had loaded well over 200 boxes by now. Connor, combination executive assistant and body builder, stayed and pitched in to load boxes. She was very strong and didn't shy away from hefting and stacking them so that they could be taken downstairs to the loading dock.

*   *   *

Murphy reached for the telephone in his hotel room. It was a little after 2 A.M. where he was. It had been a long day, and a long week. It was 11 o'clock back in San Francisco. Shalott would have to be home by now.

He dialed Shalott at home. Her phone just rang away, and as it rang, his mind wandered.

In crisis situations like this, the plan typically was to move as quickly as possible to stabilize the company. Figure out the extent of the fraud. Work with Morgan Fay's outside auditors to get them the information they needed to determine whatever adjustment to Morgan Fay's financial statements was required. It already looked like the adjustment would be well over four hundred million dollars.

In cases where the company immediately informs the SEC of the nature of the problem and that an investigation is underway, the SEC is often very understanding and supportive. They will typically want to know the scope of the investigation and especially whether the investigators planned to trap all of the e-mails. In these situations also, the SEC would want follow-up meetings in order to receive periodic updates of the progress of the investigation. Then, the lenders would need to be informed, and after that, the prosecutors in the Justice Department.

It would be a fine dance. The important thing is to keep people informed as to what is going on. The representatives of the lenders need this information because they, in turn, have credit committees and bank management who want to know what is happening. The company might be in danger of being in default of its debt covenants, promises to maintain certain financial ratios at safe and comfortable preapproved levels. The company's cooking of the books might be covering up the fact that there was no safety margin.

In situations like this, the lenders need to believe that the company's board of directors is responding in an appropriate manner. And if the lenders believe that the company's responses are rational, the company's loans might not be called due and in default. In crises like this one, that would always be an immediate concern, because if the banks called the loans, the company's only recourse oftentimes would be to file for bankruptcy protection, which is exactly what happened at Enron.

In a crisis situation like this, it was always important to maintain good relations with the SEC if the company wished to remain publicly traded in the future. And the U.S. Attorney's office would also need to remain abreast of things, for if the Justice Department believed that a corporation was acting as a responsible corporate citizen, the company might be able to remain in charge of its own fate. On the other hand, if the Justice Department believed that the company was involved in a cover-up, or was continuing with its corporate wrongdoing, then an indictment would soon follow. This in turn would force the banks to declare a default and call the loans. The company's only remaining option then would again be filing for protection in the bankruptcy court.

   Providing information to all of these important players was always the key to the survival of the corporation. Then the company could typically move on, with new management in place.

   The phone stopped ringing.

   Shalott's answering machine kicked in. "Cindy, we've been trying to reach you all night. This is Mike Murphy at—"

   Cindy Shalott picked up.

   Murphy's conversation with her was very short and to the point. "I want to know why the hell I can't have my boxes," he said. Shalott responded with more of her arguing, but Murphy was having none of it. She finally agreed to call the building manager to arrange for the boxes to be released.

CHAPTER SEVEN

"Oh, and by the Way"

"Initially it was the trade promotions that sort of kicked things off," said Jaco Sadie, a forensic accountant employed by Deloitte & Touche. He and I sat in a small conference room reviewing his role in the Morgan Fay investigation.

The notion of trade promotions has to do with those weekly specials you see in the newspaper in which your local grocer promotes a particular brand to stimulate sales. The manufacturer of the product often shares in the responsibility for these promotion costs and reimburses the grocer for the costs of these ads after the fact.

Sounds simple enough.

Morgan Fay, though, manipulated its financial statements through its accounting for trade promotions. The opportunity for fraud had resulted from the timing of events. Even though product sales resulting from an advertising campaign would be recognized in fiscal year 2000, Robin Malory and Cindy Shalott did everything in their power to see that the related advertising costs were pushed off into the next fiscal year. Having revenues appear in one period and the related expenses in the next would pump up the current year's profits, at least on paper. With the company showing such robust and inflated profits, its stock price would rise.

Robin Malory's plan was to bail out of the stock before the company's true costs of operations had time to come home to roost. The auditors at PricewaterhouseCoopers (PwC), however, became suspicious of what they were being told. Management's trade promotion shenanigans served as a trip wire, initiating an independent investigation by Morgan Fay's board of directors. The board hired special independent counsel at Caxton & Williams to advise them and coordinate the investigation.

As the investigation went along, Sadie and other forensic accountants identified other warning flags. Deleted e-mails and employee interviews led the investigators to burrow deeper into the many rat holes. The forensics team assembled for the investigation was deployed simultaneously in three different cities, San Francisco, Minneapolis, and Omaha. Individuals on the teams all had discrete tasks and specialties.

The team leaders met up periodically to compare notes. Based on information obtained from the meeting, new discrete keyword searches of the e-mails and other documents were initiated. Using a *sniffer* program, the forensic analysts searched for everything they could find on a particular subject of interest; they'd print the relevant e-mails or spreadsheets, then organize the findings by issue.

Kris Haworth would use one of several forensic software sniffers she had to undertake the electronic keyword search of the imaged hard drives. More often than not, she would use the sniffer utility provided in the EnCase forensic software.

Performing keyword searches on computer hard drives may sound banal, but it is actually an art form. Kevin Mandia and Chris Prosise, specialists from Foundstone, Inc., an Internet security firm, tell of one investigation in which employees of a corporation were suspected of skimming cash. Using search criteria provided by their client, Mandia and Prosise performed a keyword search of the suspects' laptops. The client-provided search criteria yielded over 14,000 hits every time the string search was run, far too many leads to investigate.

In a corporate securities fraud investigation, enormous amounts of data often need to be searched. The keyword searches in these investigations have to be specific or else the forensics analyst will face disaster—a 25-year project length, for example. Narrowing the search criteria is key, but over-narrowed or poorly conceived searches result in missed evidence. To get things right, specific search criteria are often developed from, and defined by: field interviews, recovered e-mails, and other recovered documents.

So the process possesses a certain amount of circularity. Recovered e-mails lead the investigators to conduct specific interviews; the interviews yield more information and specific insights, on which another round of keyword searches of hard drives can be performed. The art comes from an investigator's ability to identify the important terms on which to perform the keyword searches.

Thousands upon thousands of documents were recovered through Haworth's computer forensic recovery efforts. Alex Jarvis was one of the forensic staff tasked with undertaking the keyword searches. Alex's involvement with the Morgan Fay investigation began his first day after transferring into the forensics practice.

Kris Haworth brought him documents by the bucketful. Each and every document needed to be analyzed for content, context, and relevance to the investigation. Imagine a couple of wheelbarrows emptied out at your feet, and you'll be in the same state of grace in which Alex had found himself. Add to this the following penance: Stephen Hibbard, who heads the corporate securities fraud litigation practice at the Bingham McCutchen law firm, says that he has to read all of the documents in a case *twice* before they truly begin to make sense to him. The documents have to be read in context of the other events that had transpired in the case, as well as in relation to the other e-mails or documents recovered.

The entire process then is an iterative one and is what accounts for the high cost of litigation; it is very labor-intensive work. The requirement to reassemble the pieces of the puzzle is the real cost driver. The use of computer forensics and other forensic technology provides for the recovery of more pieces of the puzzle, helping the investigators to become more informed. In the end, however, there is always the need for a human brain to make sense of the whole. One of the exciting new developments in this field is the use of forensic technology in the analysis of information collected.

Computers simulating a neural network can analyze millions of documents and perform a *link analysis* of seemingly disparate pieces of information buried among millions of documents. This type of analysis represents the fascinating promise of the application of forensic technology, in which fabulous amounts of data can be distilled to only that which is relevant. Imagine patterns hidden among millions of documents being linked together and distilled into only those worthy of investigation.

*   *   *

The Morgan Fay investigation provides a good snapshot of how a bunch of self-serving corporate executives cooked the books, and how a dogged team ferreted out each and every element of the fraud.

There were maybe a couple of hundred thousand documents that related to Morgan Fay's securities fraud investigation, most of which had been unearthed by Kris Haworth for Alex Jarvis and other analysts to study.

The wheelbarrow loads of documents Haworth had dumped in Alex Jarvis's cubicle included e-mails, Excel files, and Word documents. These were the documents and fragments of documents discovered on the hard drives of the computers of corporate executives and employees.

First, Kris Haworth printed all of the e-mails that had been deleted by the Avalon executives when they had learned of the investigation. With this in hand, the forensics team began their investigation with the precise information the executives had tried to "delete." The forensics team developed a time line, a chronology of events. To the forensics people, it was interesting to see the time line of events as they unfolded. "You could see when they were deleted," Alex Jarvis said. "And sometimes they were deleted more than once."

I hadn't known that something could be deleted more than once. Upon reflection, I came to realize that what Alex had seen was that once a document is created, and shared with another person, the document itself enjoys a life of its own, and ends up residing in many different places. Who has seen the document, and when, can often be reconstructed from this information. The implication of what Alex Jarvis was describing was that there must have been a frenzy of activity at Morgan Fay. This would not be the first time that I would be reminded of the Enron meltdown. The image I had in my mind was that of a frenzied group of people, shredding documents and deleting e-mails, attempting to destroy evidence, and in their haste to obfuscate, completely unaware that their very efforts to obstruct would do them in.

Alex and the rest of the forensics team viewed the deleted Morgan Fay documents. This review occurred within days of the investigation's inception; in fact, it was the day after the Avalon Partners' computer hard drives had been forensically imaged. "There were hundreds and hundreds of documents that had been deleted," Alex said.

Mike Murphy had the forensics team construct a time line of deletions, beginning with the exact time the board of directors had initiated the investigation and ending when the employees implicated in the fraud had been fired.

*   *   *

After recovering the deleted documents, the forensics team needed to determine the nature of all of the other files residing on the imaged hard drives. A complete index was prepared so that Murphy and the other investigators could sort out what they wanted printed for review. The index included thousands upon thousands of e-mails, Excel documents, and Word documents, including those stored as well as those that had been deleted and recovered.

Alex and the other forensics specialists performed a keyword search of the electronic files. They started with the contents of a specific employee's imaged hard drive and used the software sniffer tool. If they were interested in the appropriateness of the year-end cut-off of revenues and expenses, they might search on the word, "cut-off." Often, the forensics keyword search would come back with thousands of hits. In the case of Morgan Fay, there were thousands of documents that had the word cut-off in it.

Alex described the effort to refine the keyword searches. "We would go through, and sometimes if it was too large of a hit, we would try to narrow it down. So, we would use cut-off together with restatement, or cut-off with another word."

Alex's process might seem intuitive to anyone who has done keyword searches online and has had to narrow their search. In the field of forensic investigations, however, the process is actually quite complex. Consider FBI Director Mueller's recent admission that the FBI's current technology would not allow agents to perform a keyword search on more than one word. They could, for example, search *flight*, or *school*, but not *flight school*. This simple example shows the complexity of such investigations, or suggests that the sophistication of technology is increasing more rapidly than a large bureaucracy can keep up with.

"We would narrow it (the keyword search) down a little bit," Alex Jarvis continued. "We'd read the documents. If it was an e-mail, we'd click on all the attachments. We'd try to get a feel for what period of time the documents related to. And if we saw a document that needed further review, we'd bring it to the attention of a manager or partner."

Though the investigation was performed using software sniffers for the searches, the forensics team printed key documents for indexing, document control, and dissemination of knowledge to others on the team. As Jarvis described it, "We printed volumes and volumes of documents, kept them in binders, and kept records of what we had looked at."

Through interviews of employees at the company's locations in Omaha and in Minneapolis, the forensic accountants determined some of the key issues. These interviews, conducted almost two thousand miles away, gave direction to the San Francisco-based investigative team's search.

"We would hear back from those employees," Alex Jarvis said, "and find out what some of the key issues were that we should be looking at on the hard drives. Those were some of the words that we determined to use in our keyword searches."

The forensics team would identify the need to do a keyword search on a specific issue; *Morro Bay*, for example. Later, the team might discover something related as a result of a subsequent investigative interview. With new information emerging, the team would re-institute a search of all of the documents, using new keywords gleaned from the latest interviews.

"And as the investigation was going on," Jaco Sadie recalled during one of our interviews, "we were finding more and more things. And then people are like, 'Oh, and by the way, we also—we cooked the books here.' And that was something to do with some specific name they'd given to some issue. Okay, there's another keyword."

The forensic accountants slowly unearthed the Rosetta stone of the Morgan Fay fraud. Discovering specific nomenclatures Morgan Fay employees used when referring to issues under investigation, the investigative team used the software sniffer to discover a new crop of interesting e-mails. Haworth continued to dump more documents on Jarvis's desk for him to plow through and assemble the abundant methods and forms of the fraud, as well as responsible employees.

I asked Alex Jarvis to describe what they saw when they recovered a deleted e-mail.

"They came in a different format," he responded. "You couldn't just read it like a normal e-mail. A lot of it looked odd," he said. "I would equate it with seeing something that looked like it was encrypted. You would see some words. And then some words would be crossed out. Some documents you would see more words that you could actually read. And then there were some documents that you couldn't even read at all (meaning unintelligible). It just looked like a bunch of jumbled information."

What Alex saw was some e-mail text fragment, or a Word document file fragment, that had been deleted but subsequently recovered by Kris Haworth, and that had been partially overwritten with other text. The overwriting was the result of continuing document processing on the part of the user. If the file fragment Alex Jarvis was trying to make sense of had been created in the distant past, there would be a much greater likelihood that the cluster in which the file fragment resided (as *free space*) would have been partially overwritten. That was why some of the deleted documents could be read in entirety by Alex and the other forensic investigators, but others might be almost incomprehensible.

Even file fragments that are mostly unintelligible gibberish can be valuable to investigators, however. Alex recalled several examples, "And so for some of those, we could retrieve enough information from it. You could see the date. You could see who it went to. And then you could see phrases of information that we could use to determine what that document was about."

Many of the documents retrieved were password-protected. "One thing I found pretty interesting," Alex recalled, "and I didn't know this before I started with the group, is how to crack a password."

When Alex encountered a password-protected document, he'd walk down to Kris Haworth's office. She would drop everything and go right to work trying to break into the password-protected file. She enjoyed this kind of a challenge, to see how fast she could crack the password.

"Sometimes I didn't make it back to my desk," Alex said. "She'd usually just call me back up, and say, 'Got it.' She'd tell me the password, and then I'd type it in and go into the file."

After initially imaging the hard drives, Haworth scans the imaged drives for password-protected files. She does this immediately after recovering any file that had been deleted; either method could have been used to try to hide something from prying eyes.

Once Alex Jarvis identified all the Excel spreadsheets he wished to view, if the files were password-protected, Kris Haworth would load the specific Excel files into a designated area on one of the servers in the lab, and would then run a *password cracker* against them. The password cracker is a software application that uses what is sometimes referred to as *fuzzy logic* to uncover passwords. Access Data Password Recovery is one of the premier password cracker applications to which Haworth will often first turn. This type of tool utilizes a data dictionary possessing a limited element of fuzzy logic. An example of how this software tool might work is if the software sees that A-M-E comprises the first three characters of a password, the fuzzy logic-based software tool will immediately try A-M-E-R-I-C-A. The software is not attempting a brute-force attack, in which every conceivable combination of characters is attempted; it will instead use logic to try to narrow down the possibilities; it will keep trying passwords until it gets the correct one. It will try all first and last names. Then it might try names of sports teams. Then, character names out of *The Lord of the Rings* trilogy, for example, or *Star Wars*. The password cracker may then try interspersing numbers and different capitalization schemes, then punctuation, or even terms from foreign languages. At a million password attempts per second, anything is fair game. According to Haworth, the vendor of this software application has a similar tool that cracks network passwords, "which they won't sell because they're worried about people getting into a network, and then just hacking into the server."

With most password-protected documents, a positive result can often be achieved quickly. Haworth often is able to go onto the Internet and download an *app* developed specifically for Word documents. These applications are downloadable for free, and very quickly will identify a password. For Haworth, the first thing then, is diagnosing which tool might most quickly crack the specific document she is attempting to get into.

After running a password cracker against the files, the passwords will start coming up on Haworth's screen. Once the password cracker application identifies a password, it will attempt that password against every other file in that space on the server's hard drive Haworth designated. "It speeds through very quickly," Haworth observed. "It'll say, 'okay, this password is the same for these other 10 files.'"

A forensics specialist may encounter password protection at many different levels. It may simply be a file that is password protected. In other cases, the forensics specialist may encounter password protected compressed files. Sometimes it is the computer itself that is password protected and, in other cases, the forensics specialist will simply face a network password.

On the Morgan Fay case, Haworth never encountered a file that couldn't be opened. Often though, she encountered what she referred to as "higher levels of security," requiring her to undertake alternative approaches. She may first "break" into the .pwl password list file. Once successfully in, she will search that file to locate passwords. However, the .pwl file may contain a significant amount of character data, and any passwords contained there may not be self-evident. Haworth will eyeball that for clues like "login," for example. The actual password may be stored in the space contiguous to that. "We've done searches just looking for things we think are likely to be the password," Haworth said.

There are other spaces on the hard drive, such as slack space or swap files, in which a simple record of recent system activity will reside. Passwords often will have been captured there, as well.

Haworth and her team will hunt through all of those areas hoping to find the passwords. According to Haworth, this method of searching for passwords is one of the more difficult approaches. This is because the investigator is trying various queries to locate passwords that may be configured differently for each application or file being attempted; such as Excel, Windows, AOL, or Lotus Notes. Peter Stephenson, in his text, *Investigating Computer-Related Crime,* likens this method of search to that used by hackers intent on identity theft, who search for passwords and other system IDs by using software sniffers.

The only difference is that the forensic investigators will instead be sniffing the hard disk using forensic software utilities. Stephenson, when undertaking this type of search for passwords, will first strip the file of what he refers to as "binary junk" captured there, using a forensic tool offered by NTI called FILTER_I. He then parses the file for probable English words, knowing that many people will simply use an actual word as their password. Stephenson then rids the file of binary characters. He then performs a visual scan for possible passwords; a tedious process.

Once Stephenson discovers a password, he then tries it everywhere possible. "It is amazing," he said, "how often people use the same passwords for everything. For example, finding a password that is used for a Windows screen saver could cause a PGP-encrypted file to yield immediately."

When investigating password-protected e-mail, another possibility presents itself. In this case, Haworth will simply reconfigure the imaged system and establish herself as the network administrator. As the new system network administrator, she will have the access right to re-establish all passwords in the system, to a password that she establishes.

For example, if the corporation utilizes a Lotus Notes e-mail system, the forensic team will 'build' a new Lotus Notes server. After this, they re-import the person's Lotus Notes e-mail into that server system. The underlying Lotus Notes application system provides for standard access control levels, and if you're the administrator of the system, as Haworth says, "You're the ruler of all."

Haworth explained the final step in this method. "So you go in and you just say, 'Okay, change this user's password,' which any system administrator can do in any environment."

Matt Larson, a computer forensics specialist based in Atlanta, recently encountered a laptop encrypted all the way down to the basic input output system (BIOS) level, which as Larson described, "is the firmware (the software code) installed on the computer's motherboard. The BIOS enables the computer to communicate with all the devices associated with the computer." In this specific case, Matt Larson was dealing with one of IBM's newer ThinkPad™ computers, where the hard drive is "married" to the laptop in question. On starting up this type of laptop, the computer and hard drive seek to recognize each other, so you couldn't just unscrew the laptop, remove the drive, and image it using a standard portable imaging unit.

Larson tried an alternative approach. He tried using the EnCase forensic imaging system to perform a forensic start-up of the suspect's computer. He then found himself staring at a screen prompting him for a password. He didn't have the password; without it, the computer wasn't going to allow him to boot up the laptop's hard drive. At this point, Larson knew the laptop had some form of BIOS-level password protection. None of the password-cracking tools that he had available to him would be of use in this situation. They required an operating system, and since Larson couldn't even get the laptop's operating system to boot-up, he was pretty much stymied now.

He tried calling IBM. After speaking with several software engineers there, he wasn't successful in eliciting a work-around. So he put out an alert to computer forensics specialists in the firm for which he works, asking whether anyone had encountered this situation before, and if so, what could be done to get around it? Another request was forwarded to listserv members from the law-enforcement community.

The answers came in. Sources from both communities recommended the same vendor, Nortek Computers, a Canadian firm that is an expert in hard drive "reverse-engineering and remanufacturing." Nortek was able to satisfy Larson that they could devise a work-around for the BIOS password prompt and could guarantee that their process would not corrupt the laptop's hard drive for chain-of-control purposes. With this, Larson mailed the suspect's laptop to Canada.

Depending on the type of computer, Nortek circumvents the BIOS-level password, by either "shorting jumpers," and/or by removing the battery powering the memory on the machine's motherboard. The Canadian vendor then encrypts the laptop with a new password. Once Larson got the computer back, he called up the Canadian company, obtained their password, and then was able to proceed with the imaging of the laptop's hard drive.

*   *   *

And there always remains the full brute-force attack. Tomas Castrejon had a brute-force attack on a password up and running in our lab in San Francisco at the time of my interview with Haworth. The password attack had been running for a couple of weeks straight at that time, the password attack simply kept crunching at the hard drive, hitting it again and again with almost endless combinations and permutations until it finds a password.

Castrejon had configured the test attack to best take advantage of the computing power assembled in our lab. He had arranged to have the numerous servers in the lab connected, one to the other; so that when server A and B and C were not in use, their otherwise unutilized computing power was harnessed to devote to the brute-force password attack. This type of attack is technically called a distributed brute-force attack. If there were a thousand machines available, the attack would be completed more quickly than if there were only 10 machines available. This is the method of last resort because it is the most machine-time consuming. If the investigation is part of a formal civil or criminal investigation, the individuals subject to the investigation may be required to hand over their passwords in response to being subpoenaed.

I asked Kris Haworth whether she had experience with those types of situations. "In my experience," she responded, "I've never had a situation where we didn't break it before they got the password back to us."

Getting into a document, file, or computer that has been *encrypted,* however, can be devastatingly difficult for the computer forensic specialist. I'll contrast the two techniques. If you simply slap a password on an Excel file, without encrypting it, that Excel file continues to exist on the hard drive in its original form; it is only your physical access to that file that is restricted by the password. Encryption, on the other hand, such as that afforded by DES, or PGP, will actually scramble the file so that it will look like gibberish unless first unencrypted.

With a password-protected file, when someone like Kris Haworth images the machine, she technically would not require a password to get into the file, because the file had been imaged. As Haworth explained, "You're reading it at this sort of DOS level. So you don't have that password sort of entryway you have to go through."

This made sense but didn't square with the situations Alex Jarvis had described to me, in which he encountered password-protected files.

"Why could he not see those files, after you had imaged the hard drive?" I asked.

"Alex was just going through electronic data we pulled," Haworth responded. "We could have stuck it on a forensics portable imaging unit and said 'Here,' but it was quicker to actually examine the files and say 'Here's your 10 passwords.'"

That made sense to me. He wasn't working with the forensics portable imaging units, driving the Encase forensics software. Alex was attempting to use the standard Excel application to view an Excel file that had been retrieved by Haworth.

"Also," Haworth continued, "things like Excel, when viewed outside of their native application, are hard to make any sense of."

"Got it," I said.

Contrast the foregoing with encryption. With encrypted data, the data itself gets scrambled. Encrypted data can only be unscrambled through the application of the pass phrase initially utilized to scramble it. The Lucifer encryption algorithm is an IBM product developed by Horst Feistel, a German émigré who arrived in the United States shortly before World War II.

Simon Singh, in his book, *The Code Book,* neatly describes the Lucifer encryption process as akin to kneading a long slab of dough that has a message written on it in chocolate syrup. The Lucifer encryption process would require cutting the dough into 64 equal pieces. Then 32 of those pieces, cut from the right side of the block, get all mushed together, and then is added to the remaining dough, and the conglomeration is then stretched to make a new block of dough. This process is then repeated. After 16 rounds of kneading, the dough is considered encrypted. Magically, if the person doing this encryption applied the correct passkey, the process can be reversed, and the original message, "I-Love-You," written on the dough in chocolate syrup can be seen again.

The number of possible keys is the critical factor in the strength of any encryption system. Before a universal encryption system could be settled on for use worldwide, the National Security Agency (NSA) stepped in and suggested that a 56-bit key become the standard length of any universally adopted DES encryption system. This would limit the number of possible solutions to the ciphered data to 100,000,000,000,000,000 (thus, referred to as 56 bits, as when this number is written in binary form it is described by 56 digits, or places). At the time of adoption of the Lucifer encryption system as a worldwide standard, in 1976, there was no computer system in the world capable of breaking such a 56-bit cipher, other than the NSA's computer systems, the most computing power assembled in one place anywhere in the world. Accordingly, in 1976, such a 56-bit system was adapted worldwide and was called Data Encryption Standards

(DES). Financial institutions worldwide to this day use DES in everyday commerce to encrypt data transmitted to other institutions.

PGP, which stands for *Pretty Good Privacy,* is another encryption tool that encrypts data with a cipher very similar to DES. The user then can transmit the encrypted data to the recipient, together with the key encrypted once more, but this time with another powerful RSA encryption algorithm.

If this all sounds complicated, it is. These encryption tools are essentially unbreakable without the application of fabulous amounts of computing power and time. That's why computer forensics specialists like Haworth can't break them.

However (there are too many howevers in this field), if a user has merely encrypted the file residing on a hard drive, there is a possibility that an *unencrypted* version of the file may also exist somewhere else on the hard drive. Ha!

I asked Kris Haworth to present an example of this and walk me through it.

"Maybe your perpetrator created a Word doc that says, 'I-did-it,'" she said. "However, in this case, your perpetrator encrypted the document (he scrambled it), then password protected it, and threw away the keys."

"So with all of that," I said (and knowing what I knew already about DES and PGP), "there is no way you are going to be able to get into that document."

"Right," Kris replied. "Because it is encrypted. But when the perpetrator opened that file later, or when he printed it, or when he saved it, the document will now have been saved in all these different places on the hard drive, and those will not be encrypted (i.e., scrambled)."

"And if that file is sitting," I summarized, "and is recoverable, in the file slack or somewhere else in the machine, you might find an image of it that's an unencrypted image."

"Correct," Kris said.

Ha!

*   *   *

Oh, yes. I almost forgot. There *is* one other way to break into encrypted files.

CHAPTER EIGHT

Mafiosi Have Rights, Too, Don't'cha Know?

On May 10, 1999, agents of the Federal Bureau of Investigation (FBI) surreptitiously entered the offices of a storefront business operated by "Little Nicky" Scarfo Jr., a Gambino family mobster. Andrew Knapik, another Gambino family soldier, had previously operated the storefront sports-book and loan-shark operation until his incarceration the previous February.

Knapik had run the operation on behalf of former Gambino family acting capo, Nicholas Mitarotonda, while Mitarotonda served out his own prison sentence. John Gotti, the so-called "Teflon Don," headed the Gambino family ever since the 1985 assassination of Paul Castellano in front of Sparks Steakhouse in Manhattan; Gotti, also in prison since 1992, continued to direct the Gambino family interests from prison through his son, John Gotti Jr.

Confidential FBI informants confirmed that "Nicky" Scarfo Jr. had approval from the Gambino family leadership in New York to assume management of the Northern New Jersey sports-betting and shylock operation. "Little Nicky" Scarfo's father had been the leader of mob operations in the Philadelphia area, and a principal player in operations in Atlantic City. The elder Scarfo was serving a 69-year prison sentence on conspiracy and racketeering charges.

Scarfo Jr. had relocated to Northern New Jersey to escape the mob political warfare in Philadelphia. In 1993, he received a seven-year prison sentence on a racketeering charge related to the distribution of illegal video poker machines. He received an early release from prison, but in 1997 was sentenced to another 13 months on a weapons charge.

Shortly before Knapik was sentenced to jail in February 1999, the FBI conducted a court-authorized search of Scarfo and Knapik while they were in Knapik's car. Scarfo was found to be carrying $10,000 in cash, and computer spreadsheets detailing gambling bets placed through different agents for that week's NFL football games. The mob had become computer literate, and was using Excel spreadsheets to keep track of its illegal activities.

At Scarfo's storefront business, the FBI surreptitiously "imaged" the hard drive in Scarfo's desktop computer. When the FBI's computer forensics specialists later viewed the contents of the hard drive, however, they found one file they couldn't read because it had been encrypted by Scarfo using a cipher program known as PGP (Pretty Good Privacy). The FBI Laboratory in Washington, DC, attempted to break Scarfo's PGP password with "a brute-force attack," harnessing all the computer resources at the lab's disposal to attempt every potential password combination possible. It was to no avail. Special Agent Leo A. Dawson's May 8, 1999, affidavit stated things succinctly: the brute-force attack "had been fruitless." The government had gotten in, but they couldn't get all the way in.

Phil Zimmerman, the creator of the PGP encryption program was later asked to comment on the situation. "I knew PGP would be used by criminals; I felt bad about that." He added, however, that "the good uses to which PGP is put are so compelling that we have to factor that into the whole equation."

The FBI was forced to come back to court to request a second bite of the apple. They were certain the encrypted file contained incriminating evidence. In fact, one of their confidential informants, identified in FBI court filings as CI-3, had stated that he was certain that "Little Nicky" kept his gambling and loan shark books on his desktop computer. The informant knew that these records had been protected with encryption, because "Little Nicky" had bragged that his code "can't be broken." To ensure that they would be able to read and/or understand the encrypted files, the FBI requested court approval for a surreptitious entry designed to "capture" the key to Scarfo's encrypted files.

But how could the FBI obtain a password they had already specifically looked for, and hadn't found? The answer to that question is found in the court order authorizing this second break and entry into Scarfo's place of business.

ORDER

WHEREFORE, IT IS HEREBY ORDERED THAT Special Agents of the FBI be authorized to enter the TARGET LOCATION surreptitiously, covertly, and by breaking and entering, if necessary, in order to install and leave behind software, firmware, and/or hardware equipment, which will monitor the inputted data entered on Nicodemo S. Scarfo's computer in the TARGET LOCATION so that the FBI can capture the password necessary to decrypt computer files by recording the key related information as they are entered.

HON. G. DONALD HANEKE
Dated: May 8, 1999   United States Magistrate Judge

When the FBI returned later in May to recover their keylogger device, they were in for another unpleasant surprise. The FBI's Lab found that the keylogger data they recovered would *not* open the file seized earlier when the hard drive had been imaged in January. Because the calendar had now run on the court order authorizing their entry, the FBI was forced to go into court once again. This time they petitioned the court to postpone the unsealing of the authorization of the surreptitious entry to give the FBI another 30 days to continue to break into Scarfo's business storefront to obtain the password they sought.

The FBI executed a total of five court-authorized entries into Scarfo's place of business in their attempt to recover a password that would work; all to no avail. The experts at the FBI Laboratory in Washington, DC, concluded that they were getting "apples and oranges." The January imaging of Scarfo's hard drive yielded the original FACTOR file, the "apple." The FBI suspected that the keylogger system installed in May was apparently capturing PGP passwords that probably opened subsequent versions of the FACTOR file, the "oranges." They believed Scarfo had changed his PGP password since the execution of their January search warrant. The high-tech approach to sleuthing was creating a mess that couldn't be reconciled.

Believing that Scarfo was still using the encrypted files, but was now storing them on removable diskettes, the FBI executed a search warrant of Scarfo's apartment in Newark, New Jersey. The agents seized a box of diskettes in the course of this search, and one of the diskettes finally yielded pay dirt. One of the diskettes contained several versions of the new FACTOR files, which could be opened using the pass phrase and key related information obtained pursuant to the May 8, and June 9, 1999, court orders. The FACTOR files yielded weekly sports-book pay and collect documents for the period September 1998 through February 1999, including copies of the identical sheets seized from Scarfo's person in January 1999. The FBI had gotten all that it needed. On June 21, 2000, a federal grand jury returned a three-count indictment charging Nicodemo S. Scarfo with gambling and loan sharking. What appeared to be a run-of-the-mill organized crime prosecution took on a life of its own from that point forward, however.

Nicky Scarfo's attorneys demanded discovery regarding the workings and method of operation of the FBI's keylogger system. Following on the heels of this first motion, Scarfo's attorneys filed another motion asking the court to suppress the evidence seized by the government through the use of the keystroke logger. They alleged that the government was aware that Scarfo's computer included a modem. More importantly, they alleged that the "pen register" the FBI had installed surreptitiously had captured AOL access telephone numbers; the FBI's pen register had recorded over 100 successful connections to the Internet. Scarfo's attorneys stated that the FBI knew that the AOL access number had been dialed "in excess of 100 times during the trap." Scarfo's attorneys pointed out to Judge Politan that the FBI had received court authorization to install the keylogger to capture keystrokes, only. They complained also that the FBI had violated the federal *Wiretapping Act* by not following the requirements of Title III, which required obtaining express permission of the court to place a wiretap on the computer modem. Scarfo's attorneys were alleging that the use of a keystroke-monitoring device comprised a "general warrant, a general, exploratory rummaging in a person's belongings," which was in violation of the Fourth Amendment to the Constitution.

In the open court hearing of these motions, Federal District Judge Politan appeared visibly unsettled about the whole thing. He told prosecutor Ron Wigler that he wanted more information regarding the details, and ordered both sides to prepare further briefing memoranda.

The press immediately picked up on the irony of Scarfo's latest discovery objections. The *New York Times'* headline read: "Organized Crime Case Raises Privacy Issues." The Nicodemo S. Scarfo case was the first time a keylogging system had ever been used by the FBI in an investigation. Mafiosi have rights, too, don't'cha know?

*   *   *

As all the legal maneuvering took place, Nicky Scarfo languished at home, under house arrest. In response to one of the discovery requests of Scarfo's legal team, the Justice Department answered that the FBI had used the pass phrase *nds09813–050* to decrypt the *PGP*-encrypted FACTOR files. Scarfo was also informed by the Justice Department that the FBI had used the Excel password 021 to unprotect the Excel FACTOR files. Scarfo had used a *double-secret* protection method. No wonder he had been so sure that his encrypted files could never be broken.

Scarfo's attorneys suggested to the court that a "dismissal of the case would be a just order. . . . At the very least this court should suppress the evidence secured by the password obtained by the keystroke recorder."

After an evidentiary hearing in open court, Judge Politan expressed his concern that the keylogger device had intercepted a communication transmitted from Scarfo's computer, in violation of Title III. His ruling concluded as follows:

> In light of the possibility that the keylogger device may have intercepted a communication . . . the court hereby orders the Government to file with the court and serve upon counsel for the defendant Scarfo a report explaining fully how the keylogger device functions.

There was no way the government of the United States would consider complying with this order. They would give up Scarfo first. The government, though, had another card to play, and the government's response on August 23 must have electrified the Scarfo camp.

The Justice Department's response invoked the "Classified Information Procedures Act." Scarfo had hit a huge nerve. The Justice Department was now asserting that the method of operation of the FBI's keylogging system was a "national security secret."

Judge Politan wryly observed that the government's response "presented a new wrinkle into what had been an already intriguing case." Judge Politan held another hearing on the issues at hand. This time though, in accordance with the Classified Information Procedures Act of 1980, only persons with top-secret government clearance were permitted to attend. In attendance were "high-ranking officials from the United States Attorney General's office and the FBI."

Judge Politan was satisfied with what he had seen and heard. He ordered the record of the hearing sealed, and ordered the FBI to give the defendants an "unclassified summary statement" of the workings of the keylogger device, in lieu of the classified information Scarfo's counsel had requested.

The court now believed it had all the information necessary to finally rule on the defendant's motions to suppress evidence collected through the use of the government's keystroke logging system. The court indicated that the Nicky Scarfo Jr. case presented an interesting issue; one "dealing with the ever-present tension between individual privacy and liberty rights, and law enforcement's use of new and advanced technology to vigorously investigate criminal activity."

The court also took specific note of the fact that the issues at hand in the Scarfo case took on "added importance in light of recent events and potential national security implications." Scarfo had been arrested in May 2001, and the court was ruling in December. The events of 9/11, however, hung in the shadow of each and every argument upon which the Judge would rule. The Administration, the Justice Department, and Congress were asking for more investigative powers for our law enforcement agencies, not more restraints.

As to Scarfo's contention that the keylogger's capturing of keystrokes provided for, in essence, a general warrant, in violation of the Fourth Amendment to the Constitution, Judge Politan reasoned that in searches for incriminating documents in a closet filled with clothing or other items, some innocuous unrelated items may be perused in a cursory manner in order to determine whether they should be seized or not. Judge Politan pointed out that the Fourth Amendment did not prohibit a search merely because it was incapable of being performed with surgical precision. He rejected this aspect of Scarfo's claim.

Judge Politan's final ruling indicated that "the principal mystery surrounding this case" was whether the government's keylogging system intercepted a wire communication in violation of the Wiretap Act by recording keystrokes of Scarfo's communications made while the modem operated. Judge Politan was satisfied with the degree of care the FBI had taken in this regard. Supervisory Special Agent Murch's affidavit to the court described the precautions the FBI had baked into their keylogger device:

> In order to avoid potentially intercepting electronic communications, . . . the KLS checked the status of each communication port installed on the computer, and if all communication ports indicated inactivity, meaning that the modem was not using any port at that time, then the keystroke in question would be recorded.

Judge Politan eloquently summarized the conflict society faces today:

> Let there be no doubt that the courts are indeed the last bastions of freedom in our society . . . The right to be free of unreasonable searches and seizures, the right to privacy and the right to a fair trial are among the most cherished of these rights . . .
>
> The amazing capabilities bestowed upon us by science are at times mind-boggling. As a result, we must be ever vigilant against the evisceration of constitutional rights at the hands of modern technology. Yet . . . advanced computer technologies and increased accessibility to the Internet means criminal behavior is becoming more sophisticated and complex. Law enforcement's ability to vigorously pursue such rogues cannot be hindered where all Constitutional limitations are scrupulously observed.

Judge Politan denied Scarfo's motions to suppress the encrypted evidence. Shortly afterward, Scarfo's attorneys struck a plea bargain agreement with federal prosecutors. The prosecutors agreed to drop the more serious charge of "conspiracy-to-commit-extortion" in lieu of Scarfo pleading guilty to one charge of "bookmaking." He faces 27 to 33 months in the federal penitentiary.

*   *   *

I remember discussing the technology the FBI used in the "Little Nicky" Scarfo Jr. case with Dave Gully, who is a technologist and specialist in e-business technology. Dave's response was "Oh yeah, that's just like the virus keylogging tool I just read about."

I wasn't sure what Dave was referring to, a not unusual predicament for me when talking with him. The consulting world in which he specializes has him brushing up against the most advanced technology in the world, most of it having something to do with the Internet. He inhales the stuff, and I usually have to slow him down a bit to find a morsel digestible for me.

Later that day, Dave sent me an e-mail containing an article that talked about a new computer virus that took advantage of a security flaw in Microsoft's Internet Explorer. The virus in question was very infectious. You didn't even need to open an e-mail attachment to infect your computer with it. You'd be toast if you even simply "previewed" an infected e-mail message. This virus also installed "a Trojan-horse" keylogging program on the user's computer. Dave Gully's Trojan-horse keylogging system was not the same as the FBI's. The FBI had to physically break and enter Scarfo's place of business to install their keylogger.

My discussion with Dave Gully occurred on November 30, 2001. Twenty-seven days later, Judge Politan ruled on the admissibility of evidence collected by the FBI's keylogger in the Scarfo case. On November 20, MSNBC filed a stunning story. According to their unnamed source, the FBI was developing software that installed a keylogging system that could be installed on a suspect's computer by way of the Internet.

According to this source, the software was code named "Magic Lantern" and the virus could be sent to the suspect by e-mail, or could be directly inserted by the FBI using "common vulnerabilities," a common euphemism for "hacking." MSNBC also reported that the keylogging system could transmit captured information "back to the FBI."

Three weeks later, on December 12, 2001, FBI spokesperson Paul Breeson confirmed the accuracy of the MSNBC news report. "It is a workbench project that has not been deployed. We can't discuss it because it's still under development." In response to a question about whether the system would require a court order for its use, Breeson said that it would only "be used pursuant to the appropriate legal process." When you line up the information available, though, things get "curiouser and curiouser" here in Wonderland.

Roll the tape back to November 20, 2001. On that day, the Associated Press reported that McAfee Corp. had contacted the FBI to make sure that the firm's anti-virus software would not "tip off suspects whose computers were being monitored remotely by the FBI." McAfee's parent company, Network Associates, denied the report, saying that the discussion never happened. The Associated Press then reiterated that their reporter stood by his story.

The technology to install keylogging systems remotely has been around for a while. The W32Badtrans@MM Internet worm was first discovered on April 11, 2001. This Internet worm spread itself through e-mail and contained a Trojan-horse "backdoor." The "backdoor" software was based on a password-stealing Trojan horse used earlier in the infamous VBS/Loveletter.BD and VBS/Funny Internet worms, both of which trapped keystrokes and stored them in a file that someone could later retrieve. If you work in a corporation with a network of any size, you might remember receiving all of those e-mails entitled, "I love you," which you needed to delete without opening any attachment if you hoped to keep your computer from being infected. Gully had referred me to a new version of this worm seven months later.

Let's complete the circle, though. The University of Nebraska reports that the BadTrans keylogger *is* detectable by McAfee's anti virus detection software. McAfee—the same company who *isn't* working with the FBI to make the FBI's remotely installed keylogging program undetectable by McAfee's antivirus software.

*   *   *

Judge Politan's court order denying Scarfo's motion to suppress evidence included a footnote that caught my eye. The footnote referred to a case in Seattle that Scarfo's attorneys had cited in one of their briefs. In this Seattle case, the FBI *had disclosed* the keylogger sniffer they used in a sting that had gone down in July 2001. Scarfo's attorneys were outraged. If the FBI revealed it in Seattle, why couldn't they reveal it to Scarfo? They argued that the government's pleading of the keylogger system as being "classified" was just a bunch of hooey; simply more garbage being thrown at Scarfo by the government.

Judge Politan concluded that the Seattle case was "of no moment." He reasoned that the keylogger used by the FBI in that "case can be purchased by anyone in retail stores," and therefore wasn't a government classified secret. WinWhatWhere is the name of the keylogger the FBI used in Seattle, and it is true that this keylogger can be purchased in retail stores. The FBI's sting, though, reads like a high-tech spy novel.

CHAPTER NINE

DumbFellas

Special Agent Marty Prewett had been with the FBI for over 14 years, focusing on white-collar crimes. During the last few years, he'd been assigned to the FBI's Computer Crime Squad in Seattle. Prewett also served as the Internet fraud coordinator for the Seattle field office. Over the last several months, Prewett had been investigating a hacker intrusion into a Seattle company. Prewett's continuing investigation had developed the nickname one of the hackers had used—*subssta*.

Special Agent Prewett would testify in federal district court that the department had also developed the name of the perpetrator. "We learned it was Aleksey Ivanov."

Prewett crosschecked the name and Ivanov's methods against the FBI's database. He found that Special Agent Ken Gray in the FBI's New Haven, Connecticut, office was also developing a case on the same Aleksey Ivanov. The FBI's New Haven field office was investigating Ivanov with regard to a hacker "intrusion into a company called Online Information Bureau."

Aleksey Ivanov was wanted for the theft of thousands of credit cards from Online Information Bureau. The FBI's New Haven office had made a formal request to Russia for information about the suspects in that case, as well as for a more recent, similar intrusion, this one into a company called CD Universe.

At CD Universe, however, Ivanov had hit the mother lode.

Thief Reveals Credit Card Data
When Web Extortion Plot Fails

John Markoff
The New York Times

San Francisco—A mysterious computer intruder has tried to extort $100,000 from an Internet music retailer after claiming to have copied its collection of more than 300,000 customer credit card files, which could be used by others to charge purchases online or by telephone.

Because the company, CD Universe, has refused to pay blackmail, the anonymous intruder has released some of the credit card files on the Internet. He also claims to have some other credit-card numbers to obtain money for himself . . .

January 10, 2000

One month earlier, CD Universe, a Wallingford, Connecticut-based Internet retailer, received a fax. A blackmailer was claiming to have stolen 300,000 credit-card files from their computer system. "Pay me $100,000, and I'll fix your bugs," the fax read, ". . . or I'll sell your cards and tell about this incident in the news."

Management at CD Universe immediately called the FBI, and then brought in a gaggle of Internet security experts to identify the weakness in the company's Web site. The company and the FBI attempted to trace the blackmailer's communications to the source. They also wanted to determine whether the hacker had truly stolen the credit card data. To do all of this, CD Universe tried to maintain contact with the corporate blackmailer and string him along to buy time.

"It was surreal," CD Universe CEO Brad Greenspan said afterwards. "I kept wondering, 'why us?'" After CD Universe appeared to be ignoring the shakedown attempt, the blackmailer sent an e-mail to the *New York Times*. In the e-mail, the person identified himself for the first time. He was "Maxim," he wrote, and was 19 years old, "and I am from Russia."

Maxim reported that he had successfully penetrated other corporate networks. Because CD Universe had refused to pay him the $100,000, the Russian said he had released 25,000 credit card files on a Web site on December 25, 1999. The other 275,000 cards could wait, for now, he said. The reporter at the *New York Times* requested some corroboration. The blackmailer supplied the reporter with the files on 198 credit cards as proof of his penetration of the 300,000 credit-card database. When the *New York Times* reporter called CD Universe to confirm the story, the company's CEO called back. "He definitely has CD Universe data," Greenspan confirmed.

Computer security experts tracked down the Web site where Maxim had posted the 25,000 stolen credit cards. The Internet Service Provider immediately shut down the Web site, but not before the site had registered several thousand hits. In a separate e-mail to MSNBC, "Maxus," aka "Maxim," indicated that part of his motivation for hacking corporate computer networks was to publicize e-business enterprises that didn't do enough to protect users' privacy.

One month later, in January 2000, Amazon.com uncovered a Russian-based plot to defraud it and other merchandisers out of $70,000 worth of merchandise using stolen credit card information. The press was now reporting that the U.S. government was finding itself hampered by the patchwork of white-collar-crime laws in the various jurisdictions around the world. "I'm not aware of any prosecutions," reported Mark Batts, special agent in charge of the FBI's Financial Institution Fraud Unit.

Special Agent Prewett pressed forward with his investigation of the Amazon.com fraud, as well as the Internet extortion attempts about which other Seattle-based companies were complaining. Prewett conferred with Special Agent Gray, based out of the FBI's field office in New Haven, about the ongoing CD Universe investigation. Prewett learned from Gray that the Russian government had not responded at all to the information request forwarded earlier by the FBI's New Haven office. Both Prewett and Gray concluded that Prewett would likely experience the same result with his Seattle investigations.

The New Haven office had now also filed charges against Ivanov in the CD Universe investigation. Ivanov, though, was still believed to be in Russia. Also, in December 1999, the FBI in Reno, Nevada, had arrested a 22-year-old student, Roustam Kamilievich, for possession of electronic goods fraudulently purchased from Amazon.com.

The fraudulent Amazon orders had been placed using stolen credit card information—orders placed using 63 different compromised credit cards. Upon his arrest, Kamilievich told investigators that he'd had limited contact with someone he knew only as "Andrei." All of the contact had been by e-mail.

Andrei had told Kamilievich he could earn a little "extra money" for receiving the delivery of the packages at his Reno apartment. A computer in Chelyabinsk, Russia placed all the fraudulent Amazon.com orders that subsequently arrived at Kavilievich's apartment.

Prewett, in Seattle, and Special Agent Gray, in New Haven, Connecticut, believed the Reno fraud was linked to the Seattle scams, as well as to the CD Universe extortion attempt. Prewett and Gray believed "Maxus," the CD Universe extortionist, was behind all three attempts. Although the Russian had established elaborate fronting IP addresses all over the world to disguise his true location, the FBI was finally able to trace their way through the maze. The Chelyabinsk address linked Maxus to all three scams. The Russian blackmailer, Maxus, aka Maxim, was a very busy young man.

In June 2000, six months after Maxim broke into the CD Universe Web site, an anonymous source familiar with that case reported that the electronic evidence was compromised. The "chain of custody was not established properly," the anonymous tipster reported, making it impossible to prosecute the case with the evidence at hand. The knowledgeable source believed the compromise of electronic evidence occurred during the initial investigative free-for-all. The company had called in three different security firms to investigate the Web site's breach of security, under the theory that when in a crisis mode, more is better.

Throughout the investigation, the FBI worked alongside the three computer-security consulting firms: Network Associates, Kroll, and Infowar.com. Afterward though, no one would accept responsibility for the mistake. In the end, prosecutors would not be able to establish that the electronic evidence had been preserved, and that the chain of custody had been documented in a manner proving that the electronic evidence had not been altered as a result of the investigation itself.

In December 2000, the FBI confirmed that it was investigating the theft of another 55,000 credit card numbers as a result of a hacking penetration of a Los Angeles-based Internet merchant-processing firm, Creditcards.com. Again, a Russian was confirmed to be the blackmailer.

The *modus operandi* in this case was similar to the CD Universe extortion plot. The 55,000 credit cards had been compromised over six months earlier; throughout that period of time, the Russian hacker had been attempting to blackmail the company's management. Failing ultimately, the Russian gave up on his extortion attempt. As in the CD Universe case, the Russian blackmailer then posted the credit card information on the Internet for others to exploit.

Ten days later, a press release put out by Egghead.com read:

Egghead.com®, Inc.
For Immediate Release

Egghead.com has discovered that a hacker has accessed our computer systems, potentially including our customer databases. As a precautionary measure, we have taken immediate steps to protect our customers by contacting the credit card companies we work with . . .

Menlo Park, Calif.
December 28, 2000

Credit-card industry sources then confirmed that Egghead had turned over the names of *3.7 million* cardholders whose cards had been compromised, "possibly."

3.7 million is not a small number, any way you look at it. At a potential average loss of $400 per card, that equates to a potential $1.5 billion fraud. That's a staggering amount of money. True, any specific individual cardholder would be indemnified so that their loss would never exceed $50. The merchants, however, had no such protection. The manner in which the merchants would be stung by the fraud is as follows.

The hacker would use the 3.7 million cards as if they were akin to a "one-time use cipher pad." In this scenario, a particular credit card would be used only once, running up a purchase balance of $300 to $500. Then the card would be thrown away, never to be used again. That way, it could never be traced back to the hacker as a result of multiple attempts.

The hacker would arrange the "ship to address" to be a central receiving point, such as a part-time student's apartment in Reno, Nevada. After enough merchandise was accumulated in this manner, the load of contraband would be consolidated and shipped by way of a container to either a former East-bloc country, or perhaps Asia; wherever the goods could most easily be resold.

The Russian hacker attacks had become an epidemic, and represented a very serious threat to commerce in the United States. It also appeared to be virtually unstoppable. Jeff Sheahan, president and CEO of Egghead.com, Inc., followed up with another press release, which was sent to all of Egghead.com's customers as well.

Egghead.com®, Inc.
For Immediate Release:
Investigation into Egghead.com Breach Suggests
No Credit Card Information Stolen

. . . Our internal investigation, led by Kroll Associates, has uncovered evidence that suggests that Egghead.com's existing security systems interrupted this intrusion while it was in progress. Moreover, reports from credit card companies we work with suggest that fewer than 7,500 credit card accounts that appear in our system have shown suspected fraudulent activity . . .

Menlo Park, Calif.
January 8, 2001

The Russian extortionist had successfully compromised corporate networks on both coasts of the United States. To establish identities with which to open a line of communication to blackmail corporate executives, the Russian blackmailer had opened several Hotmail accounts, as well as several accounts established through AT&T. The blackmailer also assumed several stolen identities by way of accounts hijacked from other companies successfully penetrated.

Jesse James, after robbing a bank, always made his getaway on horse-back, while Dillinger preferred a high-powered Ford automobile. The Russian cyber-blackmailer, though, was staging his holdups without ever having to leave Chelyabinsk, Russia, making the notion of a getaway plan seem archaic.

FBI Special Agent Prewett reviewed what he had with Gray, his coun-terpart in New Haven, Connecticut. The heat was on. The two FBI agents had been able to track the Russian blackmailer over the Internet. The problem was, though, the FBI was always a step or two behind. The two FBI agents believed they had the name of the blackmailer: Ivanov; Aleksey Ivanov. Prewett and Gray had the user name of Ivanov as well as "subssta." Sounds like Bubba, Prewett thought.

The evidence the two FBI agents needed, however, was on a computer server in Ivanov's hometown, in Chelyabinsk, Russia. The Russian gov-ernment was of no help at all, and without their assistance in making an arrest, things would remain stymied. The problem was that this "subssta" was having a field day in the United States.

Since June 2000, Prewett had participated in weekly conference calls with the FBI's National Information Protection Center in Washington, DC, where the Seattle investigations were discussed. Through these weekly calls, Prewett was able to keep up with events happening elsewhere around the country. The National Information Protection Center, in turn, kept in contact with the FBI's legal attaché in the U.S. Embassy in Moscow, and kept the supervisory special agent there informed of the progress of the multiple investigations in the United States, and the New Haven office's lack of progress in getting any assistance from the Russian government on the CD Universe prosecution.

As a result of apparent chain-of-custody problems with the evidence collected in the CD Universe case, everyone in the Computer Crimes Sec-tion knew that this case was probably not prosecutable. The FBI's best bet now was with the Seattle investigation Prewett was leading.

Prewett suggested they attempt to lure Ivanov to the United States. Once on U.S. soil, Ivanov could be arrested. To date, all attempts to arrest the hacker with the assistance of the Russian Federation authorities had gone nowhere. The team discussed whether or not to try another request for assistance from the Russian authorities. Prewett expressed a concern that the team couldn't be certain that someone in the Russian govern-ment with advance notice wouldn't tip off the hackers about the devel-oping FBI plan. The team of agents decided to go ahead without further contact with the Russian Federation. The New Haven field office gave Prewett the go-ahead to give his idea a try.

Prewett had given the problem a lot of thought. He had come up with the notion of creating a fictitious computer security company located in downtown Seattle, and offering Ivanov a job. From the communications he'd seen, Ivanov took immense pride in his ability to hack his way at will into U.S. corporate networks. Prewett had found Ivanov's resume online, and the resume contained an e-mail address where Ivanov could be contacted. Prewett decided to feed into Ivanov's vanity; tell him how impressive his credentials were as a "former" hacker and as a computer security specialist, and how he could turn those skills into a lucrative computer security consulting career. Here, in the computer security field in the United States, Ivanov would be a god.

Prewett got the go-ahead from the Special Agent in Charge of the Seattle office. The next step was easy. "We sent him an e-mail offering him a job with our company," Prewett would later testify.

The e-mail to Ivanov was sent from a "Michael Patterson," who was established as the undercover identity of the chief executive officer of Invita Computer Security Corporation, the new undercover operation.

Ivanov immediately responded. He was indeed interested in the position being offered.

Ivanov's response set off a flurry of activity. The FBI's Seattle field office sought approvals for the sting from FBI headquarters in Washington. Concurrent communications requesting authorization and approval went out to the U.S. Attorney's office in the District of Connecticut, as well as in the Western District of Washington. The approvals came in. Through the FBI's Office of International Affairs, Prewett made direct contact with the legal attaché in Moscow, his FBI counterpart in the U.S. Embassy there.

From then on, in the high-tech version of cat and mouse that played out with Ivanov, Prewett would play the part of "Michael Patterson" in the series of e-mail exchanges with the Russian hacker. Prewett would draft an e-mail response to Ivanov, but first send it to Gray, Prewett's counterpart in New Haven. The two agents would discuss the approach and come up with the best version of the e-mail to send to Ivanov; and then off it would go.

A series of e-mail exchanges ensued. Within a short time frame, one of Ivanov's accomplices, Vassili Gorshkov, would join in the e-mail exchange. Gorshkov came up with the suggestion that a demonstration hacking session be set up, where the two Russians could demonstrate their skill in successfully penetrating any security firewall that Invita Corporation could throw in front of them. Patterson (Prewett), the CEO of Invita Corporation, expressed his concern. He wasn't interested in offering up his own company's network to be hacked into by the two Russians. The risk would be too great.

Gorshkov suggested a simple expedient. Michael Patterson could establish a test computer network at Invita, and the two Russians could attempt to crack it. The test computer network would not be connected to

Invita's network, so Patterson's concerns about that risk would be taken care of.

Patterson (Prewett) agreed to get on it immediately. The CEO of Invita Corporation informed Gorshkov and Ivanov that he would set it up so that the level of security was what he referred to as "moderate," and that he would monitor the two Russians' progress. If they were successful, a much higher level of firewall security would then be established, and the two Russians would be tested a second time. Patterson e-mailed them that he'd arrange for airfare to Seattle if the two hackers were successful in getting to the "Stage Two" level of the test.

Ivanov responded that he was pleased with the discussions, but declined Patterson's invitation to have Invita pay for his flight to the United States. Ivanov e-mailed Patterson a copy of his resume in response to Patterson's request and provided another e-mail address where he could be reached, kvakin@tech.net.ru. After receiving this, Patterson suggested that he and Ivanov speak by telephone. Ivanov responded with a telephone number where he could be reached in Russia.

Another flurry of activity occurred on the U.S. side of things. Prewett was concerned that the two Russian hackers might press for technical computer information on the telephone call. The level of hacker sophistication required to pass muster might quickly plumb the depths of Prewett's knowledge.

The computer crime squad in Seattle enlisted the aid of a Seattle hacker for the telephone call to Ivanov. Prewett had Marty Leeth, one of the computer crime squad special agents, together with the cooperating hacker, make the call to Russia. If the team was successful in luring Ivanov to the United States, Leeth would play the role of the president of Invita. His business area of specialty would be that of marketing, rather than the technical side of the business. This arrangement would dry-clean him if the Russian hacker pressed him too much about the technical side of things.

Prewett learned the next day by e-mail from Ivanov, however, that Leeth had gotten through to Ivanov's partner, Gorshkov, whose number Ivanov had provided to Patterson. "You woke him up out of bed," complained Ivanov.

On the call, Gorshkov had suggested that Patterson (Leeth) simply provide a computer for Gorshkov and Ivanov to demonstrate their ability to hack into. It would be as easy as that. No problem. Why make things more complicated than that?

Patterson (Prewett) agreed. Agent Prewett immediately hired a Seattle firm by the name of Sytex to build a computer network for the undercover operation. Patterson e-mailed Ivanov back: "We set up the network to contain some vulnerabilities. We plan to watch your progress to evaluate your skills."

Ivanov and Gorshkov immediately hacked into the system, and Ivanov e-mailed Patterson providing the details of how the two Russians had successfully gotten in. Patterson responded by e-mail that the two Russian hackers had made it look easy. Patterson indicated in this e-mail that he was going to have the target network hardened. They were now moving to the Stage Two test phase. Patterson indicated that he'd like for the two Russians to attempt to hack in again, but at this second, and higher, level of firewall security. Patterson stated that this test would be conducted when the two Russians came to Seattle.

Ivanov e-mailed Patterson back, thanking him for his praise. Ivanov also indicated in the e-mail that both he and Gorshkov would be ". . . unable to travel to Seattle without an invitation letter from Invita." Ivanov stated that the two men would need this kind of letter for the U.S. consulate in Russia to provide them with visas.

Patterson (Prewett) readily agreed to supply the letter. Agent Prewett then arranged to have the FBI's legal attaché in Moscow travel to the consulate in Belarus, where Ivanov would need to obtain his visa to enter the United States. The FBI's legal attaché coordinated things with the U.S. consulate to grease the skids for the Russian hacker when he showed up with his letter of invitation to visit the Seattle-based Invita Corporation.

On November 10, 2000, Ivanov and Gorshkov arrived at the Seattle airport. FBI undercover agent Patterson met the Russians at the airport and drove them to Invita's offices in downtown Seattle.

Agent Prewett had arranged for video and audio surveillance within the Invita Corporation offices, and he listened to the meeting on the tape recording system in an adjacent vacant office. There to greet Ivanov and Gorshkov on their arrival with Michael Patterson were two other Invita "employees." Both were also FBI undercover agents, Special Agents John Cooney and Melissa Mallon. The cooperating hacker Prewett had enlisted in the sting was also present to assist in facilitating the meeting, and was introduced to all there as "Ray."

Ivanov, a pretty large young man, wore a leather coat and a driving cap. He took a seat in front of one of the two Invita Corporation computers in the room. Gorshkov moved away to the other side of the 10-foot by 20-foot room, and sat at the IBM ThinkPad laptop computer set up there on a table against the back wall. The two computers in the room were connected to each other by way of a local area network (LAN). The Invita network, in turn, was networked to the building's high-speed Internet access set up for the customers of the building.

For the most part, the discussions held were in English, although at times, Ivanov and Gorshkov would confer in their native Russian. Patterson asked Ivanov what his "nick" was.

Patterson was asking Ivanov for his computer nickname, or user name. "It's 'subssta,'" Ivanov responded.

Prewett, in the next room, made a fist and drove it forward a little in the air as he listened through his headphones. "Subssta," was the nick used by Maxus, aka, Maxim, the CD Universe hacker, who had made off with the credit information of 300,000 credit-card holders.

For Prewett and his computer crime cohorts, Ivanov's glib answer would make things immeasurably easier. The keystroke logger Prewett had installed on the computers the two Russian hackers were using would capture the entirety of their keystrokes. Now, with their knowledge of Ivanov's nick, the computer forensics specialists would know exactly where to look in the record of keystroke activity the logger would capture. Ivanov's password, the one critical piece of information he would never share, would be easily found in the morass of keystrokes. It would most likely be found in the string of keystrokes immediately following his typing in of his nick.

The undercover FBI agents had separated into two groups, one formed around Ivanov, and the second small group close to Gorshkov. While demonstrating their hacker skills, Gorshkov took time out for a moment to use an Internet connection to tap into the server in Russia that the two hackers were accustomed to using. What Gorshkov and Ivanov didn't know was that Prewett had arranged to have an off-the-shelf keystroke-logging program, called WinWhatWhere, installed on both of the two computers on which the Russians were busily pecking away.

Gorshkov's eyes lit on the prompt demanded by the *tech.net.ru* Russian server IP address:

Имя : _____

Gorshkov tapped in his response:

Имя : kvakin

The server in Chelyabinsk, Russia prompted again:

Пароль : _____

Gorshkov tapped in:

Пароль : cfvlevfq

As Gorshkov pecked away at the computer against the back wall, his back to the rest of the people in the room, he downloaded from the Russian server a program called LOMSCAN that allowed him to scan the

Invita network. At the same time he was doing this, he kept a running dialogue with the undercover agents in the room.

He described himself as the manager of the business identified as tech.net.ru, back in Chelyabinsk, Russia. In response to questions about the operations there, he told the Invita employees gathered around that there were five people that worked for him there. He indicated that there were five computers on their network at that location. Ivanov was an employee of the business, a programmer. What Gorshkov was really interested in was starting a computer security firm, and the expression of interest from Invita Corporation in doing the same would be a great opportunity to start a worldwide venture that could be lucrative for all.

The meeting went on in this manner for almost an hour before the undercover agents arrested the two Russian hackers and informed them of their rights.

Michael Schuler had been a special agent with the FBI for a little more than two years and was a specialist with the Seattle office's Computer Crime squad. Though he'd received some computer forensics training since joining the FBI, he was primarily self-taught, having played around with computers since the age of 10. His undergraduate degree was in International Relations. Now he was in "the Bigs." Using Gorshkov's user id, *kvakin,* and his password, *cfvlevfq,* Special Agent Schuler had been able to hack into *tech.net.ru,* which was the domain name for the Russian server in Chelyabinsk. The last two digits in this particular domain name, *.ru,* designated that this particular machine being accessed was physically domiciled in Russia. Schuler motioned for Prewett to take a look at the computer monitor.

Prewett leaned in over Schuler's shoulder. There on the screen he could see a directory for /amazon_com.

Schuler hunched forward a little in his seat. He scrolled around the directories in the *tech.net.ru* Russian server, looking for other familiar names. Prewett tapped Schuler on the arm and pointed to the monitor. On the lower right of the screen, /ebay_com could be seen. Below that the two agents could see: /online_information_bureau, as well as: cd_universe. Schuler scrolled some more, and several other corporate identities could be seen. These were the files containing the credit card information stolen online in the United States.

Prewett straightened and headed for the phone to call Steven Schroeder, the Assistant U.S. Attorney assigned to the case. Schroeder was on another floor in the Federal Building in downtown Seattle. Schroeder told Prewett to stand tight; he'd get back to him.

Five minutes later, Schroeder called back. He authorized the FBI agents to download all of the information. He directed Prewett to seal the evidence without looking at the contents of the files.

Using the Unix file transfer protocol (FTP), Agent Schuler began the download operation. After encountering a connection problem, Schuler called Elliot Lim, the systems administrator at the University of Washington for some assistance. Lim, responsible for the University's 20,000-computer network, dropped everything he was doing and drove downtown to meet with Schuler.

Believing they would have better odds in downloading what they wanted without experiencing another connection break if they downloaded one big file, rather than thousands of little files, they decided to use the TAR command. The TAR command is a basic Unix archiving tool and is analogous to a lawn bag. You gather up lots of pieces of files, and you stuff them into this big lawn bag. Schuler and Lim stuffed as many files as they could find that related to the stolen credit card frauds being investigated in the United States into the TAR bag. Lim believed the TAR file would download even faster if they compressed it, so he ran the G-zip command to compress the file. After the "one-big-file" was successfully downloaded, they could "unzip" it, and it would be restored to its original state. The two men then recommenced downloading the files from *tech.net.ru*, the Russian server in Chelyabinsk, Russia, by using the FTP command.

For the next 12 hours, the files containing information on not quite 500,000 credit-card holders would begin streaming over the Internet on their 12,000-mile electronic journey from Chelyabinsk, Russia, to downtown Seattle, Washington. There were a few problems with the procedure, however.

The FBI agents had neither a warrant, nor the permission of the Russian government to enter Russia and remove computer files electronically to the United States of America. New ground was being plowed here, for sure.

It took the U.S. Department of Justice two weeks to complete the diplomatic correspondence with regard to the FBI sting in Seattle, or rather, in Chelyabinsk, Russia. The Russian authorities were also notified that two Russian citizens were being held under arrest in an INS detention center in downtown Seattle. The Justice Department ran into a little problem, though.

Important and delicate negotiations had been underway over the last year between the U.S. Department of State, and its counterpart agencies around the world; the negotiations regarded white-collar crime prosecutions and any electronic evidence sought in the prosecution of those crimes. An International Guideline had been developed and approved by the participating countries. Russia was one of the participating countries. The problem was that none of the Assistant U.S. Attorneys in the field in Seattle, or anyone in the FBI's Computer Crime Section, knew that the guidelines existed. The government prosecutor on the Maxus' sting now had three immediate and pressing priorities: first, get notification to the

Russians; second, get approval for what had already had been done. After that, the prosecutor would go into federal district court in Seattle, with hat in hand, and explain to a federal district judge what had transpired, and seek a search warrant authorizing the surreptitious entry into a Russian computer and the downloading and transportation of computer files approximately 12,000 miles to Seattle, Washington, all of which had already occurred. No big deal. All in a day's work.

Kenneth E. Kanev, Gorshkov's attorney, filed a motion to suppress evidence collected and dismiss the charges against Gorshkov as a result of the FBI's use of the keylogger system to capture Gorshkov's password. In May 2001, however, U.S. District Judge John C. Coughenour rejected Kanev's motion to dismiss, reasoning that Gorshkov and his partner Ivanov were knowledgeable computer users, and as such, knew or understood that networked computer systems, such as the Invita Corporation network, often record user information; hence, Gorshkov and Ivanov should have had "no expectation of privacy."

On May 7, 2001, a grand jury sitting in Bridgeport, Connecticut returned a superceding indictment charging Aleksey Vladimirovich Ivanov, aka "subssta," with conspiring to make unauthorized intrusions into computer systems owned by companies in the United States, and with extortion.

On May 10, 2001, Ivanov and Gorshkov were indicted by a Seattle grand jury on 20 criminal counts, including conspiracy and wire fraud. On June 20, 2001, Ivanov was indicted in Santa Ana, California, for breaking into computer systems and extorting victim companies.

On August 16, 2001, Ivanov, who had by then turned 21 years of age, was charged in Sacramento, California, on a 13-count indictment with computer intrusion and conspiracy charges.

On October 10, 2001, two months before Judge Politan would rule on the admissibility of evidence collected by the FBI's keylogger in the "Nicky" Scarfo case, a Seattle, Washington, jury returned guilty verdicts against Vasily Gorshkov, age 26 of Chelyabinsk, Russia on 20 counts of conspiracy and computer fraud. Ivanov was transported to Connecticut, to await trial there.

*   *   *

Forget for a moment about the FBI breaking in and installing a keylogging system to capture the keystrokes of any one of the new breed of criminals. News accounts have reported that the federal arsenal already embraces a technology referred to as "Tempest." This refers to situations where agents, in vans equipped with sensitive electromagnetic radiation collection devices, detect the electromagnetic pulses from computer monitors, then recreate the desktop computer's environment. The press has also widely covered the FBI's system formerly known as "Carnivore," now renamed "DCS 1000," that provides for the interception of Internet packet traffic passing through a router at an Internet Service Provider (ISP). The press has also reported that federal investigators have used hidden cameras to photograph computer screens.

Try this one on for size, though.

As data is being transmitted or received through your modem, the blinking lights on the front of your modem flash. The lights you see are really light-emitting diodes (LEDs), which are extremely sensitive to changes in voltage; the intensity of the light varies with fluctuations in electrical currents. The digital data being transmitted over your modem (bits) are really nothing more than a series of electrical currents, pulsing to reflect the binary representation of the information. The light actually pulses as a result of ever-so-slight voltage variations. The modulation of these light pulses is too subtle for the human eye to discern. By intercepting and reading these pulses of light, the FBI would never even need to consider using some kind of Internet worm to install a Trojan-horse keylogger. Not possible? Think again.

Two scientists, Joe Loughry, of Lockheed Martin Space Systems, and David Umphress, a computer science professor at Auburn University, have developed a method for reading the flashes of light emitted by a computer modem. A very sensitive light detector, connected to a 100-millimeter lens used to amplify the intercepted light flashes, enables the interception of the tiny pulses of light. When the amplified light pulses are then fed into a computer, the data stream represented by the flashing lights can be reconstructed. With this configuration, the scientists were able to intercept data from a modem placed as far as 100 feet away, including, in the case of data encryption systems, unencrypted plaintext.

Connect a tiny hidden camera to this configuration and consider the possibilities.

Marcus Kuhn, a scientist at Cambridge University, reports another variation on this technique. He has demonstrated the ability to intercept and read data displayed on a computer screen by way of the light emitted from the screen, *and reflected off of a nearby wall.* Direct line of sight of the computer monitor is not even necessary. Kuhn's published paper reports that, "Not even curtains, blinds, or windows with etched or frosted glass surfaces—as are frequently used to block views into rooms—are necessarily an effective protection." Kuhn added, "A telescope could be used if you wanted to do it from another building. Although it would need to be dark outside."

How about this one, requiring a simple modification to any standard computer keyboard. Most keyboards have three LED indicators: one for the Num Lock key, another for Caps Lock, and the third for Scroll Lock. Open the keyboard and cross-connect the Scroll Lock LED to the keyboard data signal. The Scroll Lock key will now be inoperable, but who uses the Scroll Lock key anyway? Close up the keyboard again.

Every keystroke you enter on your computer will now cause the LED on the Scroll Lock key to flicker, but the flickering will hardly be noticeable. Place a tiny camera in the ceiling tile directly above the keyboard. The flashing optical output of the Scroll Lock key, containing the digital representation of the output of your keyboard, will now be available to be intercepted, as described above, including passwords and unencrypted text.

As you are reading this, countermeasures are underway. The game goes on.

CHAPTER TEN

Even a Tick Can Swell Only So Far

Enough of password-protected files, and of scrambled this, and encrypted that. No more keyloggers or Trojan-Horse Virus. No more DES, or PGP, or Lucifer, or 56-bit this, or 56-bit that. Time to reflect on the criminal mind in that very mainstream of criminal enterprises, American-style corporate accounting fraud. I was interested in Alex Jarvis's general impression of the Morgan Fay fraud, and how he saw it relating to the events unfolding almost daily in the press—Enron, World-Com—that kind of thing.

"Some of the documents that we found," Alex responded, ". . . it just amazed me that they existed. And that they would be so open and blatant . . ."

Apparently, Alex saw many documents that, for lack of a better description, simply referred continuously to the creative accounting going on. What he saw is disturbing, both in itself and its implications. Very much like Enron, and WorldCom, one way or another, many employees participated in the scheme. Not one or two. Many. Some merely facilitated the recording of fictitious entries. Others maintained a running tally of the amount of the misstatements touching on their little part of the world. Others, mostly those at higher levels of the management group, were responsible for managing the scheme. Still others, directly, or indirectly, were responsible for overt attempts to mislead the auditors.

Some, perhaps, feared losing their jobs if they ratted out their superiors. All of this is merely conjecture on our part, however. Others, possibly, seemed to feel entitled to inflate the company's bottom line results. The auditors were to be put off the scent at all costs. In fact, there probably is some coefficient that can mathematically pinpoint the degree of entitlement an individual felt, when charted against the amount of monetary value the same individual stood to gain from continuing the fraud.

The problem with all of this is that you can't put off the inevitable forever. In accounting, as in Grisham novels, the truth ultimately bleeds out.

Accounting systems have been in continuous use since the dawn of human civilization. According to archaeologist Denise Schmandt-Besserat, the first accounting system, one that was token-based, can be dated to C. 8000 B.C. The first generally accepted evidence of the use of the double-entry method of accounting is represented by the communal account books of the City of Genoa, dating back to the year 1340.

The double entry method of accounting possesses a peculiar elegance; results of operations are presented from two differing points of view—an income statement, presenting results over time, from period A through period B; the second point-of-view presented is always a balance sheet, which is nothing more than a "Kodak moment," a simple snapshot of things remaining on hand at the end of period B.

Part of the perverse and peculiar elegance of the double-entry system is that distortion of one point-of-view requires distortion in the other. Sooner or later, the distortion of a balance sheet, that Kodak snapshot, becomes visible to the naked eye. The distortion becomes discernable through various tests and measures—and audit procedures.

In other words, you can put off the inevitable, but only for so long. Six months. A year maybe. In really egregious situations, perhaps longer. If there are many parties in collusion, or if the fraud is very complex, perhaps it can be put off far longer. In time, though, the balance sheet puffery bursts of its own accord.

Even a tick can swell only so far.

Enron, though, is another story. They figured a way to beat the system.

*   *   *

Enron's management figured an ingenious method of overriding the double-entry method of accounting altogether. They simply ignored it.

In truth, it remains the simplest and most elegant financial fraud ever devised. If you get all bound up in the details—of round-trip gas trades in the Channel Islands; in the complexity of energy trading; of options and derivatives; and in the arcane accounting rules for "Special-Purpose-Partnership-Entities," the so-called 3 percent rule; or all tangled up in hedges—then you'll find yourself lost in the details.

Forget about all that stuff. They did something very simple. Enron's management was fabulously clever. They pledged Enron stock—their own stock—as collateral in the partnerships, to back-up loans the banks had made to the partnerships. The partnerships were either established to invest in speculative business ventures or to park problems so that they were out of sight of prying eyes. It doesn't really matter which of the two choices served as the underlying rationale.

As far as Enron management was concerned, their stock certificates were just pieces of paper. The sweet thing for Enron was this: when the underlying investments did well for the partnerships, Enron recorded gains. Why not? Enron was a significant investor in the partnership ventures. Enron would be entitled to record the gains. This was the fundamental recipe for success. Just add water. And replicate this formula *ad infinitum*.

Things look great. The economy is going gangbusters. It's the Internet economy. It's a new paradigm. Enron sheds its hard assets, its energy generation plants; its gas transmission pipelines. Enron's plan is to shed itself of tangible assets, those things that you can touch and feel. This is the master plan of Enron's president and chief operating officer, Jeff Skilling: to reconstitute Enron as the brokerage firm of the future. In fact, through Enron's trading desk, you could buy 30-year electricity futures, contracts to deliver or receive electricity for the next 30 years. Thirty-year gas futures. Thirty-year water supply futures. Telecom capacity; broadband this; broadband that. In fact, you could buy weather futures through Enron. And all of this is unregulated.

Never mind that there is not a supercomputer in the world that can come close to modeling fully the complexity of weather. The economy is superheating. Who cares?

The nexus of technology, the Internet, and the dot-com phenomenon change the fundamentals of the economy. Even Greenspan backs away from his early concern over "irrational exuberance," and begins musing that technology-driven productivity gains *are* responsible for driving the stock market ever upward.

During this time, Enron stock is taking off.

But as time passes, the speculative investments undertaken by Enron are failing spectacularly. Enron's management knew, by May 2001, long before the company filed for bankruptcy protection, and only a few short months before Jeff Skilling retired, that the company's portfolio of foreign assets had declined by over $3 billion. Put simply, Enron management was staring a $3 billion loss in the face.

Enron management devises a neat solution to their problems though. The failures are to be pushed off into other entities. Management figures a way to "paper" all kinds of transactions. Any downside exposure to Enron's speculative investments are to be shifted over to "off balance sheet" partnerships. They had weighted the bodies with cement overshoes and dumped them overboard. After awhile though, the bodies begin floating to the surface. Belly up. Bloated. Putrescent.

They are the decaying remains of speculative, high-risk investments. That's why they're called speculative. You put up risk capital for these kinds of things. And in Enron's case, you don't think much about it, especially if money is cheap. Or especially if it is not your money to begin with. The problem with this is that all of Enron's investments were in high-risk, speculative ventures; many were in high-risk, third-world countries.

The investments begin going bad, though; all over the world: India, South America, Asia, domestically, you name it. Management begins asking itself, "How could we have had such bad luck?"

When Enron's speculative underlying investments began failing, Enron had a simple expedient that allowed them (they believed) to avoid taking the losses. They simply issued more Enron stock to the failing partnerships. Enron's stock was still high-flying. The stock market viewed Enron as a terrific stock. The public markets had no idea what was going on in the partnerships. And this was because Enron was not revealing anything.

This is what you tell all those people who held Enron stock; take them through it step by step. First, though, review how things are reflected in a rational world of proper accounting. First, an investment goes bad. Second, a company normally "writes-off" that investment immediately (i.e., writes it off their balance sheet), and third, the resulting loss gets immediately transferred to the income statement, for everyone to see it as it really is, a loss. Fourth, the Wall Street analysts see this, they go on CNN to talk about it, the stock market in general sees it, and the value of the stock goes down, proportionate to the loss taken.

Now you need to tell the Enron stockholders that Enron didn't do any of this. They put the losing investment in a so-called independent partnership (the partnership). After a while, the bank's loans to the partnership don't look so good any more; the loans are starting to look at risk of never being paid back because of the declining value of the underlying partnership's investments. Third, Enron tells the banks not to worry; Enron will agree to contribute more Enron stock to the partnership to shore things up. Fourth, Enron issues more Enron stock to the partnership. Fifth (and this is the important one, so pay attention here), as a result of Enron's issuance of more stock, your investment in Enron stock becomes diluted. More stock out there means that every share of Enron stock must be worth proportionately less; it is, after all, a zero-sum game. Sixth, the lenders to these so-called unaffiliated partnerships are now satisfied with things; they now have more collateral (more Enron stock) securing the partnership's bank loans. By doing things this way, Enron never reflects on its own income statement the loss on its failing investments in India or Brazil. The stock market remains blissfully unaware, and Enron's stock remains high-flying, because the story management is telling sounds great.

Oh, I forgot to mention step seven, through step four thousand—Enron created thousands of these partnerships.

So, it's a simple as that. Enron hides the ball. Their stock stays flying high; it's valuable collateral to the lenders and investors who provided the underlying financing for the partnerships.

Then, as far as Enron is concerned, the recipe is leverage. Leverage. Leverage.

With leverage, you can grow the scheme almost infinitely. You keep borrowing as if there is no tomorrow, for there isn't. The tricky thing, though, is that leverage concerns lenders. They know that too much of a good thing is dangerous. It's risky. And the more you pile on, the riskier you become. The financial community will allow you to leverage to a certain extent and no more.

Therefore, the most pressing thing for Enron management now is to not let anyone know how leveraged they really are. Hide the leverage—put it "off-balance sheet." Put the off-balance sheet borrowings in the partnerships (in the exercise yard at the minimum security federal penitentiary at Lompoc, California, the guys refer to these kind of partnerships as SPEs, special-purpose entities).

There's nothing wrong with the use of SPEs, these kinds of partnerships. The use of SPEs isn't illegal. Lot's of companies use them, but Enron was out of control. According to Richard Hastings of Cyber Business Credit LLC, "the proliferation of special-purpose entities at Enron was unique in its vastness."

Vastness. Think of the vastness of the Gobi Desert, and you may begin to understand Enron's appetite for leverage.

You now have a daily pressing problem. You need cash desperately; the bloated "floaters" in the partnerships stink to high heaven. So, you begin to disguise your new borrowings. "Structure" them (that's Wall Street lingo) so that they are literally undetectable.

You do it by engaging in sham gas contracts—"round-trip" transactions. You set up the operation through one of the world's largest money-center banks. You disguise another quarter-billion dollars of another round of borrowings (another word for leverage). You call this loan an investment in power generation facilities on behalf of the great State of Connecticut. You never follow through on it, though; you never invest the proceeds that way, but nobody, including the State of Connecticut, including your lenders, is watching what you are doing with the money.

The scheme though is silently diluting the Enron stock held by its shareholders. Their stock is being diluted every time Enron issues more stock to the failing partnerships. Only the shareholders don't notice anything because none of the losses on Enron's busted investments (and the floaters are everywhere—you could walk across water on them) are being run through Enron's income statement.

You might ask, "What about the creditors? Aren't they hurt? Weren't they keeping track of things?"

Folks. Folks. Folks. The economy was superheated. The boom-and-bust cycle catches the lenders at just about the same time it catches your grandparents. Because of this, the restructuring guys at the lenders are never the people that originally made the loans. Those loans were made years ago. The ones responsible for making the loans have long since moved on, to another job somewhere else, where this part of history will not follow them.

The stockholders, analysts, and employees having all of their 401k retirement savings in Enron stock remain in the dark. And Enron's stock keeps rising, as its actual value dwindles.

Enron figured a way to keep its losses from hitting its income statement. It was ingenious. It pushed its losing investments into independent partnerships, and whenever the need arose, Enron kept the lenders to those partnerships at bay by issuing more Enron stock to the partnerships. Let's cut though all the fog, though. Enron shifted its losses directly to its shareholders. However, Enron did this without its shareholders ever realizing it, because Enron's impaired assets sat hidden from view in the partnerships. Enron never reflected the losses from these impaired investments on its own income statement. Enron shifted the losses to its shareholders, though, there is no doubt about this; it did this by diluting their stock. "Go Directly to Shareholders—Do Not Pass Through Income Statement."

Think of dilution this way: Instead of your one million shares of Enron representing a one one-thousandth ownership of the net assets of the company, it now represents one one-hundred-thousandth. That, my friend, is dilution.

Nobody notices what is happening. Once Enron's stock begins dropping in value because of other events, however, the banks begin to get nervous. As a result, Enron is forced to issue more and more of its stock to the partnerships to provide collateral to back up the partnerships' borrowings from the banks (read as more and more dilution to your grandparents holdings of Enron stock).

Okay, Enron. Issue more stock. That'll work for a while.

Enron bet on deregulation of the energy markets. The problem with this great idea was that they almost sent California over the cliff, like Thelma and Louise in that grand old convertible.

California almost imploded. The attorney general there is still looking for the manipulators of California's energy markets. Here's a hint: Look for the "choke points." The way the Robber Barons did it was by simply preempting the country's arteries of trade. California's "Big-Four" of the late nineteenth century—Stanford, Huntington, Crocker, and Hopkins— knew that the choke point for any transcontinental railroad would be its entry point into California. They also knew that there was only one pass through the Sierra Nevada suitable for a railroad grade, the Emigrant Gap at Donner's Summit. Control that one pass, and you control the entire railroad industry in the West.

Similarly today, and perversely, the energy transmission grid has been constructed such that California is once again isolated. There are only a couple of places where natural gas pipelines enter California. Look toward the Mojave Desert, in the southernmost part of the state, and again at the state's northernmost point, and you will find these few points of entry.

California's attempt at the deregulation of its energy market became a calamity. PG&E filed for bankruptcy; Southern California Edison faced a similar crisis until Governor Gray Davis brokered stopgap relief. California's then record state surplus (coming on the heels of the biggest boom since the California gold rush) was gobbled up in one summer of emergency purchases of forward energy contracts. Enron's predatory practices were in the fore of California's deregulation problems. California's Public Utilities Commissioner, Loretta Lynch, testified before Congress in April 2002 that Enron engaged in sham transactions designed to drive up electricity prices in that state in late 2000, worsening the energy crisis then plaguing the West. Federal regulators finally stepped in to cap prices in order to stave off a meltdown.

In August 2002, federal regulators were finally ready to assert that there was evidence that natural gas prices had been manipulated, fundamentally contributing to the energy crisis in the West. The report prepared by staff of the Federal Energy Regulatory Commission (FERC) indicated that Enron's operational strategies "involved deceit, including the provision of false information" in order to manipulate energy prices. The FERC noted that Enron earned almost $2 billion in profits trading energy contracts related to California and other markets in the Western United States. The FERC further pointed out that Enron's fraudulent operational strategy regarding the export of power from California to evade price caps in that market, significantly worsened the energy shortage in that market. Prosecutors have now empanelled a federal grand jury to investigate the alleged manipulation of energy markets in California by Enron and others.

Yet, with all these ill-gained profits accumulated during the two-year period through 2001, Enron still blew itself up.

Enron, a corporate parasite, broke a fundamental rule of biological diversity. In its attempt at market manipulation, Enron had almost killed its host. In nature, successful parasites never kill off the host body.

What had happened to California frightened the hell out of the other states that had been planning to deregulate, so they didn't, causing Enron significant grief. Enron's business plan was a massive bet on the side of deregulation of the nation's energy markets. Its future profits were tied to the assumption that other states would follow in California's chosen path.

A parasite requires future hosts. Enron's "future hosts" immunized themselves immediately from the harm inflicted on California. There would be no future hosts on which to suck.

Meanwhile, Enron's stock continued to slide. Sooner or later, one would expect to see the stock drop from the effect of being diluted alone. I mean the coffee's getting weaker every day. You keep watering it down, pretty soon it's not going to taste like coffee anymore. That's why somewhere back around the turn of the 19th century they named this kind of stuff "watered stock."

At about the same time, the Internet bubble burst. Then the Nasdaq went into the toilet. Technology stocks went in the tank right when some of us had begun believing that the new technology and systems bringing us "just-in-time" inventory management philosophies and other productivity gains would insure us from ever having another inventory recession. We were supposed to be recession-proof as a result.

The economy had been growing with a full head of steam; corporations were planning for 25 percent growth, period after period, year after year. If you're in sales, or a CEO, with that kind of planning assumption, you need to hit that number indefinitely or the sky is going to fall on you. Shirley Hudler, the Enron manager responsible for the *JEDI 1* off-balance sheet partnership, describes the environment at Enron, "There was so much pressure on us to make earnings . . ."

So maybe you "stuff the channel" a little bit. You ship more product than your customer wants, or needs. Has this truly been happening? You bet. Somehow, along the way, our corporate culture changed. This type of "stretching of the truth" got institutionally rationalized, at even the largest of companies, and even at the highest levels. And after institutions rationalize stretching the truth, people begin exhibiting a sense of continuing entitlement to the rewards that have ensued.

The problem with all of the foregoing is that the next month, quarter, or year, you find that you have to do that again. You have to stuff the channel again in order to replicate and even surpass what it was you had done the previous month, quarter, or year. Distasteful? You bet. But as far as you're concerned, everyone is doing it. It's no big thing. It's the new culture in business. You may also believe the situation is only temporary and that you can fix things down the line when things get better. Plus, if everybody is doing it, it's normal business practice, by definition.

The next thing that happens, though, is that the NY Stock Exchange follows the Nasdaq into the toilet and the country's heading into a full-blown recession. Each step of the way, Enron stock tumbles a bit in value, and the banks are requiring more collateral to cover their loans to the partnership. So, Enron issues more stock to the partnerships as collateral.

A curious thing results: With all of this stock issuance, Enron's investment in these partnerships starts going well beyond the magical threshold of this arcane 3 percent rule. When Enron's investment in any one of the partnerships goes beyond the level of 3 percent, the partnership is no longer deemed "independent," and can no longer be treated as "off (the) balance sheet." Don't ask me to explain the rationale underlying the rule, because it's silly and nonsensical. The upshot of it is that the partnerships now have to be consolidated with all of Enron's other assets and liabilities. The partnership losses now have to be recognized as Enron's losses. And by the way, where did all this debt come from? Holy smokes, no one knew that Enron had anything close to all this debt!

How in the world could one company have made so many bad investments? Skilling doesn't have to answer this question. He's already retired. He retired four months earlier, "when things were good." When things were in great shape. Ha!

In the end, there's no other way around it; the auditors conclude that Enron's income statement has to reflect *all* of the losses the partnerships have experienced. The scheme's success was completely dependent on avoiding such accountability, though.

The restatement announcement occurs. It's only $1 billion, give or take some, but the partnerships now finally come to light. The marketplace has been informed because the curtain has been drawn. The marketplace realizes that the emperor is wearing no clothes and banks all over the globe decide that no further credit is to be extended to Enron. To protect themselves from further credit exposure, other entities begin refusing to trade gas and energy contracts with Enron; they take their business elsewhere.

As a result, the one remaining business Skilling had decided Enron was to participate in, energy trading, comes up empty—there is no business activity available to Enron because nobody will trade with Enron anymore. Why take the risk?

Some of Enron's lenders had insured some of the *more creative* loans [my italics here] against default. As a result, these lenders call on the insurance companies to honor the surety bonds. The insurance companies respond by immediately suing the lenders for fraudulently inducing the insurance companies to issue the surety bonds in the first place. Things get weird, it's almost like a Fellini movie; one of the plaintiffs in this litigation is actually suing itself, because one part of itself is a lender, and another part of itself is an insurer.

Skilling likened it all to a run on a bank.

Rather than plead the fifth, Skilling comes up with a new *mea culpa*. He "is not an accountant," he pleads in his Senate appearance. He "wasn't aware of what was going on." Others, it now appears, will be required to testify about what Skilling did, or did not, know. The amazing thing in all of this was that there was only one whistleblower. "I wish we could get caught. We're such a crooked company," wrote Sherron S. Watkins to Kenneth Lay on August 14, 2001. "I am incredibly nervous that we will implode in a wave of impending scandals."

Sherron Watkins was dealing with a very powerful corporation, and she was accusing executives of misconduct. She was pointing the finger at powerful men, men who led by intimidation. Many, many employees at Enron, as well as former employees, have referred to this culture of intimidation bred by Jeff Skilling. He grew visibly frustrated with executives who "just didn't get it" with regard to the direction he was charting for the company. To ease these people out, Skilling implemented an employee evaluation and ranking system for everyone at Enron. Those who scored in the bottom tranche would be forced to leave the firm. The force-ranking system was ruthlessly enforced. Executives who articulated disagreement with Skilling's policies, those in his view who acted more like "cops" than people who wanted to do the deal, would be demoted and transferred.

One of Skilling's first hires upon joining Enron, way back in 1990, was Andrew Fastow. Skilling became Andy Fastow's mentor. In early 1997, Skilling was appointed Enron's president and chief operating officer. With this change, Skilling and CEO Kenneth Lay appointed Andrew Fastow head of a newly created finance department. The next year, Andrew Fastow was appointed Enron's chief financial officer. To me, the following two vignettes on Andy Fastow serve as metaphors, personifying this concept of leading through intimidation, the primary cultural factor at Enron.

A Citigroup investment banker, Ray Bowen, was sitting in a small conference room adjacent to Fastow's office waiting for a meeting. Filling the white-board on the opposite wall in the conference room was a whole series of complex equations. When Fastow came into the room, Bowen engaged in some preliminary small talk. He asked Fastow about the equations filling the white-board. "You can't tell me you understand those equations," Bowen commented to Fastow.

Fastow's response was telling, "I pulled them out of a book to intimidate people," he responded.

Fastow kept a Lucite cube on the front of his desk. Anybody sitting down across from his desk in his office would be confronted with the message imbedded within the cube. According to Fastow, the message embodied the essence of Enron's corporate culture. When Enron says it's "going to rip your face off," the inscription read, "it will rip your face off."

"Andy's boys," defined by a former Enron employee as a group of finance department employees who were exceptionally brilliant, were prepared to work endless hours unstintingly, and were ready to "follow [Fastow] down blind paths if that was required." One of them was Michael Kopper.

Fastow preferred to surround himself with ex-investment bankers who could "think outside the box." Kopper fit this bill. For meetings that had been called by others, he would not hesitate to show up late, and once there, talk over others in an effort to denigrate an idea not of his own making. With this approach to communication, he could effectively unravel any consensus a small group would be headed toward if it wasn't of his own making. This is the man that Fastow chose to run the most significant of the partnerships designed to hide, "off-balance sheet," Enron's ballooning debt.

Kopper would not hesitate to humiliate coworkers who were not prepared to deal with a subject to his level of satisfaction. "Michael did not suffer fools well," said a former employee. Others have described Kopper as being arrogant and disrespectful of others.

Sherron Watkins had a very real reason to be concerned about the corporate behemoth she had decided to challenge. At the time she wrote the memo, she was concerned about her personal safety. She was concerned enough to store in a lockbox a copy of the memo she sent Kenneth Lay. She wanted to ensure that the memo was somewhere safe, where it could not be destroyed.

With a scale of something as big as this, how can there have been only one whistleblower?

There remain many, many participants; all having some modicum of awareness of the different pieces of this puzzle called Enron.

Fastow, who had shot to the pinnacle of one of the flashiest corporations in the history of the United States, would be criminally charged with securities fraud, conspiracy, and other related charges, at the ripe old age of 40.

Kopper, Fastow's chief lieutenant in finance, would be indicted on the same charges when he was 37 years old.

*   *   *

Alex Jarvis recalled a series of e-mails that had been going back and forth between a couple of individuals at Morgan Fay.

"There were these e-mails that were titled, 'Was it really worth it?'" Alex Jarvis said. "I don't remember who they went to—or from," Alex continued. "But they were talking about the executives, whether something was going to happen to them after everything got found out. So, it was well before the investigation. But it was two employees, talking on e-mail about whether it's really 'worth it' to these executives—what's gonna happen to them."

"Meaning," I asked, "whether the executives were going to benefit from the whole scheme?"

"Right," Alex said. "'They are gonna go to jail. To get their money, was it worth them going to jail over?' That was the unspoken word of the e-mail, but that's the gist of the body."

What the forensics team discovered during the course of the Morgan Fay investigation eerily parallels what was later revealed in the unwinding of Enron.

I'm referring now to the *corporate culture* that facilitated the perpetration of the fraud at both of these companies. Though the scale of Enron's fraud far surpasses that of Morgan Fay, they are worth viewing together because the essential drivers were the same. They were both facilitated by a corporate culture of arrogance and a corporate culture of leadership through intimidation.

And the Morgan Fay fraud had many participants, who all remained silent throughout. Though some of these participants did not perpetrate the fraud, they were knowledgeable, and they were complicit in their silence.

In the Morgan Fay investigation, there was no whistleblower. Not even one.

CHAPTER ELEVEN

"Bad Tuna"

When Jaco Sadie and I first sat down around a small conference table to discuss his involvement in the Morgan Fay investigation, he immediately wanted to launch into all the "accounting shenanigans," as he put it, that he and the other forensic accountants had discovered at Morgan Fay. This part of the story interested me the least. I told Jaco that I was more interested in the investigation itself.

Undeterred by my lack of interest, he came up with the contrivance of what he would say were he "to tell the story to my mother, who lives in Cape Town, South Africa."

"Now there's a hell of an expedient," I found myself thinking. Why couldn't I think of something as creative as that?

"Fine," I said. I figured she probably loves him, but not enough to allow him to bore her to tears.

"So, if I was to tell this to my mother," Jaco began, "the one thing that I would try to explain to her, and she's not an accounting person, is all the different adjustments that was now filtering out, coming to the table . . ."

And so the interview began.

Jaco, the diminutive for Jacobus and pronounced 'Yah´-ko,' had been raised in Johannesburg, South Africa. Although he was quite fluent in English, his first language was Afrikaans, the language that had evolved over the centuries from the Dutch originally spoken by seventeenth-century settlers.

Because of the peculiarities of Jaco's Afrikaans grammar, there would often be something a little "off" in the sentences he formed in English. And as we talked, I found myself tracking on his grammatical mistakes. All of his mistakes had a certain consistency to them.

Jaco explained. "In English," he said, "you have, 'he is,' and, 'they are.'"

Jaco wasn't telling me anything I didn't already know. I could speak English. He couldn't. Then he explained that in Afrikaans you don't bother with verb conjugations. This notion began to sink in. The fact that there is a whole country that makes no distinction between the singular and plural seemed absurd. When I asked him why, he responded, "It's simpler."

Good point.

Though I began to appreciate the peculiar logic of Afrikaans, his grammatical quirks continued to make me flinch inside each time he would mangle a sentence. He'd say, "We is going," and an empty garbage can would get knocked over in some dark alleyway of my mind.

Plus, it made good old Jaco sound stupid, which he isn't. This guy is extremely bright, but he couldn't help but frame his thoughts in Afrikaans, translate the phrase mentally, and then loose the thing upon the English-speaking world.

Sometimes things got a little messed up.

He pointed out that when typing something, he'd re-read it; and then he'd often find himself thinking, "Okay, this must be an 'are' that needs to be here. Not an 'is.'"

Jaco told me he didn't worry about his grammar too much because of something that had been drilled into him in high school. "In English," he said, "there is always an exception to the rule. That's the only thing I remember," he said and he smiled with the remembrance. Whenever Jaco internally translated something, the fact that there was always an exception to the rule would cause him to experience a stab of doubt. Jaco would find himself thinking, "Now is this the exception?"

We were discussing this, again, at a farewell dinner for Jaco and his wife Anita. They and their newborn baby were transferring to our forensics and investigative practice in Luxembourg. Patti, my wife, offered some penetrating advice to the young couple, "You can always remember the singular," she said, "because it has an 's,' on the end. Like: 'has'; or 'is'; or 'was.'" I asked Jaco whether they had taught him that in school.

"They did," he said. "But the issue is figuring out whether it's singular or not."

"Well, one person is singular," Patti responded.

"It's not always that obvious," Jaco said. "There are a lot of people in Deloitte . . ."

I found myself siding with Jaco. His logic was beginning to get to me.

Jaco had met Anita, his future wife, while studying accountancy in South Africa. I asked him whether he had studied to be an Afrikaans CPA, or an English-chartered accountant.

"Afrikaans," Jaco responded.

Both Jaco and Anita had specifically joined an English-speaking firm to get international experience. Coopers and Lybrand had merged with the largest Afrikaans-speaking accounting firm, and all of their friends had joined Coopers and Lybrand. Anita and Jaco had joined Deloitte and Touche, but Jaco had run into language difficulties immediately. "The first thing they tell me is to 'foot' something," Jaco said. "Which to them means 'cast' the numbers."

"Here, it means 'to add,'" I said.

"Right," Jaco said. "Then they say, 'the trial balance.' And I would say back to them, 'What is the trial balance?' because I didn't know what the English was for a trial balance. I just know there's a proof balance. So this guy is looking at me, and I know he's thinking, 'Oh boy, I've got an idiot here.'"

Jaco was extremely bright though, and especially tenacious, which made him a perfect candidate for these types of investigations. He saw them as a challenge. He was bent on discovering every little trick Cindy Shalott's wrecking crew had devised to hide Morgan Fay's financial problems. He was equally bent on educating me, and his mother, about them.

*   *   *

"They would get so creative," Jaco said. "They would take, I think it was, bad tuna, that they had . . ."

"Bad tuna?" I asked in disbelief.

"Yeah, I think it was that. And they were trying to sell that. It was bad inventory.

"So they know it was bad inventory," Jaco continued. "And then they exchange it for advertising credits."

"Okay," I said. "So they entered into an exchange with their supplier for advertising credits—this 'bad tuna.'"

Big deal, I'm thinking. I knew that Morgan Fay's Minneapolis division included a plant dedicated to the processing of frozen fish products. This bad tuna may not have smelled so good, but nothing untoward seemed to be going on. It sounded like a bona fide business accommodation to me.

"And then if I remember correctly," Jaco continued. "They recognized profit, as if it was selling at full market value."

"Bad tuna?" I asked, because now what he was describing wasn't making any sense at all. How do you take a bad situation—maybe a ton or more of foul-smelling tuna, and turn that into a gain for financial statement reporting purposes? I was having trouble connecting the dots.

"They would book what they called a rebate," Jaco explained. "They booked $10 million of rebates as income. I think they had to do a certain amount of volume, or purchases from the supplier. And then the supplier would give them a $10 million rebate. There was no support for that. It was just, 'We'll book this $10 million rebate.' Just another way of getting $10 million."

"But a rebate is an expense, right?"

"No, no," Jaco responded. "A rebate that they're gonna get back from their supplier."

I'm still not understanding, but I persist. "So that would be booked as a rebate receivable from the supplier?" I asked. If this were the case, the "transaction" would signify "income" to Morgan Fay.

"Yes," Jaco responded.

I was getting his drift. We get a shipment of bad tuna. Don't do anything with that. Throw it out, perhaps; but leave it on the books as if nothing bad had happened, or was going to happen. And through this accounting subterfuge, convert that bad thing into something creative and positive.

"And then, would they do anything to hide that?" I asked.

"They just said to the auditors, 'Well, that's for this quarter. We will get this.' And then I think maybe for the next quarter, they would reverse it."

"And put it somewhere else?" I asked.

Jaco nodded. "Somewhere else," he affirmed.

This part of the scheme can be likened to a sidewalk shell game, where there are three shells on the table, and the peanut is supposed to be underneath one. The shells get moved from position to position, quickly, so that the player is unable to guess where the peanut is.

Whenever Morgan Fay needed to avoid recognizing a loss on some questionable balance sheet item, they would move the balance around, transferring it from one place on the balance sheet to another. They were hoping that when the balance was zeroed out on moving it, the auditors would buy their story that the thing had been collected or otherwise realized. They bet that the more they moved it, the harder it would be for an auditor to follow what it was that they were doing, or where they ultimately ended up parking the loss. Every quarter when they would be questioned about it, they would come up with a different story.

"'Trade loading' was another one they loved to do," Sadie pointed out to me.

Jaco was referring to a business practice of recording, as a sale, shipment of product into the channel—either to distributors, or to brokers, or to grocery retailers directly—product that the channel or the marketplace hadn't really ordered, or needed.

To the uninitiated, this may seem outrageous. The distressing fact is that trade loading has been going on in corporate America for perhaps the last 30 years or so. The practice got out of control in the 1990s.

Business headlines during the years 2000 and 2001, reported that corporations were taking significant inventory write-offs. Much of these write-offs had to do with "trade-loaded" product, or product that had been "stuffed" into the distribution channel. Manufacturers had shoved more products out the door (i.e., being shipped/sold to their independent distributors) than the distributors could ever hope to sell to their ultimate customers in the near future. During 2000 and 2001, these product shipments were being returned to the manufacturers in trailer loads. The ramifications of "channel stuffing" exacerbated our country's economic decline once the heady boom days of the 1990s fell away. The economy had turned, and corporations were taking inventory charges like crazy.

Morgan Fay practiced channel stuffing to an extreme. The practice of channel stuffing is particularly insidious to an auditor because the delivery of the product actually has taken place, so that the transaction looks like, talks like, and smells like a sale.

"They'd said the delivery of the product took place," Jaco was explaining to me. "So you would think that from an accounting perspective, 'Yeah, it was fine. It took place. You can record the revenue.'

"But then the product would not sell to the ultimate customer," he continued. "And so, they (the broker, or distributor, or grocer) would just ship it back to Morgan Fay and say, 'No. You have to take this back and give me a credit.'"

"And Morgan Fay would be forced to accept the return?"

Jaco nodded. "They had no choice. The right of return was part of the deal to begin with. Kind of like an under-the-table handshake."

Despite the fact of this right of return, Morgan Fay worked the whole process into one great big fraud. The product would return, and Morgan Fay would give a credit to the grocer or distributor. These two transactions would physically transpire during the first couple of months of Morgan Fay's new fiscal year. Morgan Fay would allow the original sale to the grocer or distributor, which occurred in the previous fiscal year, to stand, the effect of which was overstatement of sales and profits in the previous fiscal year. As far as the Avalon Partners management team was concerned, "next year is next year. We'll deal with that when we have to, because there's always tomorrow, and our stock options will vest before then."

Jaco pointed out a more outright fraudulent practice. "They also would sell product that they haven't shipped yet, at year end."

That's right. Morgan Fay recorded sales for product they never even shipped. They did this at the time of their ever-important fiscal year-end cutoff date.

I asked him how he determined that.

"Well, you would look at the shipping documentation," he said.

An important underpinning of Robin Malory's business plan was the acquisition of numerous "brands" from other companies—products that Morgan Fay would then have the right to manufacture and sell. The subterfuge: with each acquisition of another brand, Morgan Fay would improperly defer recognizing operating expenses it had incurred, improperly capitalizing them instead. Jaco described how Morgan Fay's Purchase Accounting subterfuge worked. "A lot of expenses would be put in the purchase accounting bucket," Jaco explained. "And the accounting implication of that is rather than taking a hit for an expense of 100 percent of that amount (today), they would then amortize it over 30 to 40 years."

Jaco was referring to the notion of the capitalization of a cost—placing it on the balance sheet, rather than expensing it on the income statement. At the time of my interview with Jaco Sadie, WorldCom's $3.8 billion fraud, which involved doing exactly the same thing, wasn't yet even a whisper on the wind.

CHAPTER TWELVE

"101 Ways to Cook the Books"

At seven o'clock in the morning, and only a short 37 days after WorldCom disclosed the biggest corporate accounting fraud in history, WorldCom's former chief financial officer, Scott D. Sullivan, and its former controller, David Myers, surrendered themselves to FBI agents in Manhattan. The next morning, the front page of the *New York Times* carried vivid pictures of FBI agents leading the two handcuffed men past a phalanx of photographers for their ride to the federal district courthouse in Lower Manhattan. Once there, the two executives were charged with accounting fraud for their roles in hiding over $3.8 billion in expenses to make WorldCom appear profitable.

FBI agent, Paul Higgins, a forensic accountant as well as a CPA, prepared an affidavit included as part of the WorldCom criminal complaint. Agent Higgins' affidavit outlined how Myers and Sullivan physically deleted over $3.8 million, excuse me, *billion,* in operating expenses from WorldCom's income statement, where the costs should have been booked. Instead, Myers and Sullivan moved the costs to WorldCom's balance sheet, where they remained "hung up" there, as if on a hook on a wall, until deducted in gradual amounts against WorldCom's income statement in future years. The *New York Times* likened WorldCom's scheme to be similar to treating these costs as akin to a mortgage, where a little bit of the debt is paid off in installments in future periods, in conjunction with each financial report to be filed in the future.

WorldCom paid "line fees" to other telecommunications carriers for the long-term lease of fiber optic lines and other facilities. WorldCom, however, had entered into many of these long-term leases in 1999, at the height of the Internet bubble. These leases required WorldCom to pay for the leased telecommunications capacity regardless of whether WorldCom actually made use of all or part of the leased capacity.

The method used in this part of the accounting fraud is so absurdly simple that it is almost beyond belief. What did WorldCom do?

They "plugged" their books is what they did.

The "plugging" of an account is an inelegant thing; it's akin to you or me forcing, or "plugging," our checkbook—resorting to this in frustration of not being able to reconcile the darn thing to the bank statement. "Plugging" is, in effect, giving up on the month-end bank-reconciliation exercise, and forcing the checkbook to agree with the bank.

How did WorldCom apply this inelegant technique?

Before having added so significantly to its fiber optic and line transmission capacity in 1999, WorldCom's operating margin had tended to approximate 40 percent, meaning that after deducting operating expenses from revenue, WorldCom would historically earn a margin of 40 percent, before back office costs and corporate overhead were figured in. Cynthia Cooper and Glyn Smith, internal auditors at WorldCom, noted an unusual discrepancy. When attempting to reconcile actual expenditures for line capacity to that reported on the company's financial statements, they found there was a $2 billion difference. Perplexed, they asked for a meeting with Scott Sullivan, WorldCom's CFO, to discuss the discrepancy. In this meeting, Sullivan stated that revenues had begun declining in the year 2001, whereas WorldCom's operating cost had substantially been "fixed" as a result of the long-term leases of telecommunications capacity signed in 1999.

The Internet bubble had begun to burst shortly after these long-term commitments were entered into. As a result, WorldCom was finding itself between a rock and a hard place, with its revenues declining and its costs increasing, "making it difficult to keep WorldCom's earnings in line with expectations by industry analysts." Because of these long-term leases, its costs were now "fixed," and could not be reduced. As reported by U.S. Deputy Attorney General Larry Thompson, "Sullivan and Myers decided to work backward, picking the earnings numbers they knew analysts expected to see, and then forcing WorldCom's financials to match those numbers."

In an e-mail sent at the very inception of this portion of the fraud, Steven Brabbs, a senior WorldCom executive in London, questioned Myers as to why Brabbs' division had its expenses reduced by $34 million. Unsatisfied with the answer, Brabbs addressed a letter to senior financial management, as well as to Arthur Andersen, WorldCom's auditor, requesting that they determine the *bona fides* of this reversal of expenses. Notwithstanding this challenge, the fraud ballooned, unchecked, to epic proportions over the next year.

On June 17, 2002, the two WorldCom internal auditors met with Myers to review the history of the $3.8 billion in questionable adjustments. WorldCom's controller responded matter of factly that WorldCom simply could not continue with the cost structure the company had entered into, and that if the cost structure did not change, the company "might as well shut the doors."

A statement I saw in the WorldCom criminal complaint caught my eye, for it harkened back eerily to something Jaco Sadie had observed in his interview with me several months earlier. The complaint summarized the results of a meeting held between Cynthia Cooper, WorldCom's Vice President of Internal Audit, certain other members of her staff, and Myers. During the course of this meeting, Myers stated that, upon reflection, "WorldCom should probably not have capitalized the line costs, but that once it was done the first time, it was difficult to stop." Myers in this meeting was articulating the same set of circumstances that Jaco Sadie had noted with regard to the Morgan Fay fraud. Once they had started digging the hole, it was too hard a thing to climb out of.

Of all the events and circumstances of the WorldCom accounting fraud, though, the one thing that I found the most distressing was something that hadn't happened. In the summaries of the meetings held by the WorldCom internal auditors, I was able to read between the lines something I could easily imagine might have happened, with the result that the fraud might have not been reported when it had. The disturbing result of this would have been that many more people would have been drawn into the quicksand of the fraud. WorldCom, though, would inevitably have staggered on its way into bankruptcy. Maybe not this quarter or the next, but soon nonetheless. But as a result of this deferral of the inevitable, many more people would be then subject to indictment when the fraud ultimately came to light. The following depicts what was unfolding in real-time.

Pressure was being brought to bear against Cynthia Cooper, to dissuade her from continuing on with the internal audit investigation. Scott Sullivan, WorldCom's then-CFO, told her that he was anticipating taking a restructuring charge in the second quarter of 2002 relating to the entries that she was auditing. Further, Sullivan stated that WorldCom would after this restructuring no longer capitalize the line charges in question. In effect, what Sullivan was suggesting was that, at the close of the next month-end financial statements, which was then only 19 days in the future, the company would take an immense restructuring charge, something well in excess of $3.8 billion, to recognize the fact that the company's cost structure could no longer be supported by operations. With this immense restructuring charge, WorldCom would be informing the stock market of the amount of loss that needed to be recognized. WorldCom would be stepping up to take its medicine and would write-off all these costs immediately. With that cleansing action, the company would put the past behind them, and be ready to face the future again.

With the treatment Sullivan was suggesting to Cooper, however, the accounting fraud that had been underway for the entire year previous, beginning with the company's filing of its Form 10-Q with the SEC on May 15, 2001, would be conveniently swept under the rug, and would be lost in all the detail of the massive multibillion restructuring charge Sullivan envisioned. The company could effect everything within three short weeks, Sullivan was implying. "Nobody would be the wiser, and we will have cleaned up our act," was the unstated premise.

Wisely, Cynthia Cooper acted immediately; she was having none of that. She initiated discussions with WorldCom's audit committee chairman, who agreed with her suggestion to meet with KPMG to determine their conclusions with regard to the entries. Her correspondence also indicated that she would "Review Andersen's workpapers related to (these costs)." KPMG replaced Andersen as WorldCom's auditor on May 16, 2002.

Over the weekend, the external auditors from KPMG, together with Cynthia Cooper, would confront Sullivan and Myers about the entries that had been recorded; the investigators would conclude there was no basis for any of the entries that had been concocted by management, nor were there even any supporting schedules, other than the entries themselves. Sullivan and Myers would within days be fired.

Cynthia Cooper, as with Sherron S. Watkins, the Enron vice president who challenged Enron's practices so vociferously, remains today in possession of her integrity, and her freedom. After Cynthia Cooper's revelations, I and one of my partners, Kerry Francis, a forensic accountant specializing in securities fraud and accounting investigations, commented about the fact that both of these people were women. We were not the only ones who had noticed, for several weeks later, Geoffrey Colvin, editorial director at *Fortune* magazine, referred to both of these women as, "Wonder Women." Six months later, Cynthia Cooper and Sherron S. Watkins would grace the cover of *Time* magazine as two of *Time* magazine's three Women of the Year.

*   *   *

During the course of the Morgan Fay investigation, Jaco Sadie and the forensic accounting team constructed spreadsheets that captured every item requiring adjustment on the company's financial statements. The forensic accountants determined the period(s) of time logically affected by each of the issues requiring adjustment. This analysis was done so that the correcting adjustment could be rolled-back (in time) to restate the results originally reported during that time frame. This required a quarter-by-quarter analysis of events during the previous three-year period, the length of time the Morgan Fay fraud had been underway.

"And that was a changing number as new information would come to light," Jaco pointed out. "But then you have to determine, okay, 'How much goes into each quarter?' And, it's trying to get back to the source of the information—as to when did the transaction take place."

The forensic accountants were tracking $400 million in corrections that needed to be made to restate Morgan Fay's financial position. But did these adjustments relate entirely to the previous quarter, or did some relate back to the previous year, or even earlier? The pieces would have to be reconstructed and put into their proper time frames. Why? Because throughout this three-year period, different classes of shareholders would have purchased Morgan Fay stock, or different lenders would have been lending Morgan Fay millions of dollars—and all of this based upon fraudulent information. All these different constituents would have a claim against Morgan Fay for fraud. What Jaco and his team were doing was identifying the amount of harm that might have been inflicted upon any investor throughout the various time frames.

*   *   *

"Now, if I told my mom this story," Jaco said, "I would say, 'This is that thick,'" holding up his forefinger and thumb for me to see—they were about an inch apart, indicating the thickness of a book.

Jaco continued with his narrative. "These people at Avalon Partners could write a book called, *101 Ways to Cook the Books*. I don't think I've ever seen a company," he said, "that tried every conceivable method of cooking the books. These people did that, not only on trade promotions. That was the biggest one. But there was $10 million here, $5 million here, and $2 million more over there. They were capitalizing expenses, doing all sorts of stuff. 'We're just a little bit short,' they would say. 'We need to do one more thing to make our number.'

"I saw more schedules," Jaco continued. "It was amazing. They would have a schedule to track what are the things they were doing to make the number. Which I've never seen that before," he said.

I wasn't really sure of what Jaco meant by this.

He clarified, "Where they actually have a system going," he said. "A system to keep track of where they're cheating." Jaco was describing another set of books. A secret set of books.

There are different rules and regulations for presenting an income statement for tax preparation purposes and these rules seem to change every time Congress gets together. Because of these differing rules and regulations, companies generally maintain a second set of accounts for tax reporting purposes. The company always reconciles this second set of accounts at the time of preparation of the corporate tax return. The differences between the two sets of books are disclosed in the footnotes to the company's financial statement, as well as in the corporation's tax filings.

Jaco, however, was describing a third set of books. "I think they probably spent more time trying to massage and manage the third account of books than the actual set of books," he said.

I asked Jaco to describe what kinds of things he saw. Not particular transactions, or specific documents, but what types of things he saw in general.

"They came up with different ways of compensating for the fact that they were not hitting their income statement."

"For example?" I asked.

"Creating fictitious invoices," Jaco responded. "As easy as that. They would do it. Because of the trade promotions, people were short-paying them."

"Short-paying them on what?" I asked.

"Say for instance they had a trade promotion with a regional grocery chain," Jaco explained. "This grocery chain would say, 'Well, I will put your product at the end of the display, and then 5 percent of what I buy from you goes toward that.'"

Jaco was describing an end-of-aisle promotion campaign. In these kinds of promotions, the grocer prominently showcases a product, for example, *Lady of the Lake* products. Because this kind of space is very visible to the consumer, products displayed on the end of an aisle tend to sell well. In this example, the grocer was negotiating a discount on its cost of the product in consideration for making this space available. The grocer would deduct this discount from the invoice price.

This type of deduction is normally treated as a trade promotion expense. Rather than treating this as an expense item however, Morgan Fay continued to reflect these deductions as if they were still owing as accounts receivable from the grocers or distributors. Using this method, Morgan Fay overstated its profits with every trade promotion negotiated.

The effect of these shenanigans was that Morgan Fay could drive their sales skyward, but a significant amount of the true costs of the sale, represented in the form of these trade promotion costs, would get hung up somewhere on the balance sheet—in this case, as a bogus accounts receivable balance.

There was one problem with this kind of deception. Morgan Fay's receivables would begin to balloon. To an astute reader of Morgan Fay's financial statements, a ballooning of the accounts receivables would imply that the receivables were not being paid on time.

With that kind of clue, an auditor would insist on reviewing the age of these balances, account by account. Looking at this kind of listing, an auditor would see that the accounts were getting old, or stale. To an auditor, accounts steadily getting older and not being paid would begin to become as noticeable as a bottle rocket going off in the sky. The first question that would come to mind is "Are these accounts receivable even collectible?" The second question would be "What's the underlying cause?"

The Avalon management team had a plan for how to deal with this. Jaco explained. "They were clever enough to say, 'Okay, maybe someone's going to find us out there.' So, they take that amount, and they create a bunch of fictitious invoices in their accounts receivable ledger. Small little ones."

"To whom," I asked. To my way of thinking, you create an invoice, you need to address it to someone, at some entity.

"To various people," Jaco said. "You make them up."

I understood now. Jaco was describing a fraud in which numerous people are being directed to participate. Many individuals were involved in this fraud at the corporate headquarters level; in this case at Avalon Partners. In addition, Morgan Fay's established internal controls were being overridden. Individuals with access to the sales and receivables ledgers at the various Morgan Fay subsidiary locations had to be creating fictitious customers, entering them in the customer master files, and creating fictitious invoices.

I ran through with Jaco the implications of what he was describing. Bogus information had been entered into the system. The system would generate invoices to be mailed. Someone had to have intercepted these so that the mailing did not occur. The same person had to have intercepted the month end statements so that the statements were not mailed.

Jaco nodded. "Right. But if you are this person, and you are sitting at home thinking about these kinds of things, the next thing you'll think about is, 'How can the auditors not find this? It's gonna age. It's gonna get to a point where it's not collectable. And it's really going to get someone looking at that.'"

With the creation of these fictitious invoices, the account balances reflected in the month-end trial balance would steadily get old, as they were never going to be paid. They would have to "age." There was no way they would ever get paid down since they weren't bona fide to begin with.

This sounds like an insurmountable problem, but the Avalon management group figured a way to deal with this problem, too.

"They would re-age things," Jaco said.

Remarkably, the computer forensics specialists and forensic accountants unearthed the very 're-aging' schedules. Jaco explained what he found. "They had assigned a specific invoice number to that fictitious invoice."

Jaco discovered that Avalon management's work-around was to simply cancel out an invoice number, and re-assign a new invoice number to an account that was going stale. This would be like resetting the clock on the receivable. With the assignment of a "new" invoice number, the computer would automatically assume the invoice was brand new.

Having discovered the technique Morgan Fay had used to hide the bogus invoices buried in the accounts receivable detail ledgers, Jaco leveraged this knowledge and used the power of the computer to hunt down each of the bogus invoices electronically.

What troubled me most about the Morgan Fay case, as with Enron, was the complicity of so many employees. Morgan Fay's management team had definitely been involved. Local management and staff at the two different divisions had helped to facilitate it. To accomplish the re-aging scheme that Jaco and the other forensics team members had discovered, the Avalon management group had directed Morgan Fay employees to consciously, and physically, create hundreds and hundreds of fictitious entries into the detail accounts. And they did as they were told. I asked Jaco how it was that so many people participated, from clerks to top management. "I think it started out very small," he said. "They were not making their number, perhaps by only a little bit at first."

Jaco was referring to the prospect of the company missing its earnings projection for a particular period. Morgan Fay, like most publicly traded companies, would have analysts from various investment banks assigned to follow the company's results of operations. Robin Malory and Cindy Shalott, as the company's CEO and CFO, would hold conference calls in which numerous analysts would receive an update on the company's current plans and strategies as well as projected earnings for the upcoming quarter and year-end. The mandate of meeting the quarterly earnings projection given to Wall Street analysts became an important cultural change in the boom days of the 1990s.

Jaco surmised that the Avalon management group reacted to the specter of missing their projections for the first time by stretching to meet the earnings target. "So we're just gonna squeeze the reserve here," Jaco suggested. "Or, push the channel a little bit here. And then it just gets worse and worse. The next quarter, we gotta do a little bit more. And then a little bit more."

Jaco's analysis of the situation at Morgan Fay was probably dead-on. The circumstances were not isolated to Morgan Fay, though. As a forensic accountant, I had found myself on more than one occasion testifying to similar situations uncovered at other corporations. In some cases, the company had been a start-up, whose future had ended in spectacular headlines and litigation. Sadly, in one other case, I would testify, in a Los Angeles Superior court, of proof that a Fortune 50 corporation, known worldwide, had falsified sales and then had sold the division in question. After Humpty-Dumpty crashed to the ground, the unsuspecting purchaser was left to pick up the pieces.

There was no jury in this courtroom on this day, as both parties had agreed to a bench-trial. I can remember the judge's demeanor as he examined the exhibits accompanying my oral testimony; it seemed so inconceivable that a company of this size and international reputation could have done what I was saying it had done. The furrows creasing the judge's forehead telegraphed his comprehension of the facts; he had in front of him uncontroverted evidence collected from third parties, including outside distributors, and including bills of lading from independent trucking companies. WorldCom, too, would be another example of this "addiction to falsification" that Jaco had alluded to. Within weeks of WorldCom's bankruptcy filing, another shoe would drop. WorldCom's fraud was not $3.8 billion, the headlines would scream; it was double that!

WorldCom became public in 1989 after acquiring a small publicly traded company. Over the course of the next 10 years, WorldCom went on a buying spree, acquiring 65 corporations during this timespan. With its 1998 acquisition of MCI, WorldCom's revenues ballooned to almost $40 billion. In 2000, however, the Justice Department disallowed WorldCom's proposed acquisition of Sprint on antitrust grounds. WorldCom's "Looking Glass" world ended that very day. Upon WorldCom's bankruptcy, former employees and analysts would come out of the woodwork to describe the acquisition "fix" to which WorldCom had become addicted.

They were talking of a "fix," as in heroin.

With each corporate acquisition, WorldCom "wrote-down" the value of the "tangible assets" it had acquired. This so called "write down," restated these assets to a value WorldCom ostensibly represented to be fair market value. On the surface, this would seem a conservative practice. However, the accounting rules for corporate acquisitions require that the difference between what WorldCom paid for these assets, as compared to their fair market values, be recorded on WorldCom's balance sheet as *purchased goodwill*. Simplified, if WorldCom paid $10 billion for a company with tangible assets (assets that can be touched, or felt) with an appraised value of only $4 billion, WorldCom's balance sheet would reflect tangible assets of $4 billion. WorldCom would record a new asset called *Goodwill* at $6 billion.

Seems logical, but there is a perversity here. WorldCom, and other corporations hell bent on growth-by-acquisition, would take advantage of rules which otherwise appear to be logical on their face.

To see the perversity of the above, you need to leave behind the point-of-view of WorldCom's balance sheet, and look at things through the looking glass of WorldCom's income statement. In the simple example I have

put forward, if the corporation WorldCom acquired had depreciated its
$10 billion in tangible assets over an average expected lifetime of five
years, that company's depreciation expense would have historically
amounted to $2 billion per year. WorldCom, after its acquisition though,
would experience depreciation of only $800 million ($4 billion ÷ five
years); an astounding 60 percent reduction in depreciation expense.
WorldCom would then amortize its Goodwill over a much longer period,
perhaps as long as 40 years. If you could reduce *your* expenses by such a
significant amount with each acquisition, *you'd* be addicted to the hit of
the "Alice's World of Acquisition Accounting," as well.

Consider this: If the price of your stock disproportionately increases
with each acquisition because of the disproportionate reduction in your
company's operating expenses, the stock market valuation of your stock is
ginning-up currency with which you may close even more acquisitions. You
no longer need to use cash, your ever-increasing and more valuable stock
is better than cash; it's even better than heroin. "The boost from postacquisition accounting was like a drug," a former WorldCom executive stated.
"But it meant bigger deals had to come along to keep the ball rolling."

The ball stopped dead in its tracks when the Justice Department put
the kibosh on WorldCom's acquisition of Sprint. WorldCom, the corporate addict, would suffer the withdrawal pangs from no longer having the
'hit' with which its income statements had previously benefited. Wall
Street, though, is an unforgiving lover. Institutional investors, the smart
money, bailed out of WorldCom stock, even as individual investors continued to hear what a good play it was from Wall Street analysts.

As far as the institutional investors were concerned, they knew the
music had ended. As described by one institutional money manager, it
had now become "a game of chicken, where you get as close as possible to
the end before getting out."

Playing chicken is a hell of a way to invest for the future. Purchase accounting principles that lead to addictive behaviors on the part of corporate management is a disease that requires treatment.

*   *   *

At Morgan Fay, after some time had elapsed with these types of things
going on, one of the divisional controllers had gotten very uncomfortable
with what he had been seeing. "He wanted to squawk," Jaco explained.
"He was ready to say, 'No. We can't go on like this. We've got to tell somebody.'" Jaco reported how the Avalon management group responded to
this threat of exposure from a potential whistleblower. "And so management here at Avalon Partners in San Francisco was offering him a position

because they wanted to merge the two divisions. And they're gonna offer him a very good position if he keeps his mouth shut."

So, in at least one case, a potential whistleblower was co-opted with a promise of a promotion. Perhaps others worried about their job security if, or when, things blew up in everybody's faces. Perhaps they were worried about their job security if they didn't go along with management's scheme.

Here was another parallel with Enron. Certain employees at Enron were concerned that the company's efforts to hide losses by moving them to other partnerships might ultimately take the company down; their concern was that continuously running those levels of losses could simply not be maintained. "We called it house-of-cards accounting and would openly discuss how crazy it was," recalled Jan Avery, an Enron accountant for eight years. She is believed to be an important witness in the upcoming civil and criminal trials. In response to a question about how upper management reacted to employees voicing these objections, Avery responded, "In meetings, we were always told the same thing: 'You have to be able to come up with a solution.' There was no alternative."

The "Skilling atmosphere" began to permeate Enron she recalled. "We were told constantly, 'Keep the debt off the balance sheets.'"

$$* \quad * \quad *$$

Jaco's fact-finding efforts during the Morgan Fay investigation revealed another amazing thing. In addition to people, an extensive amount of effort was expended to keep things covered up, requiring the participation and cooperation of managers and employees located in different parts of the country.

Jaco recalled, "Someone at 'corporate' would tell the division controller, 'Make sure that this particular person is on a leave of absence. Or takes vacation for three days. Because the auditors are coming in. Make sure she's out of the office.'"

In other words, if management was not dead certain of an employee's loyalty, they required that employee to take a holiday leave (with pay) until the auditors had left town. What a straightforward expedient! Just make sure that the person you're worried about will not be available to answer questions. I asked Jaco whether this order came directly from Morgan Fay's chief financial officer.

"Shalott, yeah," Jaco said. "They knew that person might be a little bit shaky so they had to make sure that the auditors don't get to her." Jaco recalled a series of e-mails documenting how the Avalon Partner management group coordinated efforts to mislead the PricewaterhouseCoopers

(PwC) auditors. "There was this little pile of documents that we labeled 'PwC,'" Jaco recalled. "Most of them were from Shalott. The gist of one was, 'We now have a new audit partner. And we might be able to pull the wool over his eyes fairly easily. He's a young guy.'"

I asked Jaco whether the "pulling the wool" metaphor was the way she had phrased it.

"No," Jaco responded. "That was sort of the gist of it. But it was very interesting that she would actually put this in an e-mail, and send it out to the heads of the two divisions." There was apparently a collection of e-mails along these lines; Shalott and Malory thought nothing of toying with the auditors. "I can recall an e-mail where she was sort of *prepping* these folks at the two divisions," Jaco said. "'The auditors are coming,' she would write. 'We have to get our story straight here.'"

During all of this manipulation and storytelling on the part of Morgan Fay's management, they had slipped up a couple of times. Someone hadn't been able to keep his or her story straight. As a result, the auditors were now becoming more focused in their questioning.

"She absolutely went ballistic in this one e-mail," Jaco said. "She was giving this poor guy a hard time. Telling him that 'This is not how we operate,' and that 'Anything that you're gonna tell him has to come through me. I will be the spokesperson.'"

"In hindsight," Jaco reflected, "you look at that, and it is pretty obvious that they're hiding something. And she's trying to control that. She was very controlling about how do we give the information over to the auditors."

I suspected that Jaco was sugarcoating what it was that he had seen. I pressed him a little.

He responded, "If I got an e-mail like that . . ."

He paused for a moment to reflect. He shook his head. "All I can say is you'd never get an e-mail like that here. It was nasty." There is an interesting parallel here to what was transpiring at WorldCom at approximately the same time.

A string of e-mails recovered in the WorldCom investigation reveal how WorldCom's controller, David Myers, had come down on a subordinate like a ton of bricks in order to quash any questioning of the shenanigans that WorldCom corporate was beginning to engage in. The subordinate, Brabbs, a financial accounting executive in WorldCom's London office, was confused and concerned about the reversal of $34 million of expenses, which had been directed to be made at the "corporate level" back in the United States. One thing that concerned Brabbs was that the books had already been effectively closed. Unsatisfied with the response he was getting from Myers back at corporate headquarters in the United States, Brabbs decided to bring Arthur Andersen into the picture; he met with Andersen executives in London. At this meeting, he asked them to look into the questionable reversal of expenses, as it didn't strike Brabbs as being right.

The response from WorldCom corporate was like a bolt of lightning. "Do not have any more meetings with AA for any reason," Myers directed in an e-mail warning. "Don't make me ask you again," Myers added.

Brabbs, however, reached out to Arthur Andersen once more, in early 2002, shortly before WorldCom collapsed. This time, Myers went ballistic: he wrote to another colleague about Brabbs' future with the company, "Not that I was looking for another reason to have him executed."

In July 2002, Myers was charged with securities fraud, conspiracy, and other related charges.

Jaco and the other members of the investigative team were able to string together Shalott's directions to the divisional people regarding obfuscation. The auditors at PwC must have been getting concerned about the company's treatment of their trade promotion costs.

Jaco could recall that Cindy Shalott was getting very upset with the requests for information from the auditors. The e-mail communication streams were between Cindy Shalott and the divisional controllers.

Jaco explained what he was able to put together of this history. "She was saying, 'Give him what he needs in order to go away,'" Jaco said. "It was something like, 'Read between the lines. Tell him a bullshit story. And he will go away.'"

The final result of the forensics investigation was that over fifty separate types of financial adjustments needed to be recorded in order to restate the company's reported results of operations. Morgan Fay was even having a difficult time trying to keep track of the company's false world.

The company's financial staff compensated by maintaining separate schedules for each of the areas in which management had been pushing the envelope. When the computer forensics team recovered some of these Excel files, they noted the peculiar headings on the spreadsheets. Some of the schedules had headings like, "Trade Promotions—for PwC." Other spreadsheets had headings that were significantly different, such as "Trade Promotions—for Real." Often, the forensics team discovered a third schedule that served to reconcile the Avalon management team's illusory world with the real world.

"I mean, if it comes down to the point where you have schedules labeled that way, you've gone down the path very far," Jaco said. "And the information on the real schedule is just so night and day different from that given to the auditors."

It is human nature to retain things. Even evidence pointing clearly to fraud.

I asked Jaco whether he had seen any e-mails from the divisional financial staff indicating something along the line, "We don't agree. This is wrong."

"No, I didn't see that," Jaco said. "I don't even recall any e-mails like that."

*   *   *

The indictment brought against Malory and Shalott contained charges that I was familiar with as a result of cases in which I had either consulted, or in which I had testified as an expert in court. The federal indictment against these Morgan Fay executives included the following charges that are typical in these kinds of cases:

> Robin S. Malory and Cindy Shalott unlawfully conspired and agreed together and with each other to commit offenses against the United States, namely
>
> 1. To commit fraud in connection with the purchase and sale of securities, in violation of Title 17, Section 240.10b-5—[the famous 10b-5 statute upon which most civil securities fraud cases are brought]; and Title 15, United States Code, Sections 78j(b) and 78ff;
>
> 2. To make false and misleading statements in annual and quarterly SEC reports, in violation of Title 15, United States Code; Section 78ff;
>
> 3. To falsify books, records and accounts of Morgan Fay, in violation of Title 15, United States Code, Sections 78m(b)(2)(A), 78m(b)(5) and 78ff; and, Title 17, Code of Federal Regulations, Section 240.13b2–1;
>
> 4. To defraud financial institutions [bank fraud], in violation of Title 18, United States Code, Section 1344; and
>
> 5. To make false statements for financial institutions in connection with loan applications, in violation of Title 18, United States Code, Section 1014.

These were provisions of the law with which I was familiar. These are typical charges I had seen in the various fraud investigations, and corporate securities fraud and embezzlement cases in which I have served as an expert witness. The final charge brought against Malory and Shalott blew me away:

> To make, and cause to be made, false and misleading statements to Morgan Fay's auditors in violation of Title 15, United States Code, Section 78ff and Title 17, Code of Federal Regulations, Section 240.13b2–2.

Lying to an auditor of a publicly traded company is a felony. I hadn't known that. None of the auditing textbooks with which I am familiar indicate that it is a felony to lie to an auditor of a publicly traded company. I also know that it's not taught to people entering the profession, many of whom move on to become corporate controllers, chief financial officers, or chief executive officers of corporations.

Recently, I was responsible for making some formal remarks to a meeting of my Northern California-based partners. These were auditors, corporate tax specialists, and international tax experts, risk management specialists, and a few forensic accountants. There were maybe two hundred people in the room, all possessing a minimum of 15 years experience in their chosen field. In the course of summarizing the work that we do in my department, I mentioned that it was a felony to lie to an auditor of a publicly traded company. I could hear an audible gasp rise from the audience.

The fact that my statement was so shocking to a roomful of experts in the field is very telling. It is not common knowledge that it is a federal offense to lie to an auditor. It is also therefore not in the fabric of our corporate culture. Until now, this part of the law has rarely been enforced or publicized by our federal prosecutors.

Until now that is. Enron has changed the landscape.

A record 257 publicly traded companies filed for bankruptcy protection during 2001. These companies had over $258 billion in assets at the time of their filing, shattering the previous record of 176 companies with $95 billion in assets, set during the country's previous recession.

During the first two months of 2002, the SEC initiated a record forty-nine financial-reporting investigations, almost triple the number of investigations initiated during the corresponding two-month period of the previous year.

"The bigger story is the size of the companies being investigated," Charles Niemeier of the SEC's enforcement section has told members of the business press. "We are investigating more Fortune 500 companies than we ever have."

According to a survey reported by Woodruff-Sawyer & Co., an insurance brokerage firm specializing in corporate Directors' and Officers' insurance (D&O) coverage, there were 277 federal shareholder class action lawsuits filed *during the first nine months of 2001 alone*. This represented a 68 percent increase over the annual filing rate of the preceding 10-year period.

Woodruff-Sawyer projects that the cash settlement cost of the 277 class action securities fraud cases filed in 2001 will ultimately exceed $11 billion. Compare this to the average reported settlement costs of $3.4 billion for all cases filed during the previous five-year period.

There's more.

Using an audience interactive and automated question and answer system, the moderator of an annual conference asked the over 100 corporate chief financial officers in attendance to respond anonymously to the following question:

"Has your CEO ever asked you to falsify the financial results?"

Sixty-seven of the 100 corporate chief financial officers in attendance answered, "Yes." Twelve percent admitted they had done it.

The Justice Department has finally come to the realization that monetary fines have had no noticeable effect on the shaping of our corporate culture. The current thinking is that jail time is the only thing that will get the attention of corporate America.

Cindy Shalott and Robin Malory found themselves facing a stern judge sitting high on her bench in a federal courtroom in downtown Manhattan. Shalott and Malory soon would receive a very rude awakening.

At a recent national meeting of my forensic and investigative services partners, I picked up a bit of trivia from Dan Wetzel. He had participated in the Morgan Fay investigation and he told me about his visit to the frozen fish products manufacturing plant in Minneapolis. We had been talking about the tuna processing and he described how the tuna came into the plant in big frozen slabs. Huge saws were used to cut the frozen tuna into manageable shapes and sizes for purposes of packaging.

Dan then mentioned to me that Morgan Fay had a contract with the U.S. government to provide frozen fish products for the federal prison system. He said that the workers at the Minneapolis division would routinely sweep up all the fish sawdust from around the machines at the end of every day. These floor sweepings were then compacted into filets that were packaged and shipped to the various prisons around the country.

Perhaps during the course of the 5+ year prison sentences Robin Malory and Cindy Shalott will be serving, their meals will include some of these Morgan Fay fish-sawdust filets; deep-fried.

CHAPTER THIRTEEN

"The Cider House Rules"

Tonight there would be a second raid. The forensic imaging of the computers of the division level executives was now to occur: the president, chief financial officer, and the divisional controller of Morgan Fay, all based in Minneapolis. Mike Murphy had tasked Tony Rosen with coordinating the planning.

Tony had been in Minneapolis ever since the document collection efforts at Avalon Partners in San Francisco two weeks earlier. The investigative team in Minneapolis had been working until midnight pretty much every day and, as far as Tony Rosen was concerned, coordinating this raid had been a pain. Tony had finally figured out a way through the scheduling conflicts posed by the computer forensics specialists. Kris Haworth was busy on another gig and Eric Schwarz agreed to lead this raid.

Eric and his team had flown in from Dallas earlier in the afternoon and had gone straight to their hotel. They planned to lay low there until nightfall before setting out on the task. Tony, easily excitable in normal times, was feeling a little flushed now. He looked at his watch again. It was going on 10 P.M. and they still hadn't shown up.

New to these things, Tony figured this was just one more oddity in an assignment awash with oddities. Plus, who was he to argue about when the imaging should start? He was only a lowly staffer; Schwarz was a big shot, a senior manager.

Tony looked over at the picked over pizza boxes. The conference room table in the Morgan Fay divisional headquarters offices looked as if it held the remains of a party. The only thing left of the pizzas was the cheese, which was congealed on the cardboard. The forensics team was in a rut. Not everybody liked Chinese, and they'd had pizza in every night that past week.

He'd heard a pretty good story about these pizza boxes from one of the partners back in San Francisco, but he didn't believe any of it. The way the story went was that the 35,000 or so spies who worked at the National Security Agency (NSA) supposedly generated so much paper each day that the agency couldn't figure out what to do with all of it. No way were they going to just shred all that paper and cart it to a landfill to get picked over by the Russians. So, they came up with the idea of constructing a paper pulping plant right there on the NSA campus outside Bethesda. The agency then processed the tons of discarded communication intercepts and memos through huge vats of water, where the wet mass was churned into pulp, ink and all. Supposedly the pulp was then trucked to a cardboard manufacturer where it was turned into pizza boxes. People were always trying to pull things over on Tony. No way he was that gullible.

The elevator door opened and Tony saw Eric and two other members of his team come out of the elevator. To Tony's eyes, the small group of men now heading toward him looked like a rock band. It was the good-sized rolling carts, cases, and black bags the small group of men had with them that cemented the image. That, plus the leather jackets, t-shirts, and blue jeans.

The computer forensics team unpacked their portable imaging devices and other gear. Soon, foam packaging from the rolling carts and computer equipment started filling up the work area. Tony pointed out each of the executive's offices. Schwarz sketched a rough floor plan indicating each office housing a computer that was to be imaged.

The computer forensics team began their work, taking the shells off the computers to be imaged, and hooking the hard drives of the computers directly to the portable imaging units that had been unloaded from the black cases.

Eric supervised the small team as they accessed the EnCase imaging software. Tony hung around the small group, asking Eric to explain exactly what they were doing.

As Tony watched, it didn't seem to be very exciting. All they seemed to do was connect the hardware and hit go. Then they all sat around. When he asked, "How long is this going to take?" nobody could really say. The computer forensics specialists didn't know how long it would take.

After watching nothing happen for awhile, Tony went back to the stuff he had been working on before the rock stars had arrived.

*   *   *

When I asked Tony to describe the Minneapolis Division, he recalled, "It was just amazing. After you got out of the elevator, everywhere you looked there would be nothing but *Excalibur Biscuit* boxes, and bags of *Mount Baden* bread and *Lady of the Lake* products on display and on everyone's desks. I can remember thinking I was working in a grocery store."

Beginning the assignment, the forensics team was aware that the trade promotion fraud was sizable, but they had no idea how many other things had been perverted. A fictitious sale here. Fictitious entries there. Extensive interviews conducted with members of divisional management helped identify subjects to be investigated further.

Tony recalled a weekend spent back in San Francisco. The investigative teams in Minneapolis and Omaha had flagged documents for review and the San Francisco-based investigators reviewed these as well as the interview summaries. This enabled Murphy and other team members to identify further keyword searches to be performed on the hard drives that had been forensically imaged. The keyword searches were also exercised against copies of the backup tapes of the company's servers.

The investigative team was looking for fraud by way of three separate methods: The first was interviews, which often yielded only a glimmer of a new subject area requiring further investigation. The second method encompassed having analysts study hard copies of documents. And finally, the power search ensued; keyword searches of the imaged hard drives were undertaken separately for each of the subject areas under investigation, based on the keyword lists developed by Murphy and the other team leaders. After new interviews and document searches revealed further areas of research, the whole process was repeated until each area of investigation had been thoroughly vetted.

As the assignment progressed, Tony found himself with little time to reflect on the ramifications of the investigation. The thought of people possibly going to jail as a direct result of evidence collected by him (and others) hadn't crossed his mind. The work schedule was so intense, and the need for results so immediate, that he just didn't have time to think about anything except what needed to be done that day. However, Tony did recall feeling great empathy for the Morgan Fay employees he met in Minneapolis.

"When I was there," he said, "I remember feeling sad for the people because everyone had stock options. The stock had been doing great. And everyone—the secretaries, everyone, people who had no involvement in the fraud—had just lost all this money. This was my first experience with this kind of thing. I can remember feeling sorry for them. I mean it was kind of a bad situation."

I asked Tony whether he had felt any hostility being directed at the forensics team as a result of the investigation.

"It was more that they resented management," he responded.

The full implications of the forensic team's discoveries didn't settle in for Tony until the final report started coming together: This was after the team had been almost a month into things, and after he had returned to San Francisco. One of Tony's assignments was to run point on collecting findings and the supporting evidence from the various investigative team members. As the documents and findings streamed in, Tony's point of view on the investigation changed significantly because he began to perceive the extent of the fraud. Tony began to see that the participants went well beyond the Avalon management team in San Francisco. People he had met while working in Minneapolis had been involved. People he'd had lunch with. And he was shocked by the number of issues that had been misrepresented. To him, a 22-year-old, first-year staffer, the amount of money involved was staggering.

It was maybe $200 million; perhaps $400 million, when you figured in what was going on at the other division. Enron and WorldCom still had two years of wick yet to burn before their spectacular flameouts. At that time, still only the year 2000, a $4 billion fraud would be unimaginable. Tony hadn't experienced these larger scandals: to him, the amount of money involved in the fraud at Morgan Fay was immense.

Tony wondered whether the accounting staff in Minneapolis, with whom he'd been working the whole time he'd been there, were responsible for physically entering the fraudulent data into Morgan Fay's transaction processing systems. If so, he wondered if they knew, at the time, that what they were doing was wrong. It was all confusing. Should he feel sorry for them? Were they somehow trapped into being knowing, but unwilling, participants? Or should they have stood up and said it was all wrong?

Tony recalled interviews in which some of the participants responsible for facilitating the scheme volunteered that they realized what they were doing was wrong. "They came right out and said it in the interviews," Tony said. "And they ended up getting fined, too." Tony was referring to two mid-level finance department managers in Minneapolis who were each fined $25,000 by the SEC.

Tony recalled one of the controllers with whom he had spent quite a bit of time. "He's one of the guys who's facing trial," Tony said, "and he's probably gonna go to jail."

I asked Tony what he thought about that.

"You have to wonder why he did it," he said. "You walk into his office, and you see he's got young kids. He seemed to be doing fine and was making enough money. It was my first experience into like, kind of the high level—seeing the actual chief financial officer and the chief executive officer of a major public company . . ."

At that, Tony fell silent.

Tony was silently asking the question we all have: What were these people thinking? These people at Enron. At WorldCom. These people at other companies facing indictments. These people who apparently didn't know when enough was enough.

Tony recalled being in a meeting with the controller. "I'm thinking (at the time) that he seems to have a pretty nice other life," Tony recalled. "Why would he do something like that? He seemed like a nice guy. I didn't actually partake in the interviews, but I would ask him questions. I even had lunch with him. He seemed like a really nice guy—kinda shy—kinda quiet."

Tony had a baby face, and I had noted that some days he'd come into the office without having shaved. Why not? He could get away without shaving the peach fuzz for a couple of days or so. It wasn't that he was lazy, but why shave if you don't have to?

Tony had just gotten out of college when first assigned to the Morgan Fay investigation. Over the next two years, he followed the periodic reports about Morgan Fay in the *Wall Street Journal* with great interest. He might have been only 22, but the *Wall Street Journal* was reporting on something about which he had intimate knowledge. For Tony, going through the experience then, even though it had transpired over a one-and-a-half-month time frame, to him it had felt like a year. The work just seemed like it was never going to end.

He reflected on his experience and learning. "It's obvious you could say that it just doesn't pay to cheat. It may pay off in the short run. But in the long run it doesn't." We talked about the fact that Cindy Shallot's prison sentence had been set the week before. "It took two years for these prison sentences to come down," Tony observed.

Our interview was occurring in February 2002; his work on the investigation had begun in February 2000. With this experience as a backdrop, I asked him what he thought when Enron first hit. "It's just a much bigger scale," Tony responded. "The interesting thing is how things always get 'discovered.'"

Tony had touched on a fundamental truth.

*   *   *

The "irrational exuberance" of the late 1990s was a very real thing, indeed. There was so much money poured into the telecom sector during this time frame that a vast overcapacity glut resulted; this, in addition to $470 billion of debt. Lonnie Martin, the chief executive officer of a struggling telecom company, estimates that there is now *seven* years worth of excess telecom gear, some $160 billion worth!

I'll translate. If you are a running a company sitting on two-years worth of unsold inventory, you are in deep trouble. Seven years is a staggering problem. Some corporation, somewhere, will be forced to "write-down" that excess inventory (or hopefully has already), recognizing that it can't be sold any time in the near future. These "inventory write-downs" translate into very poor corporate "margins," or outright losses; for any company that invested in building this inventory, which is now excess, and perhaps unsaleable, you will find these corresponding losses reported on the respective company's income statement. For the lenders, they now face almost half a trillion dollars of debt that may need to be "restructured." Having the need to work through problems of this scale can be a fundamental, contributing causal factor of a recession.

The issue of today is: When will we see these losses flushed through your income statement? It is not a fraud to have incurred the loss. World-Com management is not responsible for the overinvestment that happened in the telecom industry. The fraud is perpetrated (by WorldCom, Enron, Morgan Fay, and others) when they attempt to mislead investors by putting off the recognition of the fact.

The growth of the telecom sector in the 1990s has turned out to be one of the biggest bubbles ever. Suddenly, in mid-2001, it began to become clear to industry insiders that the Internet telecommunication boom "was not going to grow at the 1000-fold annual increases originally projected." The bursting of this bubble would cause the excesses wrought in those heady boom days to have to be painfully wrung-out of our financial system. An estimated $2 trillion was lost by investors who bet on the telecom sector during these time frames. The accounting frauds that had been perpetrated to prop-up the companies that were otherwise facing economic disaster only delayed the inevitable, and the delay turned out to be only a year or two at most. In WorldCom's case, it was exactly one year and a month.

WorldCom's management traded one year and a month of delayed recognition of reality for, perhaps, five years and seven months in the federal penitentiary.

Why did they do it? The losses had been sustained. It is simply not possible to hide failed investments from view forever. Scott Sullivan, the chief financial officer at WorldCom, had apparently hoped to flush the $3.8 billion in restatements amongst a planned $20 billion write-off of goodwill he was intending to take in the next quarter. The notion was that the $3.8 billion would get lost in the detail of the immense restructuring charge. In truth, he might have gotten away with this. But what was the point of the $3.8 billion subterfuge? Had he booked the inevitable major restructuring charge a year-and-a-month earlier, in May 2001, when he, and the other members of top management at WorldCom, *first* realized the company was upside down, he wouldn't be facing a prison sentence today. It's not illegal to make mistakes in business judgment, or to incur a loss, no matter how huge the size of the loss. It is, however, illegal to lie about it.

The perpetrators of any of these frauds were only delaying the inevitable. Inevitably, the house of cards would have to fall. I talked about this with two former FBI agents. Both men commented that law enforcement was encountering a similar phenomenon with some of the new recruits. And they believed it to be a "generational thing." They explained that the instructors at the FBI Academy in Quantico had received troubling responses from a class of new recruits after presenting the following hypothetical situation:

"You've got this investigation you're workin' on," the instructor says to the class. "But you know the judge isn't gonna sign off on the search warrant. Because you're missin' one thing."

The FBI instructor looks around his class of recruits. "You know for a fact that these guys you're investigatin' have committed a felony. You've got evidence of it. You've already collected some evidence. But it isn't enough to get an indictment. And you're goin' to need this one additional fact to be included in your affidavit."

The instructor raises one arm. "How many would insert this one additional thing in your affidavit, to ensure that your team gets the search warrant you need to prove your case?" he asks. "Give me a show of hands." The instructor raises his hand higher.

As he finished with his little vignette, the former agent telling me this story sadly shook his head. I took from this that the number of hands in the air must have been significant. The FBI, though, is not the only law enforcement agency having difficulty with trainees whose moral compass is a bubble off dead level center. The affidavit-training scenario is used by several agencies at the basic academy level, as well as in continuing education courses regarding investigative techniques and ethics. Counterparts at other law enforcement executive levels, whether they be sheriffs, chiefs of police, heads of state law enforcement agencies, and other federal agencies encounter the same problem in their role playing and ethics classes in their respective academies. One of my FBI sources put it this way, "At our academy as well as other academies, the instructors have noticed that over the past ten years, more students see nothing wrong with stretching the truth."

This phenomenon is confirmed by the annual ethics survey conducted by the Josephson Institute of Ethics. Of 12,000 high school students surveyed by the Josephson Institute this past year, 74 percent admitted cheating on an exam. In the 1992 survey, 61 percent admitted cheating. Consider the following statement included in the survey:

A person has to lie or cheat
sometimes in order to succeed.

Forty-three percent of the students surveyed in 2002 agreed with the above statement—an increase of almost 10 percentage points when compared to survey results of only two years earlier. This is not a good trend.

Clearly, something is happening. As one of my FBI sources noted, "These youngsters, when they become adults, will enter law enforcement, just as they do college, or the military, or education, or ultimately, the corporate board rooms of America."

I asked whether the results of the FBI training scenario was similar to when these two former FBI agents had been in the bureau.

The former FBI agent shook his head again. "No way would you risk your career over one little dumb-assed search warrant," he said. He looked across the table. His associate nodded his agreement.

The two retired agents thought that the opportunities today's generation has creates a 'no-fear' ethic. They theorized that today's generation believes that "if you push the rules to get ahead, get caught pushing the envelope a little, and got busted out of the FBI, you can always just move on to an equally attractive career somewhere else."

The culture these former agents described was in stark contrast with what was subsequently revealed about events that had occurred in August 2001. Then, the special agents in the field in Minneapolis were frustrated in their efforts to get FBI headquarters to seek approval under the FISA provisions (the counter-terrorism statutes that provide for these kinds of search warrants) in order to forensically image and search Zacharias Moussaoui's laptop. Moussaoui was the so-called twentieth hijacker who had been arrested in Minneapolis a few weeks before the events of 9/11. When the FBI later forensically imaged the computer's hard drive, they found flight simulation software, the phone number for the apartment of a Yemeni man alleged by authorities to have served as the paymaster for the hijackers, and information about crop-dusting.

This abrupt turnaround in the culture at the FBI, as compared to what the two former agents had described to me, can be reconciled. It was an apparent result of a series of events that transpired in 1999. The seven federal judges on the secret Foreign Intelligence Surveillance Court in Washington, DC, responsible for approving FISA search warrants, expressed a concern to then-Attorney General Janet Reno about an individual within the FBI responsible for forwarding requests for FISA wiretap authorizations. The judges believed that several requests pushed the envelope in terms of the red-letter limits of the FISA statute. The unintended consequence: Louis Freeh, the then-FBI director, reassigned the individual involved, and the Bureau's culture subsequently changed significantly because of changes instituted. From then on, every FISA request submitted by an FBI field office was put under a microscope at FBI headquarters; no FISA request would be submitted in the future unless it was an out-and-out, black-and-white case.

Action; reaction. Perception of risk affects what individuals in a society are willing to do. The Morgan Fay investigation revealed the risk individuals were willing to take in order to reap the spectacular economic rewards they anticipated would result. The management at Enron had taken spectacular economic risk; Jeffrey Skilling bet the ranch. The problem is that the management had inculcated a culture where bad results were never acceptable; if an investment went sour, move it off the balance sheet so that nobody can see.

This culture was deeply embedded within Enron. "Losses were never allowed at Enron, even then," Jan Avery, an accountant for eight years at Enron, was describing Enron's culture, as it was even back in 1995, to a *Vanity Fair* journalist. Avery described a meeting led by Andrew Fastow, who later became the company's chief financial officer. Fastow was standing at a grease board in a finance department conference room, trying to devise a method to move to an off-balance sheet partnership a significant loss Enron was experiencing because an Enron MTBE fuel additive plant had become almost worthless as a result of the toxic additive being outlawed by many states. "We have to be able to come up with something!" Fastow had barked to his subordinates at this meeting. "We have to construct a structure where the loss (can) be camouflaged."

Enron had invested in an MTBE plant that management hoped would yield significant returns. Events transpired to prove otherwise. Taking such financial risks often leads to substantial returns. Taking risks often leads to substantial losses, too. Camouflaging losses became a part of the culture in our country in the booming economic times of the 1990s.

Action; reaction. Living and working in Northern California during the Internet bubble, and experiencing firsthand the superheated economic climate of the time, I can remember reading then of a very specific concern that was emanating from Europe. The spectacular economic growth the United States was experiencing at the time was viewed by Europeans as a potential economic threat to their well-being. Economists in Germany and France were voicing concerns that their countries were at an economic disadvantage compared to the United States because of the lack of a "risk-taking" ethic in their respective cultures. As a result, these two countries both were planning to introduce higher education curricula calculated to inculcate the notion of "economic risk-taking" in their culture.

*   *   *

I wondered what the young and wide-eyed Tony Rosen thought about the serial revelations of corporate accounting frauds. "It actually made me think of how many more are out there that haven't been discovered," Tony responded. "And there's probably a ton."

Tony had become more jaded about human nature since Morgan Fay. "There are probably hundreds," he said. "But it affects so many people, and everyone knows how Enron's been affected. But in Morgan Fay, I actually saw the employees who lost their money. And I saw the employees who lost their jobs."

*   *   *

One of Tony's responsibilities during the duration of this assignment was to maintain a master listing of the documents the investigative team had obtained. Whenever investigators at the SEC, or the prosecutors in New York, had a question about a document, the attorneys at Caxton & Williams would get called first; in many cases they in turn would forward the question to Tony for research. "There ended up being a ton of document indexes," Tony recalled.

I knew from my experience that keeping control of a couple hundred thousand documents was not a trivial task. I asked him how many documents there were in the case. He replied that he couldn't recall off the top of his head, but that he would get back to me. A day later, I found a slip of paper on my desk. It was from Tony. He had counted all the three-ring binders. There were 83 lineal feet of documents contained in three-ring binders. Think of a pile of documents reaching to the top floor of an eight-story building, and then of the requirement to be able to locate any one of them over the course of the next two years and on a moment's notice.

With that responsibility also came the task of marshalling the supporting documents leading to the compilation of the final report, a not insubstantial task. Tony had not had occasion to meet anyone on the investigative team working the Omaha Division side of things, but he did recall, "bugging the hell out of them because I was the one in charge of the documents. I was the one who created the master report of issues. We needed to incorporate the issues they were investigating into our report." This meant taking broad and infrequent direction from Murphy.

Mike Murphy, the forensics and investigation partner directing the assignment, was responsible for coordinating the investigative efforts taking place all over the country. Murphy's team included computer forensics specialists from the San Francisco and Dallas labs. Murphy had to coordinate and meet with the prosecutors and attorneys located in Manhattan and Philadelphia, respectively. He and the attorneys periodically had to meet with the SEC investigators in Washington, DC, as well as with Morgan Fay's lenders in New York. In addition to all of this, he was directing the efforts of the forensic investigative teams in the field, in both Omaha and Minneapolis, as well as the team back in San Francisco.

Ken Avery, the PwC audit partner responsible for the Morgan Fay external audit, smiled when remembering coordinating schedules with Murphy. "We had each other's cell phone numbers," Avery said. "We were in constant communication. We'd schedule our travel plans so that we could meet up. Sometimes we'd meet in Minneapolis. Other times we'd meet in Omaha, and we'd share what we'd found to date. The forensics team was looking at every aspect of the fraud, but we (meaning PwC, the company's external auditors) were going to have to sign-off on the adjustments that had to be made to the company's financial statements."

With this amazing travel schedule, Murphy's team surreptitiously nicknamed him 'the Tornado.' "We were gonna come up with these t-shirts," Tony said. "Like a concert tour in the summer. The t-shirts would say, *'Tornado Tour 2000.'* And on the back they would have a little tornado and would say, 'San Francisco, Omaha, Minneapolis, Philadelphia, New York, Washington, DC.'"

I asked Tony if there wasn't another aspect to this tornado nickname. "They cause a lot of destruction," Tony agreed. "And then there's a calm. You don't really know what happened. It takes you a day or so to orient yourself. But we were in the Midwest. And they have tornado seasons there. Another one comes along a couple days later. It was a busy tornado season that month." Tony was red-cheeked and he smiled easily.

The investigative team faced grueling schedules to meet deadlines. At one point, Tony found he had worked 31 days straight without a day off. For a couple of the weekends, he took red-eyes back to San Francisco. Those weekends, he worked Saturday and Sunday in the office and then would take the Sunday-evening red-eye back to Minneapolis so that he could be at Morgan Fay's Minneapolis division on Monday morning. I asked him about the stress he encountered with that kind of schedule. He remembered that the team dealt with the stress by eating a lot, something you wouldn't know by looking at him, then or now: the young man is thin as a rail.

Before taking the red-eye to San Francisco on one of his Friday night travelganzas, Tony decided to ask the hotel front desk to store his huge suitcase containing all his clothing until he returned. Why lug all that stuff to San Francisco, he reasoned, only to have to cart it all back to Minneapolis on Sunday night?

That Sunday, Mike Murphy came to the conclusion that Tony's work in Minneapolis was completed. With this little hiccup in Tony's otherwise well-laid plans, he found himself on the phone the next Monday morning asking the hotel to FedEx his luggage to San Francisco. This was not the only time that Tony's travel eccentricities brought bring him unwanted notice.

There was some issue between him and Murphy regarding rental cars while in Minneapolis.

"Well the true story is that I always left my luggage back there," Tony explained to me. "After being back there a couple weeks straight, I just assumed that I was going back on Monday. So Mike had rented the car because Hertz was having a lot of difficulty renting the car to me, even though I did have a corporate credit card."

Tony had been only 22 years old at the time. Though he'd been old enough to wear a suit to work, to put in 16-hour days for 31 days straight on a special forensic investigation, and order a beer at a bar, the car rental agencies told him they would not rent him a car until he turned 25.

"So what was the big issue with Murphy?" I asked.

"When I first got there," Tony explained, "'the Tornado,' he's big on SUVs. He had rented this big Ford Explorer. But like I said, three days later he'd be gone; to Omaha or New York or something. So he left the car with me. He'd originally rented it just for the week. So I called and extended it for a week."

"Under his name?" I asked.

"It was simpler that way," Tony explained. "So I kept it. I think the second weekend was coming around and I went home. Actually, I was taking an accounting class at U.C. Berkeley Extension. The class met every Monday evening. Working like I was in Minneapolis, pretty much put a dent in that. But anyway, I went home for that weekend. I still worked through the weekend though. Then I think I flew back that Monday night on the red-eye to Minneapolis, where I picked up the car again. I had parked it in long-term parking instead of returning it."

"You didn't return it?"

"Why should I?"

"So instead of returning the car to avoid the charges on the car rental . . ."

"No, no," Tony protested. "See this is where the story's false. It was a weekly rental. It was not a daily rental."

"It had nothing to do with the fact that they weren't going to let you re-rent the car if you turned it in," I suggested.

"Exactly," Tony said.

"It had nothing to do with that," I observed. Tony flushed easily—all the time really, whenever somebody flustered him. This was one of those times.

"No," he said. "I just wanted to have it at the airport waiting for me. I'd left my luggage in the backseat. And my clothes were on the backseat of the car."

He'd almost wriggled off the hook. "What did you come home with?" I asked.

"I had clothes," he protested. "I think every piece of clothing I owned. But I left all my suits and everything there in the car."

"Because you checked out of the hotel," I said.

"Oh, sure," Tony said. "Of course I checked out of the hotel. So I go back there. Everything's fine. I don't even know when Mike discovered this."

"Well, that's the easy part," I volunteered. "It was probably a month or two later, after you finally came home. The Tornado probably got home late one Friday night, and his wife Peggy questioned him about the $50,000 charge for a rental car on their American Express bill. She probably wanted to know how they were going to pay off the account."

Frankly, the logistics of a rental car were probably not at the top of Tony's priority list. He and the others working on the investigation had been working an average of 16-hour days. Tony had submitted one time report and had immediately received a call from Cara Feldmann, a paraprofessional back at the office, "You know, you had a 20-hour day here?" she said to him. "That's gotta be an error, right?"

Tony confirmed to her that he'd actually worked from 8 A.M. to 4 A.M. that day.

*   *   *

All the time he and the others had been working in Minneapolis they were staying at the Sheraton, which was located in a large mixed-use commercial complex. The complex had a mall, restaurants, hotels, and commercial office space. Morgan Fay's offices were a short walk from the hotel.

Walking to the Morgan Fay office building morning after morning, to start another long day, Tony would pass the movie theater on the other side of the mall. For the month and a half of long days there, he constantly tried to work out some kind of break. Just take a break for two hours or so. Just enough time to catch a movie.

"A whole month there, and you never made it?" I asked.

"The first three weeks we never made it there. Finally, on one Sunday afternoon, I finally did it. Sundays we'd at least try to get out by six. The people who were assisting us from out of our Minneapolis office, they had already headed home to their friends and families.

"And on this day it was just me and Sue Quigley. We were both from out of town and we finally had a chance to go to the movies. And I remember we didn't care what we went to see. We just walked over there.

We didn't look at the any of the movie start times. We were just going to go see a movie.

"And we got over there and we ended up seeing *Cider House Rules*. And I loved it. I loved it. I loved the movie. I just remember really getting into the movie. I don't know if it was partly because we were getting away from things finally. Being able to let everything go. It was the first time that had happened.

"I still love that movie. It inspired me to read the book. I remember getting out of that movie and thinking, 'That was the best movie. That was the best two hours.' Just totally getting away from the investigation. We would go out to dinner and stuff. But you could never really get away from it.

"But the movie," Tony said. "It was just amazing to me. I can still remember that." Tony could not pinpoint exactly what is was he loved so much about the coming-of-age story of an obedient and trusting young man who slowly learns the ugly, hidden truths of people he trusts.

CHAPTER FOURTEEN

"Yeah, 'NFW.'"

I met Ken Avery, the PwC audit partner responsible for the Morgan Fay account, for the first time at the Sheraton Palace hotel in San Francisco. The hotel is a grand old building that was rebuilt after the 1906 earthquake. The restaurant where we had our breakfast meeting was ingeniously sited in the hotel's old carriageway entrance, where carriages would enter and swing around before leaving again. High above our heads, an immense stained-glass atrium let in filtered sunlight, allowing the potted plants throughout the restaurant to thrive.

Ken looked like he was in his early 40s and I found him to be a pleasant, likeable fellow—someone who'd easily fit in on the set of *Cheers*. He was a hearty looking two hundred pounds; his inner toughness, though, was not readily apparent. I mentioned a document I had seen, a letter to him from Cindy Shalott, written back in February 2000, just days before the board of directors commissioned the independent investigation. Ken's eyebrows arched and he asked how I'd seen the letter. I responded that it had been attached to a communication from Mary Jo White, the United States attorney prosecuting the case. White's letter to the court, written in December 2001, was in reference to the Cindy Shalott sentencing hearing.

Ken nodded on hearing this. "Cindy went to the penitentiary in Dublin last week?" he said.

I nodded. I had read the transcript of the sentencing hearing. The judge had sentenced Cindy Shalott to 57 months in the penitentiary.

Ken was silent. We were only 15 minutes into our breakfast meeting and this was some heavy stuff.

I asked Ken about this letter Cindy Shalott had sent him back in February 2000. The letter was sent to establish a meeting time and place to discuss Ken's concern about a memo his audit team had discovered in the course of PwC's Morgan Fay audit the week before. The memo had caused Ken's audit team concern that Morgan Fay's trade promotion expense was understated by several million dollars. Ken had authorized his audit team to extend the scope of their audit procedures, necessitating a delay in Morgan Fay's earnings release.

In the letter I had discovered in the records of the trial proceedings, Cindy Shalott, Morgan Fay's CFO, had gone on the attack:

> . . . We are aware of the tight reporting deadline required to meet our earnings release and appreciate your efforts to comply with this deadline. Unwarranted increases in the audit scope and deviations from the audit plan have caused unnecessary delays in your ability to complete your work in a timely manner are not acceptable given the level of professionalism for which we are paying. Poor planning on your part does not constitute an emergency on ours . . .

"I'd like to understand what that meeting was like for you," I said. Ken pursed his lips. I went on to say that I didn't want him to reveal any client confidences, or discuss with me any specific details. I indicated that even though the letter was a matter of public record, I was interested only in the human dynamic of the situation. I wanted to explore with him what it felt like to be in his shoes at that particular point in his life.

From other sources who had not worked on the case, I had learned earlier that Carmine Guerro, who at that time was the partner-in-charge of PwC's Northern California offices, had stood behind Ken's decision to extend the scope of the audit. At our breakfast meeting that morning I told Ken that I had heard that the rumor mill had it that during the meeting between PwC and Morgan Fay's management—the meeting referred to in Cindy Shalott's letter—that Guerro had apparently said, "Ken is the engagement partner. When he's ready to sign the audit opinion is when the opinion will be issued."

This broke the ice, for Ken smiled at this. "I had always been Carmine's 'go to guy.' I came up through the ranks under him. Whenever there was a tough assignment, he wouldn't hesitate to put me on it."

Ken told me Morgan Fay had been deemed one of those demanding assignments. One PwC partner had already been removed from the account. Ken related how he had been required to pass muster with the executives at Morgan Fay after Carmine Guerro had designated him to be "next up" on the Morgan Fay account.

"I met Cindy Shalott, and we talked," Ken recalled of his first introductions to the executives at Morgan Fay. "We got along just fine. She set up a meeting at a private luncheon club near the Transamerica Pyramid.

It was amazing. Everybody who was anybody in San Francisco at the time was having lunch there that day. Feinstein was even there." He was referring to Senator Diane Feinstein, who had formerly been a two-term mayor in San Francisco in the late 1970s and early 1980s.

"Robin Malory was there," Ken said. "He was going through the club greeting everyone. He'd apparently just had an exhibition of his Asian art collection at the Chicago Museum of Art.

"You should look it up," Ken said to me. "You'll probably be able to find some mention of it somewhere."

I nodded. I had already read about it. Malory had been compensated well over the years, and his collection of priceless Asian art was apparently something to behold.

"Anyhow," Ken continued, "this was the first time I had met Robin Malory. Over the course of the lunch, he interviewed me."

"About what?" I asked.

"My experience in the consumer products industry," Ken said. "Things like that. Anyhow, I must have passed the interview, because the next thing I heard was that Morgan Fay accepted me as the audit partner."

One year later, Cindy Shalott called the meeting I wanted to discuss at our breakfast meeting. I brought our discussion back to the letter she had written to Avery.

Ken nodded. "At the time you and I are talking about," he said, "almost a whole year had already passed. They had accepted me almost a year earlier. But now here I am, with Carmine Guerro, at this meeting Shalott had called for me to explain myself. And Robin Malory starts interviewing me all over again. 'How many years experience in this industry do you have?' he asks me. 'You act as if you're inexperienced. You're too excitable. You're over-reacting to things.'"

This was the beginning of the pressure the Morgan Fay executives would bring to bear upon Ken Avery. They were positioning things so that if Ken didn't play along, they could request another "more experienced partner" for the account. None of this, however, was explicit in that meeting.

Avery knew that this was the subtext of the meeting, though. Malory was conducting an inquisition, the subject of which was Avery's competence. Malory's repetitive, somewhat accusatory questions were being played out, real-time, in front of Avery's 'direct-report' at PwC, Carmine Guerro.

Simultaneously, some two thousand miles away, in Houston, Texas, the same little drama was being played out; in this case, though, on a much bigger stage. There, Enron's management team was responsible for the clawing of an audit partner. The partner in question was Carl Bass, one of the top accountants in Andersen's Internal Professional Standards

Group, the department responsible for Andersen's internal quality assurance. Bass had raised serious objections regarding Enron's proposed accounting practices, and was resisting compromise on what he considered fundamental accounting standards. As the impasse between Bass and Enron played out, Enron sought to have Bass removed from any review responsibility due his intransigence. Shortly thereafter, Carl Bass was removed from oversight responsibility on the Enron account and transferred to other unrelated accounts.

Here was another parallel between the Morgan Fay fraud and the Enron case, the only difference being that of scale. With PwC, Carmine Guerro chose to stand behind Ken Avery; Andersen, on the other hand, chose to cut the cord to Carl Bass and allowed him to swing in the wind. Shirley Hudler, the manager of *JEDI 1,* one of Enron's three-thousand off-balance sheet partnerships, said of Enron's relations with Andersen, "We could always bully them into getting what we wanted. We made them push the envelope."

The waiter came and cleared away the tableware. "Can you imagine what it would be like now—had you not stood your ground?" I asked.

"I'd be David Duncan," Avery said, referring to the Andersen partner on the Enron account, whom Andersen had fired after the shredding incident.

"Morgan Fay would have blown itself up," Avery continued. "Just like Enron. Only smaller. And I'd have been subjected to an ethics review. They'd review the issues and our work, and they'd probably classify it as Class 3, or maybe even a Class 4."

Ken was referring to the classification scheme the SEC assigned to the most egregious frauds that had gone undetected by an auditor when the warning signs were clear and diligent effort would have uncovered the scheme. "I'd be named in civil litigation. Milberg Weiss would have had a target on my chest."

Milberg Weiss, a class-action law firm, tracked the daily earnings releases of all of the publicly traded companies; whenever a stock suffered a precipitous decline, this law firm would swoop in and file a class-action securities-fraud lawsuit. One Florida circuit court judge compares the Milberg Weiss firm to "Squeegee Boy." In Milberg's defense, had our country's financial system possessed the proper checks and balances, together with a proper and continuing level of interest from prosecutors, there would be no economic interest for others to pursue all these class-action cases. But that would be a perfect world.

"I'd be barred by the SEC from serving as a CFO for any publicly traded company," Ken continued. "And I'd be fired from my job at PricewaterhouseCoopers. Ken finished his coffee. "Nobody has any idea how tough this job is. How tough it is to make the tough calls."

I nodded. "But you made the right call."

Ken firmed his lips for the second time this morning. "I remember walking from my office to that meeting," he said. "And saying to myself, 'C'mon. This is a $4 billion, New York Stock Exchange-traded company. And you're all bent out of shape about some one-page memo that *might* indicate the company has understated a couple of million dollars in trade promotions expense."

"But you knew that they had lied to you," I said. "They were hiding the ball. And you were on to them. You just didn't know what you were on to."

"Didn't have any idea," Ken said. "I can still remember when Mike Murphy came over with Bill Leimbach to meet with me. They were scheduled to interview me the next day. And here it was they had both flown back from Omaha and Minneapolis a day early, and were right away asking if they could come over to see me. I knew then that something was up."

I recalled my own interview with Bill Leimbach. He is a hoary old silverback audit partner who had been around the block. He knew the consumer products industry inside out. Mike Murphy had asked Leimbach to drop everything to fly out to Minneapolis. "When do you need me?" Leimbach asked; he ended up giving up his tickets to see Cal play in the NCAA tournament that weekend to take a red-eye to Minneapolis and meet with Morgan Fay's special investigative counsel from Caxton & Williams.

Leimbach and I were talking in the hallway outside my office on the 34th floor at 50 Fremont Street. "I remember walking out of Morgan Fay's operating division that Sunday," Leimbach said, "and the attorney asking me, 'How bad do you think this is?'

"'They're toast,' I remember thinking to myself. 'They're a $4 billion company,' I said to him. 'And we're looking at maybe $400 million in adjustments when we're done.'

"And I can remember the look on that attorney's face when I said that," Leimbach continued. "That's why it's so cool that they've been able to settle the shareholder litigation . . ."

"And the bondholder's litigation," I added.

"And the bondholder's litigation," Leimbach agreed. In agreeing to drop their securities fraud lawsuit, Morgan Fay's bondholders accepted an equity position in the company in return for restructuring the debt. The bondholders knew that Morgan Fay's brands were fundamentally sound; they produced positive cash flow and income, but only enough to service a reduced volume of debt. With the settlement of all of the outstanding litigation and a reduction in the amount of the company's debt load, the company moved on, as a survivor. Enron though, may be another matter. The lawsuits emanating from Enron may go on for more than a decade.

"This is going to be Wall Street's asbestos case," says Dennis H. Taylor, a former U.S. prosecutor and now an attorney with the Texas law firm Shepard, Smith & Bebel. He was referring to Enron when he made this statement; he likens the expected long-tail of Enron litigation to be as significant as the wave of breast implant and asbestos litigation claims that roiled the country the past 20 years. Donald Langevoort, a Georgetown University School of Law professor, estimates the amount of litigation exposure may range as high as $100 billion. Citigroup's chairman, Sanford Weill, has been quoted saying, "I wish I'd never heard of Enron."

*   *   *

During our breakfast meeting at the Sheraton Palace in San Francisco, I indicated to Ken Avery that I was looking forward to reading the testimony he had provided in the grand jury proceedings. He told me he hadn't even seen his transcript.

That's when he intimated that there might be a hold up in the progress of things. There might be two more cases filed, he said. The Assistant U.S. Attorneys on the case were trying to nail two more executives they believed should have been indicted. It was likely that there would be at least two more trials. The prosecutors were delaying the sentencing of the three other Morgan Fay executives who had already pled guilty, including Robin Malory, because the prosecutors were hoping to trade leaner sentences for testimony against the yet un-indicted co-conspirators. "Mary Jo White thought this was one of the most egregious cases. She definitely wanted to prosecute these people to the fullest extent of the law."

This, of course, was all pre-Enron. Mary Jo White would retire as the U.S. Attorney at about the same time Enron was unraveling. Pre-Enron, Morgan Fay was one of the most egregious cases. Since then, however, WorldCom and Enron led the daily headlines.

The prosecutor in the Enron case would turn out to be Leslie Caldwell, a criminal securities fraud specialist from the U.S. Attorney's office in San Francisco. The Justice Department investigation of the Enron fraud would be painstakingly slow and thorough. Caldwell obtained the first guilty plea-bargain almost one year to the day after Jeff Skilling abruptly "retired" from serving as Enron's chief executive officer.

On August 21, 2002, Michael J. Kopper, Enron's former director of finance, pled guilty to conspiracy to commit wire fraud and money laundering. Kopper stated in open court that he provided kickbacks to Enron's chief financial officer, Andrew Fastow, using money from one of Enron's off-balance sheet partnerships, Chewco. The kickback money was deposited into bank accounts in the names of Fastow's own family and friends. Caldwell will no doubt use Michael Kopper's testimony, and even more importantly, his knowledge of the participation of others in the Enron financial schemes, to obtain indictments of other high-ranking former Enron executives. The very next day, the authorities moved to put a freeze on all of the accounts of Fastow's family members.

*   *   *

The sentencing of Cindy Shalott was set for January 2002. The shadow of Enron lay over everything. Plea-bargaining discussions on behalf of Robin Malory and the other executives involved was occurring in March 2002. Enron's shadow darkened these proceedings as well. Every day, a new revelation would occur. Amid such a feeding frenzy, it was no surprise to Ken Avery, or me, that Shalott's sentencing was as harsh as it was.

After my breakfast with Ken Avery at the Sheraton Palace that morning, I had occasion to look up the terms of the management agreement Avalon had negotiated with Morgan Fay. This was a simple enough thing for me to do. All I had to do was go to the SEC's EDGAR Web site and retrieve the document.

It turns out that the Avalon partnership, of which Robin Malory and Cindy Shalott were principals, had a "lock-up period." The Avalon "insiders" could not immediately unload their Morgan Fay stock upon going public, until after this "lock-up period" expired. I also learned that Avalon's *Management Contract* with Morgan Fay, which named the executives at Avalon Partners as Morgan Fay's management, also had a two-year term. Both the "lock-up period" and the Avalon/Morgan Fay management contract were set to expire only months after the discovery of the fraud. Put another way, Shalott and Malory had only four or five short months until they could bail out of Morgan Fay. From their point of view, all they had to do was string together two more quarters, and the "lock-up" restrictions on the sale of their stock would lift.

All hell broke loose when Cindy Shalott discovered Ken Avery having a concern about a measly $2 to $3 million under-accrual of trade promotion expense. Because of Avery's foot-dragging, the company would miss its all-important earnings release date. Robin Malory exploded. "It was outrageous," he bellowed. "To act this way. Overreacting like this. To the littlest thing."

Robin Malory was responsible for executing his business plan; he would see to it that the company showed good earnings while the economy was superheated. And then he would bail out, and move on, to the next thing.

*   *   *

With the bookkeeping fraud they had implemented, the Avalon Partners management group had dug a hole for themselves. Every period, the fraud needed to be continued, and even increased some. They needed to buy time until their lock-up period expired. To do this, "They developed a strategy to just browbeat the auditors," Mike Murphy said.

"How could you know that," I asked.

Murphy explained that he could tell from the documents he'd seen that Morgan Fay had identified many of the issues that might be discovered and raised by the auditors from PwC. "There was this one document," he said. "The title of it was something like, *Risks and Opportunities.*"

Morgan Fay had already provided this document to the SEC and to the U.S. Attorney's office. The company had waived any legal privileges and was cooperating with the authorities; the company's board of directors had, in fact, blown the whistle themselves. Also, Morgan Fay's attorney's had previously given Murphy permission to talk about the details of this case for a panel discussion on the subject of current trends in securities fraud. Mike Murphy was certainly an expert on this subject. The document Murphy was now mentioning to me had been one of the important details about this case that Murphy had presented during the panel discussion.

Murphy continued with his description, "Across the top of the document, the Morgan Fay people had expressed a 'percentage factor.' They identified the issues where the auditors from PwC would [be expected to] hold their ground and require Morgan Fay to record an adjustment based on the information that PwC had available to them about the issue."

As to the other issues the Morgan Fay executives expected might be raised, Murphy's instincts told him that Morgan Fay had no intention of booking any adjustment for anything other than something that PwC "out-and-out" already had them "dead-to-rights-on."

To execute this strategy, Morgan Fay would withhold from their auditors any and all information that would not prove helpful to Morgan Fay. With the deck stacked like this, Morgan Fay would then adopt the position that the two parties, auditor and audited, merely had a difference of opinion. Morgan Fay asserted that when it came down to a simple difference of opinion, it was always to be Avalon's *opinion* that mattered, not that of the auditors.

In baseball, the tie always goes to the runner. In this case, all ties were to go to Morgan Fay. And Morgan Fay would see to it that the auditors would never have enough information to make it seem clearer than a simple "tie."

*   *   *

Flash back to the very inception of the Morgan Fay investigation. The whole thing kicked off on a Sunday morning in San Francisco. The Avalon Partners executives were asked to come in to the Morgan Fay corporate headquarters in San Francisco where the interviews were held. Another set of interviews were occurring simultaneously back in Minneapolis, at the Morgan Fay division there—this is why Bill Leimbach had been forced to give up those choice NCAA basketball tickets in order to take the red-eye flight the night before. Collecting stories simultaneously from the different people located in different parts of the United States would frustrate attempts to undermine the investigation.

During Murphy's interviews with Malory and Shalott, the Avalon executives in San Francisco were spinning their story. They were distressed with the way things had gone with the auditors at PwC. As far as Malory was concerned, there was no issue at all. "Ken Avery was jumping at his shadow."

After completing the interviews in San Francisco that Sunday evening, Murphy immediately hopped a red-eye out of SFO. He would arrive in Omaha first thing Monday morning and asked Leimbach to meet-up with him in Omaha. Together, Murphy and Leimbach would conduct their interviews at the Omaha division before Shalott and Malory even showed up for work.

By the end of business that Monday, Mike Murphy had collected a stack of what he considered to be the key documents. He wanted to go through them with Ken Avery.

Mike Murphy indicated that some of the documents explicitly identified "items that the auditors didn't know about."

"What kinds of items?" I asked.

"Trade promotions," Murphy responded. "Things like that," he continued. "There was one document we found during this first three day crunch. This is when people started fessin' up."

The document he was referring to apparently contained a handwritten notation in the margin that caught Murphy's attention. The notation was written in response to a question that had also been posed on the margin. The response read, "No FW."

"You mean '*NFW?*'" I asked.

"Yeah, *NFW,*" Mike responded. "And so when Bill Leimbach and I interviewed some of these people, they *told* us *what* it meant."

"Who wrote it?" I asked.

"We never were able to find out *who* wrote it."

Murphy recalled the meeting with Ken Avery. He and Bill Leimbach reviewed the key documents collected during the course of their interviews. "And so we were puttin' these in front of Ken Avery," Mike Murphy said. This was only a few days after Cindy Shalott and Robin Malory had blasted Ken Avery for 'dragging his feet.' According to the original audit schedule, Ken Avery was already supposed to have blessed Morgan Fay's earnings press release.

Murphy described walking Ken Avery through the documents he and Leimbach had collected. "And Ken," Murphy said, "he's getting more red and more frustrated with each document we put in front of him. Then we put this one document in front of him. He stared at it for some time, trying to figure it out.

"He says to us, 'Well, I understand what the percentages mean. And I understand these comments here, written in on the right margin. But what does the *No FW* mean?'

"And so, Leimbach's lookin' at me," Mike Murphy continues. "I'm lookin' at him.

"Finally, I look back at Ken Avery.

"The fuckers were writing notes to each other," Murphy explained to Ken Avery. "They're saying there's no fucking way you're gonna find these things."

CHAPTER FIFTEEN

DumbFellas Go Corporate

For revelations about corporate fraud, the month of June 2002 was a real humdinger. Rockets were going off from one end of the month to the other. Early in the month of June 2002, the New York Stock Exchange adopted a requirement for listed companies that their board of directors be comprised of a majority of independent directors. Almost simultaneously, the CEO of Goldman Sachs, Henry M. Paulson Jr., called for business reform and referred to a "crisis of confidence." And of course, there was Enron.

Congress's investigative arm, the General Accounting Office (GAO), came through with a finding in June 2002 that didn't surprise anybody living in the western United States. After a thorough investigation, the GAO found that the Federal Energy Regulatory Commission (FERC), the nation's top energy regulator, lacked the expertise and authority to oversee the electricity markets during the height of California's energy crisis during May 2000 to June 2001. That finding was probably no great surprise to Jeff Skilling and the other cowboys at Enron.

But for everything that was happening in this month of June 2002, WorldCom turned out to be the topper of them all. WorldCom hit the Street like a bomb.

* * *

In researching the manner in which the WorldCom investigation unspooled, I noticed a very odd thing. A systems access limitation had been placed on Gene Morse, one of WorldCom's internal auditors. In one of my interviews of Gene, I asked him how it was that an internal auditor's access authority would be limited to the point that he wouldn't be authorized to make a simple inquiry of an income statement account. He explained that when he had first started as a finance associate with WorldCom he had full access rights within the company's financial system. He could make any inquiries of any account, and at any level of detail. It was when he first started fiddling around with a powerful new data-mining tool that he found his wings getting clipped.

WorldCom had grown dramatically by acquiring other companies. As a result, the financial reporting systems and ledgers at WorldCom were a hodge-podge of legacy systems, holdovers from WorldCom's spate of acquisitions. To cope with this cacophony of financial systems, WorldCom began to run Hyperion Essbase on top of its numerous and diverse financial reporting systems. Essbase, a sophisticated data mining application, allowed for the integration of these multiple data sources. Users could script simple but powerful queries of the multiple data warehouses, and get back answers that would provide greater insight about lines of business, suppliers, customers, and markets. Gene loved learning about powerful new tools, and soon became one of WorldCom's "power users" of the Essbase data exploration tool. He began using the tool as part of a new cash flow modeling exercise when he first joined the company and had rotated into the treasury department. The use of the powerful data exploration tool immediately got him into trouble. He was wandering into places that others, higher up in the organization, did not want explored.

"I was working on a cash report for the treasurer," Gene said. "And I tried to get some information from the general accounting department. About a week later, they reduced my access level." The Essbase data interrogation system with which Gene had been working provides security layers—from server and database levels to even individual cell-level locking. A corporation's systems administrator is typically responsible for establishing system access level for network users. I asked Gene if he believed the IT department had been directed to reduce his access. "Yeah," he replied. "It was either Buddy Yates or David Myers."

David Myers was WorldCom's former Corporate Controller. "Buddy" Yates was the former Director of Accounting there. By the fall of 2002, both men would plead guilty to criminal conspiracy and securities fraud. In the court hearing in which David Myers pled guilty, he stated to U.S. District Court Judge Richard Casey that he had been "instructed on a quarterly basis by senior management to ensure that entries were made to falsify WorldCom's books to reduce WorldCom's reported actual costs and therefore to increase WorldCom's reported earnings."

In entering his guilty plea, Buford "Buddy" Yates, "a portly man with a goatee," refused to identify who had directed him to file the false reports to the SEC. In response to another question from the court, Yates told U.S. Magistrate Judge Andrew Peck, "I concluded that the purpose of these adjustments was to incorrectly inflate WorldCom's reported earnings to meet the expectations of securities analysts and mislead the investing public of the company's financial condition." Those in attendance in the courtroom that day reported that Buddy Yates spoke quickly and in a barely audible voice. Gene Morse spoke of a very different side of Buddy Yates.

In late 1999, Gene had built a financial model to assist the company in making more accurate cash flow projections. The company's treasurer had asked Gene to reconcile the data he was using with that reported in the company's financial statements, and Gene was following up a discrepancy with regard to the reported line cost expenditures. His numbers were off by a little over $1 billion. He headed up to the general accounting department and soon found himself in Yates's office. "What do you need?" Buddy asked without looking up. Everybody around the office that ever worked with Buddy knew him to be a bulldog of a fella. "I need to understand more about these numbers," Gene said.

Buddy looked up from what he was working on. Gene was holding some papers out for Buddy to see.

"Where'd you get those?" Buddy asked.

"San Jeev Sethi gave them to me," Gene replied. "I just want to understand where the numbers come from," Gene added. "You know, where they're going. Stuff like that, how they interact with one another."

Buddy fixed Gene with his eyes. "Gene, nothin' personal," he said coolly. "But, I'm not gonna tell you anything about those numbers."

Gene, the little associate, stood there, holding his couple of pieces of paper in his hand for Buddy to see.

Buddy remained deadpan, his eyes still fixed on Gene's. "And if you show those to our goddamn auditors," he continued, "I'll throw you out the motherfucking window."

Gene believes his recollection of the incident is pretty accurate, though he might have mixed up the expletives a little. "It was either damn and fucking," Gene said. "Or goddamn, and motherfucking. I can't remember."

After leaving Buddy Yates's office, Gene headed back to meet with San Jeev Sethi, the senior manager to whom he reported at that time. Gene related what had transpired in Buddy Yates's office. On hearing the story, San Jeev gave a look of disbelief, and then went over to Yates's office.

San Jeev returned 30 minutes later, looking kind of flustered. "Leave the accountants alone," he said.

And so Gene did. Until the spring of 2002.

*   *   *

"We'd gotten an e-mail regarding some unusual capital expenditure activity," Gene Morse said. One of the accountants in the field had noted that some of the operations people had begun *expensing* capital expenditures rather than capitalizing them, because they had run out of capital expense budget room. Mark Abide had sent the e-mail to Glyn Smith, a senior manager in the Internal Audit Department, suggesting, "This is worth looking into from an audit perspective."

A capital expenditures operational review was in the process of being wrapped up, and Cynthia Cooper, the company's vice president of internal audit, asked Gene Morse to read the report and provide her with any comments he had on it. The operational review was focused on looking at procedures surrounding the issuance of something the company referred to as "AFEs," or Authorization for Expenditures. No money could be spent on any capital expenditure unless the item had previously been budgeted for, and an AFE had been initiated and approved. As Gene read through the report, he noted an oddity.

The document he had in front of him summarized the dollar amount of capital expenditures coming out of the AFE system. Another table in the document reflected the amount of capital expenditures reported in the company's financial statements, which are reported to the SEC. Gene could see that there was a $2 billion difference between the two reports. The difference was attributed to something called "corporate adjustments." Gene was familiar with the AFE system and the procedures surrounding them. The document in front of him didn't make sense; the data implied that some $2 billion in capital expenditures hadn't gone through the normal AFE process.

Cynthia Cooper and one of her senior managers made several inquiries of San Jeev Sethi, who by now was the company's director of financial planning. San Jeev was buried in attempts to attract critical bridge financing the company required, and couldn't spare the two of them any of his time. The company was running out of cash, and this was his highest priority. He did, however, indicate that the $2 billion in "corporate adjustments" had to do with something he referred to as "Prepaid Capacity." Stymied, Cooper decided to take up the subject with Scott Sullivan, the company's CFO, but without providing him with the details that the internal auditors were trying to reconcile.

She came back from the meeting, reporting that Sullivan had asked her to put off her review until the next quarter, as he was expecting to record a significant restructuring charge at that time. Sullivan had also directed that, when she and her staff *did* perform the review in the upcoming quarter, they were *not* to review any activity in any of the prior periods. Gene noted that Cynthia Cooper looked a little spooked. Even though Cynthia had dotted-line reporting responsibility to the company's audit committee, an important committee of the company's board of directors, she also technically reported to Sullivan. Gene inwardly hazarded a guess that dealing with Sullivan must be very difficult for Cynthia. A little bit of history between these two was now coming back to roost, and this time it might be payback time for Sullivan.

Only one month before, Cynthia had taken on Sullivan in a heated exchange that had to be adjudicated at the board of director's level. That month, Cooper had directly challenged Sullivan. He was attempting to reverse $300 million in bad debt reserves in order to pump up World-Com's earnings for that quarter. As far as Cooper was concerned, there was absolutely no foundation for that kind of adjustment. John Stupka, the head of the company's Wireless Division, whose earnings were being manipulated, felt the same way. Cynthia Cooper appealed directly to the board's audit committee, and both Sullivan and Cooper were invited to make presentations to the committee. After debating the issue for some time with the audit committee, Sullivan ultimately backed down and agreed to not reverse the $300 million. The next day, Sullivan drew a line in the sand. Unable to reach her directly, Sullivan called her husband in order to get her cell phone number. Sullivan caught her by dialing her cell phone, reaching her at her hair salon. No, it couldn't wait. He made it explicitly clear to her on this call that she was *not* to interfere in the Wireless Division's operations ever again.

The $2 billion difference in capital expenditures identified by Gene Morse, however, was a financial statement issue. A bright line had previously been established between what the internal auditors were responsible for and what Arthur Andersen was tasked with. The outside auditors were to audit the financial statement balances, and the internal auditors were charged only with performing operational reviews—there was to be no duplication of effort.

The problem was that Arthur Andersen had just been indicted by the Justice Department. The foundations were crumbling at Andersen, and Cynthia Cooper was concerned that nobody was minding the store there. She made an executive decision on the spot. She directed the internal audit department to immediately change focus. They would take on the responsibility of reviewing the appropriateness of the company's financial statements. "We've got to start looking more at the financial numbers," she told her team. There would be no corporate-wide announcement of the shift, she told them, and Sullivan would not be informed of the change.

The internal auditors stood down for a couple of days as a result of the Sullivan directive. They hadn't given up, however. They continued to attempt to find out what "prepaid capacity" was, and nobody in the company seemed to know. Whatever it was, a $150 million entry in the third week *after* the end of the fiscal third quarter certainly smelled. Cooper was finally able to get a meeting with San Jeev Sethi, the company's director of financial planning. They sat down and Cynthia turned to Gene Morse, "Gene, do you have any questions?"

Gene asked San Jeev a simple prefatory question, got an answer, and then asked another. Gene had worked directly for San Jeev for six months during one of Gene's rotations through different finance departments. The two men knew each other pretty well. Gene posed his third question. "San Jeev, can you tell me about prepaid capacity?"

"For the fourth time," San Jeev replied. "I don't know what prepaid capacity is, you'll have to ask David Myers."

And so that was that. Another dead end. San Jeev hadn't seemed too concerned about it, but he had kicked them upstairs. David Myers was the second highest-ranking finance official in the company; the only people higher than him in the pecking order were Scott Sullivan, the company's CFO, and Bernie Ebbers, the company's CEO.

Cooper and her team met in her office. She knew that if she went to David Myers with questions on prepaid capacity, she would find Scott Sullivan coming down on her again like a ton of bricks. She came up with an alternative approach. "Let's call Mark Abide," she suggested. Everyone in the room knew Mark Abide to be a very professional individual; he was always helpful, and never a roadblock. Abide was a manager in the area of Property Plant Equipment, and if anyone knew what it was, it would be him. So they placed the call, and Cynthia posed the question.

Mark Abide responded that he didn't know what it was. "Those entries were made by Buddy Yates's shop." He was referring to general accounting in Clinton, Mississippi.

Cynthia then asked Mark if he knew which accounts the entries had been posted to. Mark responded that five "natural accounts" in property plant and equipment had been hit. He ticked them off: "transmission equipment, communication equipment," and three other similar accounts, but then indicated that there were hundreds of detailed accounts under each one of those headings that had been hit as well.

The three internal auditors got off the phone. Mark Abide had provided them with a few more clues; they now knew where the prepaid capacity had been parked. Cynthia turned to Gene Morse. "Go see if you can find out what it is," she said.

Because of the access limitations that had previously been placed on him, and which were still in effect, Gene Morse would be working with one arm tied behind his back. Scott Sullivan and David Myers did not want this internal auditor snooping around.

Flash back a couple of months, to the fall of 2001. Shortly after Enron had imploded, Gene Morse noticed that, once again, his computer access had been further reduced. He was now in the internal audit department and having reduced access was extremely frustrating. He no longer had any account access above a certain level in the income statement. He called his buddy Jerry Lily in the IT Department. "What is the deal?" Gene asked. "I keep bumpin' into this. Y'all reduced me again."

Jerry acknowledged that Gene's access had been reduced, again.

Gene sat forward at his desk, with the telephone to his ear. "Who reduced me?" he asked. "Buddy?"

"Higher," came the response over the line.

Gene reflected on this. "Well, I don't need to know," he finally said into the receiver. As far as he was concerned, there were only two people higher than Buddy Yates in WorldCom. One was David Myers; the other was Scott Sullivan.

Even though Myers or Sullivan had reduced his system access, Gene Morse had an advantage; he had technology on his side. He had become an expert in data mining, a power user of the Hyperion Essbase data interrogation tool. Myers and Sullivan had pretty much wiped out his access to the income statement. So what? He could at least look at one side of the entries, the side that hit the balance sheet. He'd figure where to go next after that when he got there. His use of this data interrogation tool would soon place him in personal jeopardy; it would take him as close to the edge of the cliff as it was possible to go.

*   *   *

Gene Morse received his undergrad degree from Mississippi College, just across the highway from WorldCom's headquarters in Clinton, Mississippi. After a few years of work experience, trying and failing for a while in several different careers, he came to the realization that he was more interested in the analytical process of finance. In 1995, he decided to enter the MBA program at Tulane University. Upon finishing that program, he interviewed with WorldCom on campus. Gene Morse sat in on a presentation from Scott Sullivan, the company's CFO, and a Q&A session with Bernie Ebbers, its CEO. David Myers, WorldCom's Controller, interviewed Gene on campus. Myers described a new financial management program for young executives that WorldCom was implementing. It was a special "management-track" program, in which new finance associates would work four to six months in one area of finance within the company, and would then rotate into another finance area. After two and a half years, the finance associate could select the department in which he, or she, wanted to make a career.

Gene started with WorldCom in 1997, and thrived on the variety of experiences he was getting in the different departments. While at World-Com, he enrolled in a CFA program that was offered at night and on week-ends. He completed that program during his first couple of years at the company, and had become a Certified Financial Analyst (CFA), in addition to having his MBA. After his two and a half years of rotations, he accepted an offer to join the internal audit department, and then studied at night to become a Certified Internal Auditor (CIA) as well.

Over the course of his rotations, Gene learned to use the various tools and technologies that were becoming available. He took advantage of the internal training programs on Excel and the Access database tool.

He also realized that unless one actively used applications like those, the skills would wither away, so he looked for opportunities to use them. Upon settling in the internal audit department, he became the most pro-ficient user of the Hyperion Essbase data interrogation tool. His desk was only 12 feet from Cynthia Cooper's door. Whenever Cynthia found herself wanting to know something about the ledger, or anything on the more technical side, or with a need to do data mining on a database, she would walk straight to Gene's cube.

Now it was time to go hunting through the system. Nobody knew what the hell "Prepaid Capacity" was. Gene Morse knew, however, that he could use a new tool to figure it out. His buddy in the IT department, Jerry Lilly, had given him access to a new technology that would provide him with enhanced data interrogation ability when working in Essbase. This new tool had been designed for Buddy Yates's shop, but it hadn't been used yet. Gene Morse would be Jerry Lilly's beta tester. The new Essbase add-on application Jerry had developed could provide Gene with a hyperlink on a document number. That capability was hot off the press. With this, Gene would be able to double-click on the hyperlink, and immediately drill down to where he hoped he would be able to find the actual entries that had been made. Or at least trip across "one side" of them; the access limits imposed on him by Myers and Sullivan would still hamper him. But what the hell, it was worth trying.

*   *   *

Okay, Gene said to himself. They told me it hits these five accounts. Gene knew there were literally hundreds of accounts underneath each one of these. He fired up Essbase and decided where he would start. He'd get all the activity in each of the five accounts for each month of the first quarter of 2002. He'd start there.

WorldCom was a very difficult animal; with all the mergers and acqui-sitions the company had gone through, there were now over one hundred fifty legal entities that would need to be searched. The company's servers updated their database four times a day, so the information Gene would get back was virtually real time.

He started looking through the account detail that had been returned. He was looking at the account for computer equipment. Looking for unusual activity. For two of the months in the quarter, the account had only a million dollars of activity, or so. However, in March 2002, there was activity for some half billion dollars and change. Gene was aware the company had no cash, and had supposedly curtailed its capital expenditure spending. What he now was seeing didn't look right. He now wanted to find out what all this spending activity was about. He drilled down into the detail. He found a nice round $500 million entry in one of the detail accounts, effecting an increase in computer equipment. But this one was weird, because it was in a Network Services Depreciation Profit Center account. It didn't make any sense. A nice round number—500, with a lot of zeroes behind it—where one would expect only to see credits. Gene could see that the entry had come from the company's Intercompany Account. The problem with that was that 350,000 entries hit that account each month. The trail had gone cold.

Gene headed into Cynthia's office and explained what he had found. The next thing he knew, she had gathered all of the internal audit department senior managers and directors into a small conference room, and Gene was diagramming what he found for them on a white board. He described to them how the $500 million was part of a $1.6 billion entry, but that the trail had become completely obscured within the asset clearing account. He had followed all the pieces back from there. There was a $150 million increase in switching equipment. There was a $50 million increase in furniture and fixtures. Then there was another $300 million increase in fiber-optic equipment; $100 million in network power; and the original $500 million in equipment that he'd first tripped across. Everything was in nice round zeroes.

But that was as far as he was able to take things.

*   *   *

Gene Morse sat in the lunchroom having lunch with some of his peers. After finishing lunch, he got up from the table with his tray. The others were still finishing their lunch, but he had an Essbase data interrogation query outstanding and was anxious to get back to his cube to take a look at the results. This time he had plowed through the Intercompany Asset Clearing Accounts. Who cares if there were 350,000 entries hitting that account every month, he thought. He was using the power of the computer servers to crunch through that. He wanted to get to the other side of the series of entries he'd discovered adding up to some $1.6 billion.

He dumped the contents of his tray into the trash, and loaded the tray on the conveyor belt.

Scott Sullivan was standing behind him when he turned around.

"What kinds of things you working on?" Sullivan asked Gene.

"A report on International Capital Expenditures," Gene replied. It was a lie, but he came out with it as if it were as true as the fact that the sun had set the evening before. Cynthia had prepared him for the possibility that Sullivan would confront him, wanting to know what it was he was working on. Scott Sullivan had made it clear as could be to Cynthia Cooper earlier that he did not want anybody on her staff working on the increase in domestic capital expenditures. "International was safe," though, she had said, and she had instructed Gene to respond this way.

"It was pretty much finished up a month-and-a-half ago," Gene added. "Cynthia just asked me to give it a glance before we issue it 'final.'"

Sullivan nodded, and walked off.

*   *   *

Gene got back onto the system and started looking for his Essbase data interrogation files. He realized they weren't running. All of his requests were dying. His reports were dying. There were error messages everywhere. Gene picked up the phone and called the IT department. His buddy Jerry Lilly wasn't there. He finally got hold of Randy Lominick, with whom he'd worked before and who was Jerry Lilly's boss.

"All my reports are dyin'," Gene said into the telephone. "What's going on?"

"Whad'ya mean 'what's going on?'" came Randy's voice over the line. "What're you doin'? You're killin' the server."

Gene knew his requests were taking a couple of hours to run. In order to hunt down the origins of the entries he was looking for, he was having to run serial interrogations of the files. First, he'd have the system run the query of the Intercompany Receivable Account. The servers would plow through all the 350,000 entries hitting that account every month, then download the results into a massive "comma-delineated file" for easy import into an Access database that Gene could query. After doing his analysis in Access, Gene would then have to run another Essbase request, this time running through the other side of the entry, tracing it into the Intercompany Accounts Payable Account. Both of the Intercompany accounts were massive, each comprised some $800 billion of cumulative activity.

Gene had been finding the pieces he was looking for all over the place. Almost $500 million of it had been hung up in a "Suspense" account. It was a laborious process, and what he was trying to do was not too dissimilar to searching for evidence of money laundering, where the dollars were being laundered through all these Intercompany accounts and suspense accounts, and then transferred into asset accounts and then parceled out to specific assets. "These routines are important," Gene said.

"No one else in the whole company can log on to Essbase when they're runnin'" Randy complained. He sounded irritated. "That's why I'm killin' all of them."

Gene could see the problem. Hell, when he downloaded the files to his own PC, he was causing his own PC to crash a couple of times a day. Gene knew that there were thousands of people in the company who used Essbase on a daily basis. That thought paralyzed him for a moment. His Essbase inquiries were causing chaos, and getting people all up in arms. Gene froze, paralyzed with the next thought that came through his head. He pictured Randy Lominick, on the telephone in his office.

Lominick's office was next door to Buddy Yates's, and on the other side was David Myers's office. And here Lominick was killing all these Essbase requests 'cause good ol' Gene Morse is causin' the servers to crash all over the place. And everybody's complaining they can't get onto Essbase.

"Would I hurt anything if I ran them at night?" Gene quietly asked.

"No, nobody'd be using it at night," came Randy's response.

That's when Gene decided to work nights.

*   *   *

By mid-June 2002, Gene Morse had captured enough information that he thought he knew what was going on. He then began pulling down the company's income statements and balance sheets for the last several quarters. On a pro forma basis, he started reversing the bogus adjustments he had discovered. He wanted to see what would happen. "Our line cost went from around 42 percent to 51 percent," he said.

And this was happening every quarter. It was surreal.

By this time, Cynthia Cooper and Glyn Smith were in direct contact with Max Bobbit, chair of WorldCom's audit committee. Cynthia related to Bobbit that she and Glyn Smith planned to go over what they had found the next day with Ferrell Malone. WorldCom had a new accounting firm, KPMG, and Ferrell Malone was the senior KPMG partner on the account.

The evening of June 25, 2002, the world of WorldCom would shatter into 3.8 billion pieces.

*   *   *

_____x

UNITED STATES OF AMERICA   )
-v-   )
)
Scott D. Sullivan, and   )
David F. Myers,   )
            Defendants   )

_____x

SOUTHERN DISTRICT OF NEW YORK, ss.:

Paul J. Higgins, being duly sworn, deposed and says that he is a
Special Agent with the Federal Bureau of Investigation ("FBI") and
charges as follows . . .

. . . WHEREFORE, deponent prays that the above-named defendants be
arrested and imprisoned or bailed as the case may be.

                        PAUL J. HIGGINS
                        Special Agent
                        Federal Bureau of Investigation

Sworn to before me this 31st day of July 2002.

CHAPTER SIXTEEN

The Lexicographer and the Dormant Accounts

BEGINNINGS

The *Independent Committee of Eminent Persons* came into being in 1995 for one purpose only: to address the treatment of "dormant accounts" in Swiss banks believed to belong to victims of Nazi persecution. The investigation that resulted included the most exhaustive use of *data mining* in a forensic examination, ever.

Paul Volcker served as the chair of the Independent Committee of Eminent Persons. In addition to Volcker, the former Chairman of the U.S. Federal Reserve, the Independent Committee included representatives appointed by the Swiss banks, as well as Jewish organizations.

The fact that the Swiss banks agreed to subject themselves to such a comprehensive examination demonstrated the "willingness in Switzerland to undertake this review with 'fresh eyes,' and with the expectation that the review would be both objective and fair." The fresh eyes, this time, though, would be those of forensic accountants.

$$*\qquad*\qquad*$$

Switzerland, a declared neutral, surrounded on all sides by Axis Powers during the years leading up to World War II, found itself in the most delicate of positions. The people of Switzerland, then, as well as now, adopted a view of themselves as a people who had strived to maintain their long-held values of neutrality, democracy, and banking probity, despite the turbulent events of those times. As the years clicked away after the end of World War II, that uncritical self-view became subject to a growing number of calls for an independent assessment by others. Documents were being unclassified in the United States, and the fall of the Iron Curtain was making new information available—information that might prove helpful in reconciling the record of the events of those past years, and the role that Swiss banks might have played.

The forensic accountants signing on to the multiyear assignment of the Independent Committee were charged with discovering as much of the truth as possible regarding the fate of those accounts. Their challenge was to discover, after the passage of 50 to 60 years, not only the original ownership of the accounts, but also the subsequent treatment of them by the Swiss banks.

Perhaps the event most responsible for the feasibility of such an undertaking was the invention of the personal computer. Frank Hydoski, the principal architect of the data-mining approach used by the investigators, put it very succinctly. "Without the computer, you couldn't have done it. It would have been impossible."

By the time the analysis undertaken by all the forensic accountants involved was completed, they would cover over 82 percent of the Swiss banking system existing in 1933 through 1945. The 254 banks examined accounted for substantially all of the deposits of foreign account holders in those turbulent days.

The records the forensic accountant investigators sought were in three different languages: German, French, and Italian. Amazingly, the investigative teams were able to actually locate records for almost 70 percent of the accounts in existence in 1945. Over 4.1 million accounts were reviewed by the investigators and placed in their computer databases.

At its very peak, over 650 forensic accountants were bent at the task of completing the record. To put it to rest; with care, once and forever.

*   *   *

After World War I, most countries in Europe established exchange controls in an effort to curb the flight of capital from their respective economies. The breakdown of the gold standard in 1931 resulted in a reinforcement of this notion. The exchange controls in Germany, though, even before Hitler, were the most stringent.

After Hitler's rise to power in Germany in 1932, the exchange controls imposed in Germany became even more restrictive. This was in stark contrast to many of the other countries in Europe, which began loosening restrictions on the movement of money and goods. One aspect of Hitler's worldview embodied the notion of making an "expanded Germany" entirely self-reliant. With the taking of *Lebensraum,* adequate living space for its peoples, a greater Germany would be able to generate self-sustainable agriculture, raw material commodities, manufacturing, and commerce. With this, there would no longer be a need for foreign exchange. After 1936, the Nazi regime's commitment to rearm in preparation for the upcoming war, together with a corresponding level of domestic consumption, threatened hyperinflation and economic catastrophe; the level of government debt had tripled. The control of capital necessary to finance the competing needs became a fundamental necessity.

By the mid-1930s, all movement of capital and goods out of Germany required a permit. During this period, a Capital Flight Tax was imposed on any significant movement of capital or goods. The introduction of a new law in Germany in 1937 illustrates the seriousness of this notion to the Nazi regime; beginning that year, the death penalty was imposed for exchange control violations.

At the very back of the final report on the forensic investigation is an appendix that I found simply numbing in the sterility of its detail. The historian, Helen Junz, had compiled the appendix for the use of the forensic accountants. Some excerpts:

1933

April	Germany	Law . . . barring "non-Aryan" instructors in all public educational institutions: as officials and employees of the Imperial railway administration, of . . . gas and electricity works, of . . . banks and, insurance companies, of the postal service, of . . . other public agencies, and . . . as police officers and . . . employees of the army.
May	Germany	Licenses of "non-Aryan" tax consultants, judges, professors, instructors, and lecturers in universities . . . revoked.
September	Germany	Exclusion of Jews from agriculture.

1935

March	Germany	Jewish attorneys disbarred . . .
September	Germany	Nuremberg Laws passed. . . . Jews denied citizenship and reduced to status of "subjects."
November	Germany	Jews prohibited from being stockbrokers.

1936

April	Germany	Jews barred as veterinary practitioners.
April	Germany	Jews denied admission to . . . qualifying exams for public accountants.

1937

February	Germany	Jews barred from acting as notaries public.

The chronology had been compiled from OSS files, the precursor to the CIA, maintained in the U.S. National Archives. By 1938, the laws spread to newly annexed countries.

1938

March	Austria	Jews excluded from professions.
July	Germany	Licenses of Jewish physicians revoked.
September	Germany	All activity of Jewish lawyers terminated.
October	Germany	Passports held by Jews declared invalid.
November	Germany	Decree prohibited Jews from owning retail businesses, or mail order houses, from owning export businesses. . . .
December	Slovakia	Jews excluded from public service.

1939

January	Germany	Licenses of Jewish dentists, dental technicians. . . revoked.
March	Protectorate	Jews . . . ousted from civil service, professions and businesses.

As Hitler's armies marched across Europe, one could almost trace the expansion of the Third Reich by the spread of the confiscatory laws:

1940

January–February	Bohemia-Moravia	Jews forbidden to maintain any business enterprises.
	Poland	All Jews to register property.
	Slovakia	Jews excluded from all business enterprises.
September	Luxembourg	Jews barred from professions . . . Jews required to register property.
	Slovakia	Registration of all Jewish property required.

| October | Netherlands | Registration of all Jewish property. |
| November | Belgium | Jews ordered to register . . . property. |

1941

| May | Occupied France | Jews completely eliminated from economic life, barred from all trades and professions. |

*   *   *

The ever-increasing restrictions placed on Jews living in Germany in the 1930s, as well as in areas controlled by the Axis Powers, caused many Jews as well as other people to attempt to move assets to countries deemed safe havens—countries like Switzerland. "The Bank Secrecy Law in Switzerland goes back to 1933 and 1934," Frank Piantidosi explained to me one day. He had been one of the lead partners at PwC directing a significant portion of this forensic accounting investigation.

I learned through my reading of documents in the public records that the numbered accounts were accounts for which a special number or code was used to identify the depositor. A bank might maintain its record of account numbers and corresponding account balances in one ledger; information regarding customer identity then typically would be kept secret in separate ledgers stored under lock and key. Only designated bank employees were to ever have access to information regarding customer identities. In addition, hold mail fees were assessed by the bank for mail held at the bank at the customer's request.

I later described to one of the investigators I interviewed how fascinating it was for me to learn that the notion of numbered accounts had originated in Switzerland in the early 1930s, to facilitate people . . .

"—hiding their identity," the investigator said.

"Right. Hiding their identity," I said. "To help the Jewish people in a sense, then."

"It was a marketing tool," the investigator said.

*   *   *

I first learned of the investigation of the dormant Swiss Bank accounts in October 1996. On that day, Hydoski was sitting next to me in a Price Waterhouse conference room in Los Angeles. Hydoski passed around the scope of work outline for the others in the room to see. He was clearly enthused about the proposed project.

I can remember glancing through the Independent Committee's Request for Proposal, and silently thinking to myself that it would not be a very interesting project. It would involve opening up a lot of old and dusty ledgers. They wouldn't have anything in them except numbers. It was 50 to 60 years after the fact. Who would still be around to answer questions about the documents, let alone have knowledge about procedures in place from 1933 to the present? I was aware of the self-examination recently performed by the Swiss banks themselves. They hadn't been able to come up with much of anything and had been criticized for it. I remember thinking that I wanted no part of the project, thinking it would likely turn into another public relations nightmare.

Six years later, I found myself interviewing Frank Hydoski in a hotel room in New York City. As I sat with him, learning of his role as the architect of the largest forensic data mining investigation ever, I found myself turning 180 degrees in my point-of-view.

On the one hand, I had been right. The forensic accountants involved in the investigation had immediately attempted to go to the dusty old ledgers, where they could learn hardly anything of value.

The intuition of Hydoski, however, turned the adverse results of these initial pilot projects into an approach that ultimately succeeded. Hydoski was the one who insisted, "No, we're not going to keep trying to do it that way. We're going to these external sources first. We'll load all the information we find from these external sources into databases. The last step we'll undertake is to go to the banks to find what they have. We'll load that into the databases, and then let the relational database software perform the matching process."

As Hydoski described how he had gotten the thing turned around, the whole notion floored me—it seemed so counterintuitive. Everything he had proposed seemed to be in the wrong order. His notion was to first scour the world, collecting everything possible to know about potential victims of the Holocaust; to then throw all of this into a massive database; and only after the completion of this massive effort, prepare to go into the banks. His plan was brilliant and produced a wildly successful result. I was interested in how he had come upon the seemingly unorthodox approach.

He explained that he relied on his previous experience in using technology to assist in investigations. "What you come to realize," he said, "is that one of the best ways you can use the computer is to emulate what we do in our heads when we learn about something on one day, and then when we talk to somebody else, and learn another fact, and don't immediately realize that those two facts go together. It's only on reflection that we sort of put those two things together. And then we begin to see the problem a little differently."

"It usually requires an interval of sleep," I said.

Frank laughed. "Right," he said.

My comment about sleep, though, was not in jest. The human brain, the most complex neural network in existence, gathers tables and tables of data every day. The process of absorption and assimilation, though, happens when we sleep. Neurons fire while we are in the REM stage of sleep, sifting through what we have collected and archived during our waking hours. It is only when we dream that our brains reconcile things, and the neural connections between synapses and neurons become hard-wired. We wake up, the next day, or maybe months later, with insights that build on information learned previously. That's why students pulling an all-nighter studying for an exam fool themselves. They may get by on the exam, but the information they study hasn't had a chance to get locked into long-term memory with the absence of that all critical deep sleep element of REM.

Hydoski recognized that the huge scale of the Swiss Bank dormant account investigation required the use of a "relational database." He would load the computer database with tables and tables of disparate data. Human brains could later direct the analysis and comparison of the different tables. He wanted the "process" of the forensic investigation to approximate that of a neural network, but in this case, one that would be created to fit the need.

I then found myself considering the brain that conceived these complex databases. Frank Hydoski completed graduate school at the University of Chicago in 1975, where he had finished his PhD—in Philosophy, of all things.

His dissertation centered on the French Encyclopedists of the eighteenth century, the developers of the famous *Encyclopédie of Diderot and Dalambert,* 18 huge folio volumes intended to cover everything known in the world at the time. To me, this was hardly the stuff of excitement, but I pressed on, for I was curious. How was it that Hydoski, who had completed his doctorate in Philosophy, became *the* world-class expert in the application of data mining to forensic investigations? *The* expert who just happens to be available when one of the most complex data mining exercises in the history of forensic investigations comes along his way. *The* investigation that, without the insight he brought to the project, could have resulted in a colossal exercise in number fumbling.

After completing his dissertation, Hydoski had gone on to four different teaching positions at different universities over the next five-year period. He realized that he needed a change; the life of an academic did not suit him. He had been trained as an analyst, he realized. An academic PhD program trains an individual to analyze. You are trained to break a problem down into its constituent parts, reassemble it as a solution, and go on.

He found himself going through the *Washington Post*'s classified section one morning. A consulting firm was looking for a lexicographer. The consulting firm specialized in document management for law firms engaged in large-scale litigation. Hydoski had studied encyclopedias and systematic languages. He had some academic preparation for that kind of job. He was hired. The little industry in which he now worked was in its infancy in the early 1980s. This was well before the proliferation of the technology enabling the "imaging" of documents, the scanning of a document into a database through the use of OCR, optical character recognition.

The dictionary defines lexicography as the writing and editing of dictionaries, and as I sat there listening to Hydoski and his story, I was reminded of *The Professor and the Madman*. The book narrated the symbiotic relationship of an American doctor, William Chester Minor, confined for life to Broadmoor, an English mental institution, for having committed murder. Minor, who was schizophrenic, also happened to be a lexicographer. A man whose singular competency and contribution to society was the invaluable assistance he provided from his Broadmoor cell to James Augustus Henry Murray in compiling the *OED*, the *Oxford English Dictionary*; assistance that transpired unfailingly over an 18-year period from 1881 to 1899. Today, in its second edition, the *OED* is a 20-volume fountain of lexicography; its 22,000 pages include 2.4 million quotes illustrating the use of 500,000 words.

In the context of document management systems for the legal industry in the 1980s, the lexicographer was the one who created the "index" to the subject area in question; its "lexicon." In order to find a relevant document in a massive case, the subject matter index was used to systematically search the body of documents. Hydoski's first assignment involved a nuclear power plant. His job required him to learn enough about the industry so that he understood the relevant terms and their relationships to one another.

The lexicographer would capture certain elements of a document, and place that into a computer database as a "record." That record might have five, ten, or fifteen fields. The "fields" were the terms that the lexicographer defined as being relevant and important. Hydoski got the opportunity to learn something about litigation and how computers were used in litigation.

He became expert in the field of document management and litigation. He experienced a couple of computer revolutions. The minicomputer revolution had occurred, making information more accessible due to the reduced cost of systems and storage. Microcomputers eventually came onto the scene. Each succeeding revolution made information more accessible and easier to manipulate. It also made the document management aspects of the legal industry more of a commodity type of service. The need for a dedicated lexicographer for this type of work was diminishing daily.

Hydoski found yet another niche in which he could apply his skills. He became a litigation consultant with Price Waterhouse, where he became an expert in the design of large-scale "claims databases," for claimants in bankruptcy cases; and after that, claims databases for large-scale class action cases, such as the breast implant and toxic tort cases. In the 1990s, forensic accounting investigations started coming into the forefront, along with securities fraud litigation. In order to provide the forensic accountants with the information they needed to do their job, he became expert in discovering different ways of drilling through mountains of data. He knew just how to do this, using computers, and through the use of data mining.

It simply required a subtle turn of mind.

* * *

The idea of using the computer to create a record of what happened to the dormant accounts became an intriguing challenge for Hydoski. There, residing within the confines of archives located around the world and within the underground vaults of 254 Swiss banks, was a 70-year encyclopedia of history; one that was written in at least four languages, ready to be catalogued and explored.

On such an expedition to unearth events of the past, where does one begin? The three firms who began planning the undertaking—Price Waterhouse, Arthur Andersen, and KPMG—immediately formed large complex teams to attack the problem.

Some team members, calling on their earlier experiences, believed they could find helpful insights through the use of interviews. Others argued for the use of questionnaires, believing that developing a great, long questionnaire to give to each bank would provide the insights necessary to discover where to look next. No road map was available to follow because no investigation of the scope or scale of this one had ever been attempted. Frank Hydoski, the trained lexicographer, was working out the problem in his mind from a database point of view.

Hydoski called together a small group of Price Waterhouse investigators to help work out the problem. They met on a lovely day in December 1996 on the back deck of his home in Pasadena. Hydoski outlined his thinking to the team. He outlined what they knew and what they didn't know. They knew they would be collecting information from archives. Everyone agreed on that. They knew the banks had computerized systems and that they would be dealing with massive amounts of documents.

What they didn't know, yet, was how to attack the names of the victims. That day, this small group of forensic accountants and data-mining specialists sat in Hydoski's backyard and sketched out the various inter-linking tables of an Oracle database that would support this investigation. The design they mapped out turned out to be eerily similar to the one the investigators finally ended up with, five years of painstaking work later.

The conceptual design did not have all of the fields identified, but it successfully identified the path Hydoski wanted to take over the next years. One part of the database would be called the *account table,* and that table would be populated with all the facts that the investigators could collect about specific accounts. A separate table would serve as the repository for facts collected about Holocaust victims. This would be the *person table.*

In the end, there would be many such tables, all designed to contain the disparate pieces of information collected. The computer could later interrelate all these seemingly unconnected facts and figures. The lexi-cographer, though, was adamant. He wanted all the facts the investiga-tors collected to be segregated, and placed into the appropriate buckets.

The data-mining specialists made another key decision on that sunny winter afternoon in Pasadena, California. They agreed that they would collect the account information, and the person information, exactly as they found it. During the information collection phase, they would avoid attempting to piece together the "story" of the particular piece of infor-mation collected. It would just be collected.

Later, they would use the power of the computer relational database to remove duplicate records. After all of the information had been col-lected, they could use the computer to identify every fact that "related" to a particular victim, and allow the database to consolidate everything into a single record about that victim.

A MINE, FILLED TO THE BRIM WITH DATA

One of the most significant tasks the forensic accountants undertook dur-ing the first phase of their investigation was to survey and research what was known and written about the Holocaust. They wanted to learn every-thing there was to learn about the victims, and about where the victims came from. They wanted to know which banks the victims were most likely to have used, and what conduits they might have used in order to get money into Switzerland. The investigators attempted to obtain all the rel-evant information available in the public domain, including any books that had been written on the subject.

"We went to the Holocaust Museum," Frank Piantidosi explained. "We went to the Reichs Museum in Germany. We went to all the Swiss public archives to try to gain as much information about what was known about what happened." The researchers gathered several hundred texts and numerous articles and microfiched copies of archived documents. One staff person was assigned per text.

The forensic accountants read about victims who had brought their belongings and money with them to the concentration camps, and of how the Nazis then stole them. I asked whether the investigating teams attempted to deal with the issue of the money that went into the camps.

"We tried every angle," Piantidosi said. "We tried to see if there were names from the camps," he explained. "When the Allies won the war and took over Germany, all the German archives were boxed up and sent to the United States." He was referring the Operation Safe Haven records.

Prior to and during World War II, the OSS and other U.S. and British intelligence agencies intercepted messages leading to a belief that assets throughout Europe were being looted by the Nazi regime. These concerns led to a joint U.S. and British undertaking referred to as "Operation Safe Haven." Any information about the looting that was happening in Europe was to be archived for purposes of future reconstruction and restitution. Beginning in 1996, much of this information was finally declassified and consolidated in the U.S. National Archives located in College Park, Maryland. Another key factor to the success of the investigation was that access to the German and the Russian archives became possible after the fall of Communism.

Very little of the information had been computerized, though, and it didn't take the investigators very long to realize that the index systems at the various archives in the various countries were not likely to lead to the type of information the investigators were interested in collecting. The forensic investigators went back again to the archives to examine the indexes, looking for possible points of entry. They established a data room in Zurich. The information collected, though, was in different languages. "So we had French speakers," Piantidosi said, "Italian speakers, German speakers." At the inception of the assignment, 20 forensic accountants would work in the data room, gathering information.

The researchers combing the Safe Haven Records, for example, might find a document that listed account holder names. The Safe Haven Records also yielded communication intercepts detailing accounts transferred into various banks within the Reich at the direction of the Nazi regime. This provided the investigators with the name of an account holder, or perhaps an account number, and the amount of the transfer. They collected that information and stuck it into the lexicographer's steadily growing database.

The investigators attempted to determine the likely origin of the money deposited in various branches of the Swiss banks. Other reference sources provided the investigators with information about the neighborhoods in which depositors most likely lived, providing an important clue as to addresses for the investigators to use in the matching process that would occur later. Piantidosi explained one of the initial challenges. "One of the first bits of information that we received was that there were middlemen that would collect the money and deposit the money in the Swiss banks."

The forensic accountants found numerous references to the phenomenon of middlemen in the archived records. The experience in Poland provides an illustration. In early 1936, though anticipated for some time, the Polish government announced the imposition of strict exchange controls. During this same time frame, numerous advertisements touting the services of middlemen began appearing in the newspapers serving the many Jewish communities in Poland. Not surprisingly, the investigators' research revealed that the banks in Poland began experiencing steep declines in savings deposits during this same time period, and this, after steady year-to-year increases having been experienced. These events were inextricably connected, and caused consternation for the forensic accountants. "At first," Piantidosi explained, "we didn't know whether we would find accounts under the names of individual victims, or under the names of the middlemen they had used."

After the passage of 50 years, it struck me that the question seemed insoluble. Had the middleman made the deposits in his (or her) name, or did he (or she) open up individual accounts using the names of the actual owners? Frank Hydoski provided clarification.

"At that time," he said, "they were referred to as representatives. Sometimes they had legal status and powers of attorney and sometimes they didn't. Sometimes they'd put the account in their own name. They may have come from a village somewhere, and they had the assets of 10 people and they put an account in their [own] name. That is a fascinating phenomenon and one that we were not able to figure very much out about by the end of the day. In some cases, we nailed it."

However, this was not always the case. "We couldn't reliably figure out whose assets were in these accounts unless you had some other fact, like an affidavit from somebody. If they were honest, they would have put that as part of the account record. It would go into the customer dossier, and then that would tell you that this asset really belonged to somebody else." The researchers' database ultimately included a table of all known, suspected and possible intermediaries.

Into the database, then, went the names of Swiss intermediaries used by victims of Nazi persecution to hide funds in Switzerland. The forensic accountants also loaded the names of Swiss lawyers who had facilitated the laundering of Nazi assets toward the end of World War II. They also loaded the names of intermediaries who facilitated ransom payments to the Nazi regime in return for safe passages to neutral countries.

The forensic accountants' attempt to trap all known and possible intermediaries was exhaustive; they loaded into the lexicographer's tables the name of attorneys listed in Swiss telephone books during the period 1930 through 1950; they loaded the names of attorneys listed in the Registry of Swiss Lawyers and in the Swiss Federation of Lawyers during the same period of time. They loaded the names of intermediaries identified during earlier investigations made by the Swiss Compensation Office, and intermediaries identified during a 1962 survey of Swiss banks. The forensic accountants even interviewed a retired Jewish banker who was a relative of one of the founders of a private Swiss bank. Into the lexicographer's database went the names of potential intermediaries gleaned during this interview. Into the lexicographer's database, too, went the names of high-ranking Nazi officials; the names of Swiss companies allegedly owned by Germans; the names of noted European Nazi collaborators and informers; the names of galleries, dealers, and individuals who allegedly had received looted art during and after the war; the names of banks and finance companies allegedly hiding German assets during and after the war; the names of holders of "enemy assets in Switzerland," that had been identified by intelligence agencies during World War II; and the names of "enemy individuals who allegedly transferred assets to Swiss banks." The FDR library even yielded the names of officials in German financial institutions.

A total of 4,025 potential or suspected intermediaries were identified and loaded.

When the threads of this list were later matched against the account data recovered from the Swiss banks, the resulting woven fabric told quite a tale. The forensic accountants were able to positively link one intermediary, a Dutch lawyer who appeared to have been involved in a large number of "ransom for safe-transit transactions," to six specific accounts (read "people"). The forensic accountants also linked 5,800 accounts at one bank to the table of identified intermediaries; at another bank they found another 8,200 accounts under the names of some of the same intermediaries; and another 1,300 accounts at a third bank.

Sadly, the forensic accountants identified over 1,900 individuals associated with the looting of dormant accounts. The forensic accountants positively identified accounts transferred to third parties without the account owner's consent, or transferred under duress. One thing was clear, the asset looting intensified as the Nazi regime invaded other countries. The forensic accountants learned of Nazi espionage undertaken in Switzerland. Espionage oriented toward one thing: finding any and all accounts hidden in Switzerland.

When the final matching process was undertaken, the lexicographer's database queries revealed almost 1,700 numbered accounts

linked to victims of Nazi persecution; accounts that had been transferred to high-ranking officials in the Nazi regime, as well as other European collaborators.

Even with this effort though, perfect clarity could not be achieved
with regard to every account identified. As the investigation moved into
the year 2001, significant controversy arose as to whether the names identified with all dormant accounts possibly related to victims of the Holocaust should be published. The forensic accountants wanted the entire list
to be published. The sticking point had to do with the powers of attorney.
The forensic investigators prevailed in their arguments to have those
names published as well. Frank Hydoski explained the reasoning.

"If some family member had a record . . . that said, 'my dad put his
money into representative so-and-so's hands.' And representative so-and-
so, indeed, shows up as having an account and we published the name,
they [the rightful heir] can claim against that account. That could then
ultimately result in a successful claim."

When one got down to the account level, and then to the subject of
possible middlemen, and powers of attorney, and affidavits of this, and
affidavits of that, it struck me that one could easily lose sight of the big
picture. An account balance with $10,000, or even $250,000 was not the
issue. And a potential disagreement whether that account balance should
specifically go to this individual, 50 years later, or to another, could easily appear to be simply a quarrel over money. With this kind of disagreement, you might lose sight of the fact that the account holder had died as
a victim of the Nazi regime. The forensic accounting investigation showed
that society cared enough to give it our best shot, to have left no stone un-
turned. To know that the victims were not numbers, whether that be the
number of a Swiss bank account, or the number tattooed on the inside of
the wrist of a victim of a Nazi concentration camp. The forensic accountants needed to know that they had done their very best to bring closure
to the subject of victims' dormant accounts.

People can always argue about money. Memories, though, are another thing altogether. One cannot argue about the memory of a life
now extinguished.

*   *   *

The forensic accountants were not immune from the depressing effects
of the research they were conducting. "We really had to get into all the details of what happened," Piantidosi explained. "That was very tough, to
read about the Holocaust, and about the victims, and what happened to
the victims, and where their money might have gone."

The readings caused despair because the investigators could see the plight of the people. "There were despairing moments," Hydoski recalled. "Certainly."

Someone on the forensic staff discovered a book written by a French historian. The book was about French children who had been murdered by the Nazis. "And the book [contained] a little biographical sketch of each child and a photograph or two," Hydoski said. "And it's one of the most despairing books you could possibly look at."

"Because you are looking at children," I said.

"Children, yes," Hydoski confirmed. "Somewhere between newborn and 13 to 14 years old. Pictures of their normal life prior to incarceration and death. Just a very affecting thing. We ran into that sort of thing over and over and over again."

There was another aspect to the anguish the investigating staff experienced. There was just too much work to do. "We can't possibly get it done." Hydoski described how these two faces of despair in the end had a common nexus. "It produced in many of the staff, and certainly in me," he explained, "a feeling that 'I gotta get it done because it's really important to do.'" A mental image described by Hydoski brings into focus these two seemingly conflicting emotions. "On the one hand, I have this mental image of this child," he said. "And then on the other, I have this mountain of work. And you know you need to address the mountain of work in order to address the situation of the child. It was tough emotionally, I think for everyone."

*   *   *

In 1932, advertisements appeared in a Swiss newspaper offering "loans" to employees of Swiss banks. The advertisements were part of a scheme to purchase information from bank employees. The Nazi regime was interested in learning the names of Germans having an account in Swiss banks. Upon the provision of the requested information, the Nazi agents paid a commission based upon the account balance. One bank employee, arrested for espionage by the Swiss authorities, had revealed to the Nazi regime the ownership information of 74 accounts. By the time this individual was arrested, the balance in 20 of the accounts had already been repatriated to the Nazi regime in Germany.

On March 14, 1938, Adolf Hitler entered Vienna to the accompaniment of unending cries of, *ein Volk, ein Reich, ein Führer.* On April 10, elections were held in Germany and Austria. Ninety-nine percent of the population in both countries voted *Ja* to the Anschluss, the political joining together of the two countries into a "Greater Germany."

The researchers, assisted by historian Helen Junz, located in one of the Austrian archives a census of Austrian Jews, ordered taken shortly after the Anschluss by Austria's new government. The census recorded all property of Austrian Jews, including whether or not an Austrian Jew had Swiss bank accounts. Shortly afterwards, the account balances were transferred from Switzerland to the Austrian authorities. Exactly 50 years later, Hydoski, the lexicographer, ordered the record of this census to be loaded into his database.

"And they kept a record of all of this?" I asked, incredulous.

"An unbelievable amount of records are still around," Frank Hydoski replied.

I found this puzzling. "Why would they have kept a record?"

"They didn't think of them as nefarious," Hydoski explained. "First, there was a law in Austria that said that Jews had to complete the census. Part of the census was a registration of their assets. And then there was a law that said that if they were holding assets outside the country, there'd be a 100 percent tax on those assets."

During the late 1930s, the transfers of accounts in Swiss banks back to "Greater Germany" could only be effected upon the presentation of seemingly "proper" powers of attorney, affidavits, and other releases signed by the account holder. After the years passed, though, accounts were often simply repatriated based upon lists presented by officials of the Third Reich. The record isn't clear.

Fifty years hence, however, the forensic accountants found records of these transfers in archives located around the world. The information was collected, to be put into the massive database the lexicographer was having populated.

Suppose a person who had once lived in Munich, or some other city in Europe, had an account at Credit Suisse, or Swiss Bank Corporation. The numbered account might have had 5,000 francs in it that ended up repatriated. Although that may be all the researchers could know from that particular record source, the information would be called an "account," and loaded into the lexicographer's database for future assimilation with other partial information.

The forensic accountants looked for this type of information in both foreign archives and Swiss archives. Every once in a while, the investigators found a little treasure trove of information. One of the peace accords at the end of the World War II required the Swiss to freeze all Axis Power accounts, including accounts originating from areas now thought of as Eastern European and Northern European countries, as well as parts of France and Italy. The Allies wanted to determine whether or not the account holder was a Nazi. If, for example, an account holder was a German, the Swiss separately administered the account over several years following the war. The account may eventually have been appropriately released to its rightful owner, but Hydoski would have located another nice record of a Swiss account to load into his database. The name, account number, amount, whatever information could be identified, would be loaded.

The forensic accountants collected this type of information from various archives located all around the world to build a record of some of the accounts before they began their investigation inside the vaults of the Swiss banks themselves. This was the keystone to the Hydoski data-mining plan.

To build the list of victims who had died in the Holocaust, the investigators attempted to collect names from every source they could find. They discovered that no single list was "complete." There was no agreement among the various authorities on the subject about the number of Holocaust victims. "The numbers that you see published are estimates," Hydoski explained.

I learned from reading the report of the forensic investigation that one million victims were killed by firing squads in villages in Eastern Poland and Russia. I also learned that no record of those killings existed. The people had simply disappeared from the face of the earth. At the end of the war, synagogues and other agencies developed lists of those who had disappeared. They had birth and death records for the people of their respective communities. By a process of elimination, they could identify the names of people who had vanished.

The lists were compiled synagogue by synagogue. "Some of these were rolled up into country lists," Hydoski explained. "Romania has a country list, for example." But this would not be true for all countries. There had been many other attempts to develop the names of Holocaust victims, resulting in hundreds of lists. No one had ever assembled a single comprehensive list. "All the lists are partial, for a variety of reasons, I think," Hydoski explained. "There are some very deeply held beliefs in some parts of the Jewish community that it's inappropriate to make a list like this."

*   *   *

Fifty years had passed since the end of the war. Frank Piantidosi knew that banks had acquired other banks. The Swiss banks had expanded regionally, across cantons. Piantidosi insisted that one of the database tables needed to include everything known about all 254 banks from the 1920s through the end of the century. Hydoski readily agreed. There would be a "bank history database."

The researchers learned that the Swiss National Bank published an annual report on banks doing business in Switzerland. The investigators collected every annual report published between 1920 and 1999, and then compiled the first comprehensive historical view of banks in Switzerland. This analysis detailed which banks existed during the relevant period, which bank had been absorbed, and by whom and precisely when, allowing the investigators to ascertain precisely what had happened to the deposits in banks that had been acquired by other banks.

IN THE BANKS

It was time for the forensic accountants to unearth what could be unearthed about accounts existing in 1933 through 1945, from within the 254 banks themselves. Once in the banks, and once they were able to develop a record of accounts that existed between 1933 and 1945, the forensic accountants developed an understanding of what had happened to these accounts, all the way up through the present time. The investigation involved much more than the tracking of numbered accounts.

"There are very few numbered accounts; that's a misnomer," Hydoski explained. "In a Swiss bank, a commercial bank with several million accounts, the number of numbered accounts is gonna be less than 100,000." The investigators looked at all the accounts. That was the only way they could determine which accounts needed to be investigated; the task was truly monumental.

In addition to the archives at the headquarters of the major banks, the forensic investigators found bank-specific archives. Major archives were located in both the French and Italian sectors. Archived information was also found at various bank branches located throughout Switzerland.

Once an archive was identified, the forensic accountants took a complete inventory of its contents. The process included a shelf-by-shelf examination to determine the information that was relevant to the investigation. According to the Independent Committee's final report, the banks themselves "devoted significant . . . manpower to assist . . . to convert paper and microfiche records into computer databases and to assist in the research of the matches."

*   *   *

Once in the banks, the forensic investigating teams from the different participating firms pressed forward with the various techniques they believed might work best. Those advocating the use of questionnaires almost immediately ran into insurmountable obstacles and were forced to abandon the notion. Other forensic teams encountered difficulties with the interview approach. That investigative approach was unsuccessful for a number of reasons, the biggest being that there were very few people possessing the requisite knowledge of events and bank procedures going back fifty years.

The investigative teams pressed on though, learning what could be learned about the accounts. They requested a "dump" of the computer systems in use at each of the banks being examined. Even such a seemingly routine request yielded unforeseen headaches. Almost all of the accounts in each of the banks' computer systems had incorrect "dates of origin." The oldest accounts that could be located through this method all seemed to have been created some time in the early 1970s.

Every once in a while, the forensic accountants would hit pay dirt. "The Swiss government's records on accounts that had been frozen in 1945 were very useful," Hydoski said.

During the late 1930s and early 1940s, two of the Swiss banks had transferred deposits to the United States, allegedly for purposes of safekeeping in the event Switzerland was overrun by the Nazis. In 1941, those assets were frozen by the New York Banking Authority because of concern that they included German assets.

"And later, there was some interest in the idea that they may have had some victims' assets in them as well," Hydoski continued. Immediately after the war, pressure was put on the Swiss banks to similarly put a freeze on all assets held in Switzerland by Germans, or anyone connected to the Nazi regime.

"So we got those records," Hydoski said. "Those were very useful for those two banks. They told us some several thousand accounts in each bank."

Procedures had been established in the United States for applying for assets frozen in the United States. Fifty years later, the forensic accountants would go through these files and would discover letters from victims, pleading to have the money sent to them or to pay bribes to try to get them out of a concentration camp.

*   *   *

The forensic accountants went through 270 kilometers of archives. Make the conversion; that equals 168 miles of archived materials. In an archive at one of the banks, the forensic accountants might actually locate customer account cards. For the lexicographer, these proved to be treasure troves of information. They provided addresses; the nature and number of accounts held; account origin dates, and any changes made—a veritable history.

Piantidosi's investigative team was provided space in the vault of the old private bank—their gold room; five levels underground. "It was sealed with security like you just can't imagine," Piantidosi said. "And we were the only ones that ever got into that archive. They were reluctant to open it up. And you can well understand that."

The forensic team took over the space completely. They established a proprietary network in the vault in which they worked, including data-base servers and computer workstations. "It was a very insular network," Hydoski said.

I asked him whether the bank wanted the investigative team located down there because it was convenient to the records, or whether they wanted the forensic accountants down there so that they would be out of the way, and out of view.

"Both," Hydoski replied. "They wouldn't have to move their records around as much because we were next to their temporary archive, which was a staging area, and it was more secure than having us in offices with windows." At the peak, the Price Waterhouse investigative team comprised over one hundred investigators. According to Piantidosi, 45 percent of the complement came from the forensic and investigative practice group in the United States. Many of those staff members were bilingual. "We pulled from the French firm," he said. "Canada, French speaking."

Many of the staff also came from Germany. There were bilingual staff participating from the British firm, as well as staff pulled from the Italian firm. "Anywhere we could find staff that had the language capability," he described, "we would recruit 'em, and train 'em, and put 'em on the staff."

Piantidosi described the process once the investigative teams moved on to sifting through the data found at the banks themselves. "Well, we pulled a ledger out," he said. "Blew the dust off it. Start flipping through it. See what it represented. If we found account balances on a particular date, we would later attempt to match it with names." These were num-bered accounts, so in most cases, the only information found in the ledgers would be an account number and a record of activity.

* * *

The investigators would use their computerized relational database to at-tempt to match names possibly associated with a numbered account. The final report on the investigation describes the software technology the investigators developed specifically for their task:

> The firms used exact-name and near-exact name matching algorithms. Near-exact name matching involved matching vowel equivalents for a, e, i, o, and u, as well as for double consonants.

Frank Hydoski had also included a name-matching test incorporating the use of "fuzzy logic." The final report on the investigation described the software algorithm.

> . . . Additional testing was conducted using a fuzzy logic matching technique. Fuzzy logic matching uses a phonetic algorithm that matches names that sound alike but are spelled differently, as opposed to exact name matching which requires the same spelling of the first and the last names on the account as is in the victim database . . . matches [were placed] into one of four categories depending on the accuracy of the match.

Iterative research was the key in this world of forensic data mining. The team of researchers put together by the lexicographer to accomplish all of this was impressive. "I had a very capable senior manager, Mary Jane Schirber, who worked with me," Hydoski said. "At any given time, we had a total of 16–20 database specialists working with us. Mary Eton was another senior manager whose work was very critical to our success."

The team of database specialists developed an initial theory regarding a specific matter of inquiry. They then "queried" the Oracle relational database in order to get a picture of what the data might reveal. Invariably, after getting back the preliminary array of data, the investigators would realize that the form of the query wasn't quite right in one respect or another, and they would try another.

The database was used to identify accounts deemed highly correlated to victims of Nazi persecution on the basis of evidence of an address in an Axis or Axis-occupied country. The strength of a match was determined based upon possible agreement of street address, birth date, surname, middle name, city, and country. The forensic accountants assumed that "numbered accounts" (hold-mail accounts) were opened by foreigners. Conversely, accounts positively identified to have a Swiss address of a permanent nature were excluded from further research, as were accounts identified as having been disbursed to an account holder who had survived the war, or to the heir of an account holder. Based upon a country-by-country analysis of accounts closed during 1933 through 1945, the computerized database also allowed the forensic accountants to identify and exclude from further analysis accounts that had been closed before Axis occupation of the country of the account holder.

The forensic accountants knew that at each of the banks there should have been some kind of record relating to accounts that had been closed, or suspended, due to the absence of activity. In their interviews, they learned that inactive accounts had been transferred into collective accounts. The forensic accountants had to fight through a morass of confusion with regard to what had happened to these dormant accounts. It all had to do with the notion of *escheating*.

Escheating is an obscure word, indeed. In medieval England when a person died leaving no legal heir, or when a tenant was outlawed, feudal law provided for the property of the deceased to revert to the feudal over-lord. Because of the particular laws regarding the practice of escheating in Switzerland, the record of what had happened to the dormant accounts would be as obscure as the definition of the word itself.

I once testified as an expert witness in litigation brought against a title company by the state of California, and so I had a passing famil-iarity with the notion of escheating. The lawsuit I am referring to was over the legal right to interest on customer deposits held by the title company. Did the interest belong to the customer, or to the title com-pany? Because of my involvement in that case, I knew that, at least in California, dormant customer accounts were to be forwarded to the State, for "safekeeping." If the depositor, or customer, could later prove the funds were theirs, by law the State was required to remit the "es-cheated funds" to them. This would be the case no matter how many decades had transpired. I was mistaken in my assumption that proce-dures were similar elsewhere.

"Switzerland is different," Frank Piantidosi informed me. "In Switzer-land, escheated funds go back to the bank."

"Except for in some of the French-speaking cantons," Frank Hydoski clarified.

The two men were saying that under Swiss law, if a depositor's account had gone dormant, the bank had the right to absorb the funds. Whereas the law in France regarding the treatment of dormant accounts was simi-lar to that in the United States, other countries had laws on their books that were similar to the Swiss laws; specifically the U.K., Germany, and Belgium's private banks.

The forensic accountants investigating the treatment of Swiss Holo-caust accounts yielded records of specific instances where dormant ac-counts had been closed and the funds converted to income. "It was a major issue that we were dealing with," Piantidosi said. "It was very tedious."

*   *   *

The lexicographer's database matching process yielded almost 300,000 positive matches of accounts held by victims of the Holocaust. The foren-sic accountants identified another 100,000 accounts to be further sub-jected to painstaking research due to circumstances indicating a likely possible relationship to victims of the Holocaust. For example, although a positive match had not been made, the data mining exercise may have yielded other positive indicia, such as a concentration camp address being found in the files, or perhaps some kind of notation being found in the files indicating that the account holder had died in a concentration camp. Almost $1 billion has been escrowed against claims from lawful heirs.

*   *   *

The forensic accountants found that there were over 6.8 million accounts that had been open in the 254 Swiss banks during the period 1933–1945. The investigators found records relating to 4.1 million accounts, an astounding accomplishment considering that 60 years had elapsed. The obverse, the 2.7 million accounts for which records no longer exist, represents an unfillable gap that can never be analyzed for any relationship to victims of Nazi persecution.

There is, however, another manner in which to regard the two opposing faces of the available record. We now know everything that is knowable on the subject of the dormant accounts of victims of the Holocaust. The history has been completed. The book can now be finally closed on this subject, in order that it can be put to rest, on its shelf in the library of happenings to mankind since the beginning of recorded history.

*   *   *

Thirty-four million continental Europeans died in World War II. Even as I write this, I need to pause to reflect on the significance of this number.

Thirty-four million people—who once existed.

*   *   *

I found an odd quote today. Stalin once said, "The death of an individual is a tragedy. The death of a million people is a statistic."

How can one respond to such a statement? Of 3,300,000 Polish Jews, only 440,000 managed to survive the war.

CHAPTER SEVENTEEN

"I'm So Glad You're Here"

Frank Hydoski had demonstrated the use of data mining as a forensic tool. With its use, 60 years after the Holocaust, he and his team of investigators had been able to use the power of the computer to piece together the millions of clues pointing to ownership of accounts that still lay dormant in Swiss banks. A few short years after this, in easily the most significant corporate fraud investigation in the United States prior to the corporate meltdowns of Enron and WorldCom, investigator Jim Littley used data mining in another way. He used computerized data mining as a forensic "sniffer." Littley and the others on his team were seeking fraudulent entries "booked" by the corporation's former CEO and his cronies.

Littley believed that the bogus entries he and the other forensic accountants were looking for just might end in nice round numbers. To test his hypothesis against the six-year time span under investigation, he used data-mining computer technology to look for all journal entries "with a bunch of 000s on the end of them." Littley was betting that neither the former CEO, or the company's former CFO, were smart enough to think to use a series of randomly generated numbers in the entries the two men devised to manipulate the corporation's financial statements. In the year 2002, the same subtle blunder would tip-off a savvy young forensic accountant, leading him to piece together the shenanigans of Scott Sullivan, WorldCom's former CFO, who is now charged with several felonies for the manipulation of WorldCom's financial statement.

Gene Morse, the internal auditor at WorldCom who first discovered the massive fraud there in the late spring of 2002, knew for sure he was onto something when he discovered "one side" of an entry booked to World-Com's fixed asset account. The entry, for something described as *Prepaid Line Capacity,* was for an even half-a-billion dollars.

When Gene Morse started nosing around the corporation a bit, he was repeatedly told, "You have to ask Dave."

Dave Myers, WorldCom's corporate controller, however, wasn't about to provide Gene Morse with anything Gene could work with. Gene Morse knew the thing smelled, though. He knew it at first sight before he started receiving the runaround. Why? Because the entries he was seeing were all booked in nice round increments; a half a billion here, a half a billion there—and they were always in big round numbers.

Gene Morse, at WorldCom, just like Jim Littley a few years earlier, knew from gut instinct that big round numbers being booked to a financial statement account didn't seem to pass a reality test. Both men relied on common sense. Littley also had an advantage; he knew that statistical analysis supported his belief. He knew of Benford's Law, and he devised his computerized investigation data-mining efforts to include specific tests based on Benford's Law.

Mark Nigrini, who has written extensively on the subject, first came across the notion of Benford's Law in his graduate studies; it was his indefatigable pursuit of data that enabled him to ultimately prove its validity to financial statements. But he needed lots of data, reams and reams and reams of data, to prove that the law had validity in detecting fraud in a financial statement, or in a tax return.

As a student, Nigrini intuitively believed that in a financial statement, which is nothing more than an accumulation of thousands upon thousands of financial transactions, that any number or "digit" had an equal probability of occurrence. A "nine" for example, had the same chance of occurrence as a "two," or a "one," for that matter. He was amazed to learn in his studies of statistical theory that this was simply not the case. Nigrini knew that a financial statement of a publicly traded company could be imagined as being nothing more than one of the world's largest adding machine tapes. What he learned was that, in truth, in any large series of sums, or data, or transactions (such as a financial statement), a one was six times more likely to occur than a nine.

James Benford had discovered this principle while working for General Electric in 1938. Benford's research led him to conclude that 31 percent of the time, you would expect to find a one appearing as the first digit in any series of numbers. Benford found that the frequency of distribution of numbers follows a logarithmic function; a curve, that gently curves downward; a two had a lower probability of ever occurring as the first digit in any series of numbers, only a 19 percent probability. The distribution function of numbers he discovered, his downward sloping curve, sloped downward so far to the right that a nine only had a 5 percent chance of *ever* occurring as the initial digit in *any* large series of numbers.

Nigrini's work with Benford's Law was oriented toward discovering whether the law had any validity in large transactional data sets. It does. Nigrini's work proved that the odds were against the likelihood of a transaction having a zero in the second position of a number, and that the odds were again against a zero being in the third position of a number; the same thing for the fourth position in a number. In fact, the odds were 88 percent against the likelihood of a zero occurring in the second digit. They were 90 percent against a zero showing up in the third digit; and they were also 90 percent against a zero showing up in the fourth digit. The odds against a last-three-digit combination being 000 are a long-shot bet; it's exactly 999 to one, against. When people estimate, however, they typically use round numbers. When you read that 64,000 people were at the Rose Bowl game, you intuitively know that the number is an estimate. Littley knew about this. He devised his data-mining queries to look for transactions with lots of zeroes in them.

A sophisticated data mining forensic tool, called *D-Tect,* builds Benford's Law and other sophisticated tests for indicia of fraud into an immense anomaly detection search engine; one which is able to query massive corporate databases to identify fraudulent patterns. One Fortune 500 corporation deployed this anomaly detection tool against its procurement databases; the data mining quickly covered over 600 office locations, 10 different computer data-processing centers, and $30 billion in disbursements. The software examined 70 million records automatically. The computerized software applied 150 separate analytical tests to each transaction, including a whole series of Benford's Law tests. The software then scored the transactions tested, indicating where a transaction, or series of transactions, failed multiple tests, indicating a higher probability of fraud.

Transactions relating to over seven million invoices that had led to five million checks being disbursed to 500,000 different vendors were tested in this manner. The software identified the need for follow-up on 6,000 duplicate payments that were each in excess of $100,000. The software also flagged some 3,000 checks that had somehow been disbursed even before the date on the invoice. This corporation has over 170,000 employees. For good measure, the software was used to cruise through the corporation's payroll database. One of the more valuable utilities provided in this age of the Internet is that the software can be used to test the validity of a payment by polling independent open sources of third-party data. For example, when the database was polled and compared to an outside database of valid social security numbers, the software identified payments to many employees whose social security number matched that of individuals who were deceased; follow-up research was definitely warranted. The software also identified some 4,000 employees who continued to receive regular salary after their termination date.

This company's internal controls and procedures are no better, or worse, than 99 percent of corporate America. The executives there are not embarrassed by the findings. They believe the diligence of the examination speaks for itself. Anomaly detection software such as this also can be utilized to scrutinize databases comprising sales and accounts receivable, procurement and accounts payable, inventory, and payroll. The types of fraud that may be detected through this kind of analysis include: kickbacks, ghost employees, falsified hours or salary, and embezzlements using fictitious vendors or diversion of payments.

*   *   *

John O'Connor, a forensic accountant who specializes in white-collar crime and procurement fraud, has seen it all. As a former senior financial investigator for the U.S. Attorney's office in Boston, as well as for the Massachusetts Attorney General's office, he has worked exclusively on complex financial crimes. During his tenure as an investigator with the U.S. Attorney's office, he was responsible for locating assets hidden offshore by people who had already been convicted. He became a forensic accountant as a result of an interesting turn of events.

As a young man recently out of college, O'Connor had hoped to join the FBI as a special agent. Back in the 1980s, however, it took almost 18 months to complete the application process. During those 18 months, his forensic accounting job at Price Waterhouse blossomed. He found himself working every day with the FBI on joint investigative matters. He soon came to believe, rightly or wrongly, that he was receiving a richer experience than he might have had as a new agent. He was supervising teams of people and providing input to the FBI in very significant cases. He thought that he would not have had a similar opportunity as a new agent because the FBI was at that time a very hierarchical organization.

At the end of the 18-month application period, O'Connor received his FBI Academy class start date, but decided to turn the offer down. That was painful for his dad, a former FBI special agent. "That was probably the hardest thing I've done, in terms of disappointing him," O'Connor explained. As an FBI "legacy agent," John O'Connor Jr. would have received a special honor upon graduation from the Academy. His father would have been invited to come to Quantico to personally present him with the badge his father had worn. "I think he had kind of played that movie in his head," John said, "and so when the time came when I didn't do it, it was a tough message to deliver. It was a tough one to receive. But I will tell you now, he thrives on hearing the types of stuff that I get involved with."

Some of the most outrageous cases of procurement fraud he has seen in his career as a forensic accountant, however, have been in the private sector, investigating cases in which corporations have been stung by employees. He believes that the way the typical corporation views its buyers is significantly different than how the corporation's vendors view the same buyers. In his experience, a corporation's purchasing agents, or buyers, are viewed by others within the organization as middle management. "They're typically tenured employees, and are paid reasonably well," he said.

Most of these middle managers have little opportunity to climb much higher up the corporate ladder. "They have a lot of responsibility, though," O'Connor explained. Several of the corporations who have retained him each spend upwards of $60 billion annually on the procurement of products and services in support of their business operations. A typical buyer in this scenario might be responsible for $40 million or more in annual purchases.

From the perspective of the corporation's vendors, however, that corporation's buyer is the senior-most corporate official the vendor will ever deal with. O'Connor's point was that as far as a vendor might be concerned, "the corporation's buyers are the guards at the gate into the company." The primary objective of the vendor is to obtain business from the corporation, and through the vendor's eyes, the buyers are the key.

John provided the example of a vendor trying to sell into a $60 billion company for the first time. Initially, he explained, the vendor might just simply try to sell into one of the company's smaller subsidiaries. With that accomplished, the vendor will have been legitimized as a corporate vendor, finding it perhaps easier now to sell into other subsidiaries owned by the corporation.

"I interviewed a broker in Florida once," O'Connor said. "It was about some kickbacks that were going on. I was standing in this guy's office asking some questions and he stopped me. 'You know, John,' he said. 'Some people are money people, and some people are TV people. Of course, I don't do this stuff, but you just have to figure out what people want.'"

The broker in this case was a middleman who brokered the sale of product, and was a significant vendor to O'Connor's corporate client. The "but" in this broker's statement negated everything that preceded it. The broker, of course, had been referring to kickbacks—figuring out what it was that a particular purchasing agent, or buyer, within a corporation might prefer to have. Although the interview with the broker, the president of a brokerage company, was in Florida, the broker was conveying to O'Connor, in his

Bronx accent, that you've got to give these buyers whatever they want. If it's a TV, then give him a TV. If it's a stereo, then it's a stereo. Some might just want the cash. "He was laying it on the line," O'Connor said. "He knew I didn't have much against him, and he was pretty confident." O'Connor believes there are a lot of vendors out there willing to do just about anything to open a door into a blue chip company.

There is another aspect to the internal procurement frauds experienced by corporate America. When individuals possess some level of procurement authority, if the appropriate controls are not in place, the procurement process can be initiated using fictitious vendors. The individual possessing the authority to procure some level of product or services arranges for sham transactions to be initiated, with the result that monies are paid to the fictitious vendor without any services or product having been provided to the corporation. O'Connor described a procurement fraud perpetrated within the bowels of a very large company.

"A guy named Larry Swanson was the director of training for this company," O'Connor said. "He was in a position to approve the procurement of services for this department. It doesn't have to be the people making the widgets," he emphasized. "It can be anyone with that kind of authority. Particularly people at a higher level, because they can sign off on fake invoices."

This individual was prosecuted for embezzling several million dollars from the Fortune 100 corporation. Since the controls in place within the corporation somehow had not precluded Swanson from being able to approve payments to fictitious vendors, I mused that his biggest challenge must have been figuring out a way to hide the bogus expenditures so that they wouldn't stick out in the company's financials. The guy didn't need somebody asking, "Why are we spending 15 times the amount we're supposed to in this area?"

John O'Connor disabused me of this notion. "Larry actually *budgeted* for his fraud so it didn't stick out," he said.

O'Connor explained that upper level management was accustomed to seeing a certain level of expenditures for the department Larry managed, and they assumed of course that the expenditures were legitimate. When the annual budgeting process was underway, Larry would say, "I'm looking for a 6 percent bump this year in our spending." When the budget received approval from corporate headquarters, good ol' Larry effectively received approval to "bump" his take.

I asked O'Connor how this ultimately got discovered. The answer was a little complicated and bizarre. "Larry got very comfortable with approving payments to these fake companies," O'Connor said. It turns out that each of the payments Larry authorized would individually be under the threshold of the limit of his authority. Therefore, no one else had to approve them, or even see them. "He could sign up to 10 grand," O'Connor said. O'Connor's recollection was pretty close; an affidavit filed by the FBI in support of mail fraud and money laundering charges indicated that all the checks were for amounts less than $5,000.

Our fellow Larry apparently knew how to pump the volume through. "He was cranking out up to 20 checks a month to himself," O'Connor said.

Larry arranged to interpose an intermediary, or two, so that the disbursements could not be traced to him. "The first intermediary was his son's girlfriend," O'Connor said.

I thought that he was pulling my leg. "Really?" I asked.

"You can pull it up in the news," O'Connor said. He was very sincere when he said this. "I mean, you'll be amazed," he said. "This is gonna be hard to believe, but when you pull it up on *Lexis/Nexis*, you'll see that what I'm saying is true."

"Go on," I said, making a mental note to check it out.

"Larry convinced this woman that he was actually a secret agent," O'Connor said.

O'Connor's story was true. Larry Swanson somehow convinced this young woman that he was a secret agent whose undercover identity was as a training manager at a nationwide chain of convenience stores. He was fighting the war on drugs. Larry explained to her that there were monies that needed to flow, and that they (his covert operation, I assume) needed to legitimize these funds, and make them look as though the corporation he worked for was helping. He instructed her how to endorse and deposit checks that he would make payable to a fake company. He would mail the checks to her address. She was to simply deposit the checks, and immediately turn the money around by writing a check to Larry, net of a fee.

I found the story to be curious. It's always a curious thing when two or more people are in collusion. What binds these people, one to one another? "Were the checks made out to her, in her name?" I asked.

"No," O'Connor responded. "They were made out to a fictitious company name that he had created."

Swanson, however, was an unbelievably thorough thief. He arranged to always meet with his intermediary at a hotel in the area. Once the connection was made, the two would move off to a private area. When the woman handed over the check to him, Larry provided her with a cassette, or a computer disk, which was always crudely wrapped in tissue paper. She was then instructed to take it to the ladies room, drop it in the trash, and then walk immediately out of the hotel. He told her the disks would be picked up by other agents. She was not to look back and she was to immediately leave the premises.

I asked John if she believed what she was doing was wrong.

"No," he said. "She had no idea that it was wrong."

The secret meetings and handoffs went on like this for some time. Ultimately, there was a falling out between Larry's son and this girl. She told Larry that she didn't want to do it anymore.

Her mother was aware of the whole operation, however. The young girl related to Larry that her mother had said, "Well, I'll do it then."

Larry had his next intermediary. It was as simple as that. From that point forward, the young girl's mother would receive the couple of hundred dollars for each clandestine meeting. It was the patriotic thing to do.

Larry had been with the company a very long time. He ended up reporting to a new boss and they had a falling out. It was time for Larry to move on, a mutual decision. Now he'd have time to go and get his PhD. The company gave Larry a grand walk off into the sun.

Larry's assistant was very nervous about the transition of Larry's retirement. The company hadn't had time to find a permanent replacement for Larry, and Larry's assistant would have to handle the month-end close. She hadn't performed many of these functions before.

Larry could see that his assistant was very nervous about the transition. Larry had been processing all these payments to himself. The checks were made out to one of his fake companies for services rendered, although there were no services rendered, of course. The checks had gone out in volume. There were 15 of them this month already; and there were another 20 the month before; and another 20 the month before that. It would take a little time for all these checks to clear the bank. A month, or two, at least. "I'll tell you what," he told his assistant. "I'm gonna be retired," he said, "but, next month, at month-end close, why don't you call me. I'll come in and I'll help you through it."

His assistant agreed with this plan, and Larry left. His mind was at ease. This way he could seal off the final bulk of payments.

Over the course of the following month, his former assistant noticed some of these payments to these companies. She didn't believe anything was wrong necessarily, but she wasn't familiar with any of the companies. She asked others in the department if they had ever heard of these companies. No one had. One thing led to another, and O'Connor received a call, asking him to have a look around.

O'Connor put a call into Wendy Schmidt and Lisa Dane in New York who lead a business intelligence services desk for the large accounting firm O'Connor worked for. O'Connor wanted the two to gather business intelligence data on a fellow named Larry Swanson. O'Connor wanted to know what the man owned, where he owned it, and anything else that might be knowable from public sources. O'Connor was asking for more than a simple background check on the man. He knew Schmidt and Dane would begin their work by interrogating the various corporate databases maintained by the Secretary of State's office. They would also research the various databases maintained by different county recorders in the state. O'Connor was looking to match any hits they might come up with against the corporation's master vendor database. If they found any corporations registered to Swanson, O'Connor would have his team run a match against the corporation's vendor master file. If the vendor master file contained addresses related in any way to Larry Swanson, O'Connor wanted to know this. O'Connor concurrently opened his second investigative track. He brought in Bill Farwell, his Boston-based computer forensics specialist, to image Swanson's computer.

O'Connor and his team found more than one company registered to Larry Swanson. The forensic accountants queried the accounts payable and procurement system and found every payment made to these companies.

Swanson refused to take a meeting. "He was retired," he said.

The case was referred to the FBI and Swanson was ultimately indicted. He chose to plead insanity at his trial, unsuccessfully. He is now serving time in prison. Over $430,000 in checks had been cut to the daughter; $588,000 in checks were mailed to the mother.

O'Connor wasn't finished with his investigation, though. He showed up at the mother's house one evening and knocked on her door. He'd done many surprise interviews before and he knew that you could never predict how they would go. One time the door gets slammed in your face. The next time, you're getting yelled at. O'Connor liked the uncertainty of it all.

The woman's mother opened her front door.

O'Connor introduced himself. He was a forensic accountant who had been retained on behalf of the company Larry Swanson used to work for. He gave her his business card.

She glanced at the card and looked up. To her, the forensic accountant standing in front of her must have looked a lot like David Caruso, from the television shows *NYPD Blue* and *CSI—Miami*. And now he's a forensic accountant. "I'm so glad you're here," she said.

O'Connor stood there with his hands clasped in front of him. Surprise, surprise, he said to himself.

She opened the door wider. "Come on in," she said.

O'Connor entered the small apartment. He looked around. The place was humble, sparely furnished. The TV was on, tuned to the *Home Shopping Channel.*

She went over to turn the volume down on the television set. "Because I got something from the IRS that I don't understand," she said.

"Yeah, that would be a 1099," O'Connor responded.

The mother had received a Form 1099 reporting $680,000 in income and she was dumbfounded. It was all over the newspapers that Swanson was being pursued by the FBI, and she had been calling Swanson asking for tax advice. She didn't know what to do about this $680,000 on this 1099, or whatever the thing was. And Swanson had been no help at all.

She pulled out all her bank statements for O'Connor to see. Her bank books, too. O'Connor went through the records with her, right there in that humble apartment. He spread the cancelled checks out across the kitchen table and went over them individually with her. From what O'Connor could see, 80 percent of what she netted out of the scam had gone directly to the *Home Shopping Channel.*

CHAPTER EIGHTEEN

"More Valuable Than Heroin"

Larry Swanson had received a wake-up call. On December 5, 1995, the granddaddy of wake-up calls was delivered in Silicon Valley. On that day, a combined strike force raided Avant Corporation's headquarters in Sunnyvale. The Santa Clara county investigators and FBI computer forensic specialists were looking for evidence that Avant, which makes software used to design computer chips, had stolen proprietary technology from its archrival, Cadence Design Systems of San Jose.

Four former Cadence engineers, who claimed they could make faster chips than Cadence, had formed Avant in 1991. In 1994, however, law enforcement computer forensics specialists found Cadence's source code in the home of a former Cadence employee and found evidence that the former employee was being "paid off the books" to write code for Avant.

In December 2001, four executives of Avant Corporation, including cofounder Stephen Wuu, received prison sentences for stealing Cadence's trade secrets. Prosecutors alleged the former Cadence employees had stolen the source code from Cadence beginning in 1991, and had used it in products Avant had sold from 1993 through 1998. The executives were ordered to pay $8 million in fines, and Avant was ordered to pay a $195 million restitution fine.

For the past 25 years, many have remarked on the vibrancy of innovation and the creation of new intellectual property in Silicon Valley. One factor contributing to the output of this remarkable engine is the fact that it is nestled between two world-class universities, Stanford and UC Berkeley. Before the Avant/Cadence brouhaha, another prevailing point of view had been that the high pace of innovation in the Valley also resulted from the high incidence of job-hopping that occurred there.

It has taken almost 10 years for the Avant/Cadence dispute to wend its way through the criminal and civil courts. Contrast the Avant story of the 1990s to the recent events experienced by SpectraSwitch.

In August 2001, criminal charges were filed against Xinkun Wu, a former Corning research scientist, who had downloaded Corning technological trade secrets before leaving to take a new job with SpectraSwitch in Santa Rosa, California. The research scientist admitted to downloading the product design data during an interview with FBI agents in Northern California.

SpectraSwitch, however, had expressly instructed Wu to *not* bring any proprietary information belonging to Corning with him to his new job, and had assigned him to work on different technology in order to avoid even the appearance of any impropriety in his hiring. SpectraSwitch immediately rescinded its job offer to the research scientist after reviewing the evidence in the case.

Nick Lawrence, the founder of SpectraSwitch, had the following to say, "Hiring a worker who brings proprietary information from an old employer is asking for trouble. A prudent company would never accept anything like that from an employee. Most high-tech companies wouldn't touch anything like that with a 10-foot pole. First, it is illegal. Second, it is unethical. And third, it is stupid. If a corporate culture encouraged that, then all they are doing is putting themselves at risk."

Perhaps there was more than meets the eye here, however, for Wu immediately disappeared after his initial interview with FBI agents. The FBI now believes he may have returned to his native country, mainland China.

In a survey undertaken by the National Counterintelligence Center in 1995, 73 corporations reported 500 separate instances of suspected economic espionage. Few had referred these incidents to law enforcement, fearing negative publicity and stock market impacts.

"Certain business information is more valuable than heroin," FBI Special Agent Larry Watson has said. Larry Watson heads the FBI's Awareness of National Security Issues and Response Unit.

The National Counterintelligence Center has reported to Congress instances of corporate break-ins in which laptops and computer disks have been stolen, when other more valuable items that were in the same vicinity went untouched. The same report refers to "bag ops," surreptitious break-ins of hotel rooms in foreign countries for the express purpose of collecting sensitive corporate information. To facilitate this, the intelligence agencies of several countries have apparently convinced hotel operators to provide access to visitors' rooms, or stored luggage.

The U.S. intelligence community in 1998 reported that eight countries were most actively targeting U.S. trade secrets and critical technologies. An earlier FBI study of the situation revealed that 57 nations had covert operations underway targeting advanced technologies developed by U.S. corporations. In fact, France is reported to have successfully planted moles in many U.S. companies, including IBM, Texas Instruments, and Corning. Douglas Pasternack, in an article in *U.S. News & World Report,* stated, "Indeed, countries such as France, Israel, and China have made economic espionage a top priority of their foreign intelligence services." Five months later, Senator Arlen Specter made certain to have this article made a part of the Congressional Record.

In a Senate hearing in 1996, Norman Augustine, the president of Lockheed, reported that 100 percent of the aerospace corporations surveyed believed that domestic and international competitors had used intelligence techniques against them. Senator Arlen Specter stated it succinctly, "For years now, there has been mounting evidence that many foreign nations and their corporations have been seeking to gain competitive advantage by stealing the trade secrets, the intangible intellectual property of inventors of this country."

The American Society for Industrial Security publishes an annual survey of Fortune 1000 corporations and 300 other high-growth companies. During the last several years, the reported losses attributable to the theft of intellectual property have ranged between $59 and $300 billion. The corporations estimated their losses utilizing traditional financial analytical techniques that were based on: (1) either the investment that had been made in the technology, or (2) the lost profits that would ensue as a result of the misappropriation of the intellectual property by a competitor.

As the concerns mounted over the years about the magnitude of these losses, Congress passed the Economic Espionage Act in 1996, criminalizing, for the first time, the theft of trade secrets. These types of thefts, however, are sometimes infinitely more difficult to prove.

*　　*　　*

Julia Karenina pulled into the tree-shaded parking lot opposite the old Mission in downtown San Rafael. One of the original reasons why the old Spanish mission outpost, located on the north side of the San Francisco Bay, had been established in 1817, was that the Spaniards were becoming fearful of the expanding Russian outposts on the Pacific coastline. The Spaniards were concerned that, if left unchecked, they would soon be facing Russian domination of the coastline as far south as Marin county.

The new Mission's name explains the second reason for the establishment of the compound of adobe structures on the north side of the bay. The Spaniards dedicated their new Mission to San Rafael Archangel, the saint of healing.

Something odd had been happening to the Indians working at Mission Dolores, the existing Mission on the San Francisco peninsula. The Mission Dolores annual death rate exceeded 40 percent, far exceeding that of any other Mission in California, and the operation of Mission Dolores required many Indians. Something had to be done, and quickly, before the labor supply was exhausted.

By 1824, Mission San Rafael was up and thriving. There, nestled in the little valley at the foot of Mount Tamalpais were weaving rooms, a chapel, workshops, dormitories, and houses for single women. There were nine buildings in all; each constructed of adobe. In addition, there were over 1,000 Indians, together with over 4,000 sheep and 3,000 cattle.

Otto von Kotzebue, the world famous Russian explorer, passed by the Spanish Mission grounds in his travels that year. He wrote in his journal, "It is a great pity we were not here before them. The advantages of possessing this beautiful bay are incalculable."

But this morning in the year 2002, it was it was a little before eight. It had taken almost an hour for Julia Karenina to get to downtown San Rafael. Julia Karenina was part of a small team led by Kris Haworth. The small group had gathered earlier at the office—in the high-rise financial district of downtown San Francisco—and they had carpooled from there to San Rafael.

As Julia Karenina's car pulled into the parking lot across the street from Mission San Rafael, Kris Haworth checked her watch. It was better to be early than late. Everyone was to meet up in the parking lot by 8:30. The raid the team of investigators was to undertake at Baldur Technologies was scheduled for 9 A.M., and Baldur Technologies was another 20-minute drive up Highway 101 to Petaluma.

Kris Haworth sat in the front passenger seat of Julia Karenina's car. Lisa Galloway sat in the back. Julia was a good one to bring on this raid. The whistleblower from within Baldur Technologies was supposedly Russian. Julia was from Russia, too, and could find out who he was, hopefully. After that, maybe she could learn a little bit about the specifics—about how it was that Baldur Technologies was surreptitiously using Pegasys Semiconductor's trade secrets. At least that was the plan. Larry Hooper and his security team from Pegasys Semiconductors would be here soon. When he got here, they'd convoy up the highway to Petaluma.

A moving truck pulled into the parking lot, which was odd. At this hour, there were no cars in the lot other than Karenina's. The moving truck stopped 10 yards away.

*   *   *

In rapid succession, the four black Suburbans pulled into the parking lot of the Petaluma low-rise office complex. Larry Hooper, Pegasys Semiconductor's Director of Security, eased himself out of one of the Suburbans and headed inside the low-slung office building. He came out after a long while and went over to talk to his staff members gathered around the four black Suburbans. The little gathering of men broke up.

Larry Hooper came over to the passenger side of Julia Karenina's car. From inside the car, Kris Haworth rolled down the car's front passenger window.

"They've called the press," Larry Hooper said. "We're just going to have to sit tight for a while. See what happens."

Kris nodded, and Pegasys Semiconductor's Director of Security headed off to talk to Lou Pichini, an investigator from the Philadelphia office that Kris Haworth had enlisted to help lead the engagement. Pichini was a former prosecutor with the U.S. Attorney's office and was terrific in coordinating this kind of effort with law enforcement.

Kris rolled up the window to the car. So much for the element of surprise. They'd all been sitting in the parking lot of Baldur Technologies's corporate headquarters for the last twenty minutes. *No wonder* they'd called the press, she thought. You pull up in four black Suburbans, with another four cars filled with people right behind, and with a moving truck for all their documents. Who wouldn't think it was the FBI making a raid?

She sat back in her seat. They could wait.

The day before, Pegasys Semiconductor had cancelled their manufacturing outsourcing contract with Baldur Technologies. In response to this devastating action, the Baldur executives immediately laid off 300 of their employees. Larry Hooper thought there was only a skeleton crew inside there this morning. He'd been told that the attorneys were working things out. They told him they believed he'd be able to get his people inside within the next 15 or 20 minutes.

*   *   *

Kris Haworth was still running on adrenaline and coffee. These gigs usually took the better part of a day, but this one was now almost into it's second day. Yesterday morning, David Wilson, who headed up the computer forensics lab in the Dallas office, had simultaneously gone into Baldur Technologies's manufacturing plant in Austin, Texas, with a separate team. His team had imaged just about all the computers they found there.

She and David had spoken around four in the morning, and he was just finishing up. Their discussion had occurred a couple of hours earlier. His part was under control.

But ever since Kris and her team had been allowed into Baldur Technologies headquarters in Petaluma, she realized the magnitude of data needing to be forensically imaged. And now, Kris was getting an uneasy feeling. She wasn't sure how much more time they would have before their access would be taken away. The forensic imaging team was targeting the highest people on the food chain. Haworth and Pichini had developed an imaging work plan based on a copy of Baldur Technologies's organizational chart. The two investigators decided which computers would get imaged, and in what order.

Luckily, Julia Karenina had found the whistleblower. They were both of Russian descent and had bonded right off the bat. Based on what he told her, the forensic imaging was now a little more tightly focused. They had now been on this raid for 26 hours straight. They were using all four of the portable forensic imaging units, but it took a couple hours to image each machine. Forty computers were a big job to image.

Meanwhile, the Pegasys Semiconductor security people had been walking around, filming and talking to people. Apparently they'd done some dumpster diving as well. They'd already discovered some documents containing a Pegasys Semiconductor Plan of Work, but with some other company's logo on it. The environment had turned hostile after that discovery.

Kris and her team had full security protection, but there was this one Baldur Technologies person who had followed them around all night long, just staring at them with his arms folded across his chest as they imaged machine after machine. He had moved physically closer to them as the hours went on, trying to intimidate them. The situation was intense and emotional.

Pegasys Semiconductors had the right to go into Baldur Technologies at any time to see how their intellectual property was being used. This had been negotiated as a fail-safe provision seven years earlier as part of the Settlement Agreement imposed on Baldur Technologies, when the company had been caught red-handed. The Baldur executives had taken the blueprint process designs Pegasys had provided them under a Non-Disclosure Agreement(NDA), and had sold the designs into the marketplace as if they had been their own. "This time we're not cutting them any slack," Larry Hooper told Pichini when they began the planning for this raid.

When the first raid occurred seven years earlier, Pichini had been with the U.S. Attorney's office in Philadelphia and Hooper had been with the FBI. Both men had since retired and moved on to corporate executive positions in the Philadelphia area. Five years earlier, Baldur Technologies had been a sole-source provider. The only option Pegasys had at that time was to keep Baldur Technologies in place, and to handcuff them as best they could. This time around though, Pegasys was better prepared. They now had two other suppliers who were fully qualified. That's why this time "Baldur Technologies was toast."

By now, Haworth's team had imaged over 40 computers, laptops and desktops, and had gotten a full backup of Baldur Technologies's computer server. The Baldur executive team had provided several assurances to Kris that they had provided her with a full backup of their server. Knowing she had this now in hand, Kris made the decision that it was time to leave. Things were getting just a bit too hostile. Her team had collected enough data and had the backups they needed. By now, the team had collected so much data that they would be spending the next couple of weeks trying to sort it all out. They were sure to have everything they needed by now.

*   *   *

Kris's servers back in the San Francisco computer forensics lab kept going down because of a huge virus attack. The way the lab was set up, all the servers were physically "secure." There was no physical connection to the firm's network, and there was no connection to the outside world by way of the Internet. No one could get into the lab without an authorized code.

Tomas Castrejon had said there were over 500 viruses, though. If Baldur Technologies's system had something like that going on at the time of the raid, it would have been down for sure. Tomas believed someone at Baldur Technologies must have launched the virus just before the computer forensic team arrived. Maybe that was why Baldur's top executives had seemed so smug. Maybe that's why they had been so open to all the computer forensic imaging that was going on. They kept saying that they would provide Pegasys with full access, that they hadn't done anything wrong.

Well, they had managed to crash all the servers in the computer forensics lab. Kris knew that if an imaged computer contained a virus, the virus became part of the evidence collected. She did not use the Norton Anti-Virus Software because she did not want to change the physical evidence by eliminating the virus. It was a fine balancing act.

With 500 viruses running amok, however, all the servers in the computer forensics lab had been brought down, crippling the investigators. So the team had activated the anti-virus tools. They'd brought the servers back to life. They then had pulled out all the sales data, recovered all the deleted e-mails, and now were running some keyword searches. Laurel Sutcliffe's reconstruction of the Oracle database was planned as the next point of attack. The team decided that they would have to adopt a reverse-engineering approach to the problem. Laurel was the forensic lab's database expert, and she knew Oracle cold.

In fact, almost everything they'd imaged from Baldur Technologies's server in Petaluma was in Oracle. The people at Baldur Technologies had assured Kris that she and her team would be able to quickly query it. The backup tape Baldur Technologies provided, however, was only a partial backup, despite what Lou Pichini and Kris had been told by the Baldur executives. Kris was thankful to have Laurel Sutcliffe's expertise available to the other computer forensics specialists in the lab.

"Don't worry about it," Laurel had said. "We can figure it out on our own."

*   *   *

Pegasys Semiconductor was suing Baldur Technologies to recover lost profits on the sales Pegasys would have made "but for" Baldur Technologies's "infringing" sales to third parties. One of the outcomes that complicates these types of cases is that the shenanigans pulled by a company like Baldur typically will facilitate unauthorized competitors to enter a market on the cheap. This results in financial losses, which are referred to in the litigation world as *damages*. One aspect of the possibility of new entrants flooding into a marketplace on the cheap is that the price at which the product may be sold may start to come down. These new market entrants don't have to price their products to cover their research and development costs associated with the product—they don't have any R&D costs because they stole the R&D. They got it on the cheap. The result of this chain of events often is that the price at which all participants in the market sell the product starts coming down. This phenomenon is referred to as *price erosion*.

In patent infringement cases, the injured party typically has invested a significant amount of money in developing a technology, and someone else has attempted to reap the reward. The classic remedy for the injured party is to go to court to seek relief for the financial damages it feels it is experiencing as a result of the infringement of its intellectual property. To do this, the injured party generally has to prove two things: (1) that the infringer had actually converted the injured party's trade secrets for their own use, and (2) that infringing sales to customers had occurred.

Once one of these cases of high-tech thievery ends up in court, the steps one undergoes to prove damages have been well established over the past 20 years or so. It goes this way. If the fact that the technology had been stolen is proven beyond a doubt (the *liability phase* of the trial), the case enters the next phase: proving the amount of damages suffered by the injured party (the *damages phase* of the trial). For forensic accountants, determining the amount of infringing sales and resulting profits is simply a process of measurement. You find and count the infringing sales, and you calculate the resultant profits. The challenge is boiling down the complexity of the whole thing for a jury to be able to understand. Proving high-tech theft, though, requires high-tech sleuthing.

To make matters worse, a patent infringer often may initiate a countersuit—saying, in effect, "We didn't do anything wrong. You owe us for the inventory we built for you, and you shouldn't have put us out of business."

Corporate litigation often is an extremely expensive proposition. This type of litigation, however, may often serve as a kind of lubricant for our economy. If something is wrong, corporations go to court, and they either get it fixed, or they recover damages for the economic harm they have suffered. Then everybody moves on.

Somehow it works.

To prove liability in a patent infringement case, the injured party must prove that the defendant had used the injured party's technology for their own benefit. In the case at hand here, there were at least two ways to show this. The first way was to go into Baldur's system and look at the stored AutoCAD files. The reason for this step was to identify instances in which Baldur Technologies had doctored Pegasys Semiconductor's AutoCAD files for their own benefit. This would be the smoking gun. The second way to prove liability was to go to the traveler database, essentially a "bill-of-materials" file, and find the smoking guns there.

Laurel described a traveler: "It describes the steps involved in the chip manufacturing process. It included information such as: part number, sequence number, machine set up time (how long it took to set up a machine), the process steps that that particular machine would handle, and other process steps involved."

The problem, however, was that the travelers didn't "exist," in the sense that you or I might expect. Because of the nature of Baldur's Oracle data processing system, the travelers did not exist as a tangible thing or document. The travelers were not something that had been saved and could be located residing in a file. As a result, they couldn't be touched or found anywhere in Baldur Technologies's data files. Their elements existed in a sense, however, in the Oracle database. Laurel would have to figure out how to recreate the travelers. Her plan was to do this using the Oracle database.

With the traveler files, Matt Larson and Laurel Sutcliffe were searching for instances in which Baldur Technologies had used the process-design-steps originally created by Pegasys, its intellectual property, to create the semiconductor chip technology that Baldur Technologies had repackaged as its own and sold to third parties. "So there's two pieces of intellectual property," Matt Larson said. "The first is the drawings themselves, and the second is the steps toward making this process work."

To prove this, the team would look at the AutoCAD files, the drawings, to see if they were changed and then used and sold to a different customer. To determine that they were used in a sale to a third party, they would have to look at the travelers, as well. The traveler is akin to a bill of materials, but in the high-tech world, it is the document that outlines the technology used in the 55 steps involved in the semiconductor chip manufacturing process. After this, Matt and Laurel would gather the relevant data from the sales database of Baldur Technologies. With this approach, they could specifically identify how much of that material had inappropriately gone out the door. The next step, as in any classic analysis of damages in a patent infringement case, would be to determine the dollar amount of revenues associated with those sales transactions. Pegasys wanted those sales back.

*   *   *

In his remarks to Congress in 1998, FBI Director Louis J. Freeh indicated how lost profits resulting from the theft of intellectual property can be enormous even for one company. He described the arrests of Hsu Kai-lo and Chester Ho, both U.S. naturalized citizens.

The two men were charged with attempting to steal the cell culture technology of *Taxol*, a new powerful anti-cancer drug that had been patented by Bristol-Myers Squibb. Their plan was to deliver it to a Taiwan-based multinational conglomerate. Louie Freeh estimated Bristol-Myers's revenue stream for its Taxol product to be $1 billion annually. He also estimated the amount of potential lost profits Bristol-Myers could have suffered had this technology been successfully stolen. The total foreign market share for Taxol was estimated to be $200 billion. With that, the "potential losses could have been in the billions of dollars over the 10-year period Bristol-Myers holds the patent for the plant cell culture technology," he said.

The harm to our economy from the theft of intellectual property can be devastating. Our corporations spend trillions of dollars annually on R&D. Many ideas and efforts will be abandoned before even one product ever makes it to market. The *only* way for a corporation to hope to recover its investment is through profits on successful products.

*   *   *

David Sikorski, another member of Kris Haworth's computer forensics team, began a separate hunt through the Baldur computer files. He attempted to use one of our standard forensic tools to perform a keyword search of the AutoCAD files. He was searching for instances in which the suspect's name or logo appeared in any of the AutoCAD files. The suspect in this case was Baldur Technologies.

The AutoCAD files were the intellectual property of Pegasys Semiconductor. AutoCAD is computer terminology for Computer-Aided Design software. Pegasys had used computer-aided design tools to sketch out their manufacturing processes and had provided these computer-aided design drawings to Baldur Technologies under their Non-Disclosure Agreement. David Sikorski was now going to look for specific instances where Baldur Technologies illegally converted these computer-aided drawings for their own use by inserting their own name on the CAD drawings.

He struck out immediately. The keyword attempt died. It wouldn't work on AutoCAD files.

He did a Google search on "AutoCAD searching text." Google took Sikorski on a search around the entire globe and returned to him a *Dr.DWG,* of all things—in Pleasanton, California, about 25 miles away as the crow flies, on the other side of the Bay. The tool cost him 30 bucks, and provided him with the capability to modify the keyword search software, DT Search, so that it could go in and take a look at the AutoCAD drawings. David's use of Google to find a tool he desperately needed is an illustration of how the use of the Internet immeasurably improves the productivity of a forensic investigator. Without the use of the technology and tools that are so easily findable today, what the investigative team was attempting to do in this case would have been prohibitively expensive, or given the time constraints, close to impossible. Who could have guessed that there was a *Dr.DWG* out there? This is an illustration of how the Internet has opened up the marketplace for the development and sale of tools that otherwise would have had too limited a market to be economically viable to create.

AutoCAD software programs allow the user to use the computer to do the drawing of plans, whether architectural designs, or engineering drawings for parts or structures. The plans drawn using this system are integrated with one another; for example, a set of architectural drawings might contain a plan view of the floor, a roof elevation, side elevations, and front and rear elevations. For the Pegasys Semiconductor drawings, all the parts were designs in miniature. Certain parts had the same structural elements, so the software would access a base, or foundation layer of drawing, and automatically overlay on that the structural modifications specific to the specific part being drawn. This is much like how some architects work. Using tissue paper over an existing hard-line drawing, Ed McEachron, a fabulous architect I know, can sketch umpteen versions of what it is you are describing to him, while you sit there having a discussion. An Auto-CAD program goes one step better. It will then integrate the drawings into a hard-line version, and change every other drawing in the file that is related somehow to the new drawing that is made. The analogy to this would be that—with each sketch Ed made of a floor plan—the roof, side, front, and rear elevations would also be automatically updated.

The tool that David Sikorski found, *Dr. DWG,* first indexed everything. He then simply entered his search terms and it took him to the specific drawings in which Baldur Technologies had illegally converted Pegasys Semiconductor's intellectual property. It narrowed down the field. Out of some 30,000 drawings, it narrowed down the violations to some two dozen drawings.

*　　*　　*

One of the challenges Laurel Sutcliffe had to deal with on this case was that she had only the backup tape of Baldur Technologies's database files with which she could work. Baldur's Oracle database was in a proprietary format. The travelers were somewhere in there, but they couldn't be viewed without installing Oracle together with the specialized programming applications specific to Baldur Technologies's system. Laurel was faced with the need to recreate the entirety of a working database on the computer servers in the forensics lab. Once Laurel did this, she could visually see the tables and the structure of the database. There were over five hundred tables in the database; it was very complex. To Laurel, it seemed as if she was looking for the proverbial needle in a haystack, and she was reminded of Kris Haworth's comments on how smug the Baldur executives had been that day of the raid. They were thinking, "There's no way anybody's going to be able to find this stuff in here."

But Laurel had a trick or two up her sleeve. She planned to use a third-party software utility called PowerDesigner. This tool enabled Laurel to reverse engineer the database. Using it, she was able to view all the tables. She printed out those tables upon which she needed to perform further research, and printed out the table structures and the relationships between all the tables. With this, she could figure out how it was that the database related one table to another, and how Baldur Technologies used the system.

I can remember walking into the computer forensics lab one day. Laurel was there, with a small team huddling around her in front of her computer monitor. That wasn't anything unusual. What was unusual was what was covering the walls of the lab. Computer printouts covered the walls, as if they were wallpaper. The papers plastering the wall were at least six feet high, and they ran 10 feet down one wall, and then returned on another wall.

"That was probably only 50 tables," Laurel said.

Laurel is a tiny thing, and she wears wire-rim glasses. And she is a walking incongruity, for the other thing you would see whenever you walked into the lab would be a framed picture under glass hanging on the wall. The picture is of Laurel, all 5'2" of her. In this picture, she's hunched over a racing bike that probably weighs close to what she weighs. She's in protective gear from head to toe, so you just have to accept her representation that it truly is her. She's leaning into a turn on the bike, and the two of them are at something like a 45-degree angle, going I suppose about 100 mph, because she's on a banked turn at Sears Point Raceway, now called Infineon Raceway.

But this day, Laurel was poking around in the database. She was physically looking at a hard copy of a traveler, on which she could see a part number. Looking around at the structure, she noted that there happened to be a table that was called "Components." That's the hunt-and-peck methodology she was forced to employ. She was just using common sense.

She started dumping the contents of the tables in the database using Structured Query Language (SQL). With this, she was able to begin to get an idea of the data physically residing in each table. Some of the requests she submitted returned an avalanche of data, which exceeded even the ability of the Excel software program to print. Excel has a 65,000-line limitation. This gives one a sense of the enormity of data that the team was faced with sifting through. As a result, Laurel decided to perform the analysis using Microsoft Access. This was another database that would be easy to use, but would not have the same 65,000-line limitation.

Laurel began with a process of elimination, eliminating those tables out of the 500 that did not hold data. This enabled her to slim down the number of places where she would have to look.

Her biggest challenge though turned out to be that the process steps contained in the travelers were built and stored in a binary format. Her SQL requests of this data were returning a "hexadecimal kind of garbage number," she said.

The numbering system in which we are used to working is a decimal based system, containing the digits zero to nine. Laurel was receiving back hexadecimal-based data, based on 0 to 16. By way of comparison, computer bits are binary, a system utilizing only two digits, zeroes and ones, representing whether an electrical charge is either off or on.

Things weren't simple. She had already identified tables where other data resided in text-readable form. The last few tables were accessed by way of preprogrammed "links," a program identifying the relationship of one table to another. This represents the horsepower provided by a relational database. With these clues, she was able to deduce that the hexadecimal data represented the process steps for which she had been looking. She wrote some code, using Oracle's proprietary programming language called *PL/SQL,* to translate the data from the hexadecimal format so that it was readable as text. With this, the team was then finally able to locate all of the data that comprised a specific traveler.

Laurel was able to build the traveler associated with the transaction using the Oracle database. The team was then able to use the database to accumulate the total amount of infringing sales. They could quantify the amount of parts that had gone out the door, and the sales value associated with the transactions.

No one said it was going to be easy. To prove the theft of high-tech intellectual property, the investigator is required to engage in high-tech sleuthing.

The use of computers by the intelligence community to collect the information needed to perform their job, however, is of another order of magnitude altogether.

CHAPTER NINETEEN

Hunting the World's Greatest Outlaw

Our National Security Agency (NSA) intercepted Osama bin Laden's radio-satellite telephone calls on a regular basis during the 1990s. These communication intercepts had become so commonplace that the NSA even entertained visitors at its Fort Meade, Maryland, headquarters with taped conversations between bin Laden and his mother. Sometime in 2000, however, the NSA intercepted a disturbing communication from an al Qaeda member boasting that bin Laden was planning to carry out a "Hiroshima" against the United States.

The Hiroshima intercept was all the more disturbing as bin Laden's network had successfully attacked the United States on several occasions during the 1990s, including the bombing of two embassies in Africa, as well as the U.S.S. Cole. The Hiroshima intercept set off an exhaustive search within the U.S. intelligence community.

On August 27, 2001, a Palestinian leader was assassinated in Ramalah. Press reports indicated that Israeli signals intelligence analysts had been able to locate the Palestinian through the wireless signals emanating from his cellular phone. From that time on, Osama bin Laden avoided the use of cellular or satellite telephones and relied on human couriers to relay his instructions.

*   *   *

That the NSA was specifically intercepting bin Laden's communications became public knowledge during the criminal trials of participants in the 1993 bombing of the World Trade Center, and was reinforced by disclosures in subsequent trials of individuals who participated in the bombing of American embassies in Africa. Other writings in the late 1990s, including a special report prepared by the European Parliament, simultaneously revealed the scope of NSA's immense communications intercept capabilities. These documents describe a global, electronic signals-intercept system, code named *Echelon*.

Echelon comprises a vast network of electronic communications-intercept stations located around the globe. The NSA supervised the implementation of the network, with the help of four other participating countries: Australia, Canada, Great Britain, and New Zealand. Together, these five countries are responsible for the operations that occur at these sophisticated earth stations.

The scope of the Echelon system is truly amazing. Nearly every wireless communication sent at any moment around the globe is subject to interception by this phenomenal system. The notion is staggering. Every cellular telephone call, every e-mail (sent utilizing wireless communications), every fax, and every telex.

Positioned in geostationary orbits 22 thousand miles above the earth, 24 *Intelsat* communications satellites link together the world's telecommunications networks. One of the more recent of these satellites is able to relay 90,000 telephone calls and data transmissions simultaneously.

These satellites carry the majority of all satellite-relayed phone calls, e-mails, faxes, and telexes throughout the world. During the 1990s, this communications backbone began to be supplemented by fiber optic cable laid around the world to help transmit the expected Internet Age data avalanche. During the 1970s, however, *all* the Intelsat satellite downlink transmissions were subject to interception by the NSA.

This communications interception was accomplished by powerful 90-foot diameter radio dishes at two earth stations. The first is located in the southwest of England, at Morenstow, near Cornwall. The second is located near Yakima, Washington, at the U.S. Army Yakima Firing Center. Today, a total of seven earth stations located strategically around the globe enable the interception of virtually all satellite-relayed wireless telecommunications traffic originating anywhere in the world. Echelon exists, but consider the challenge of sifting through trillions of messages.

In the year 2000 alone, seven trillion e-mail messages were sent. Now add to this, cellular telephone calls—not just in the United States, but also around the world. And not only for this current year. The NSA archives many, many years of this data. Imagine this stored collection. How can any government intelligence agency, no matter how big, ever hope to make sense of the cacophony? The answer is computers, and the use of data analytics.

The key to making sense of this humming, buzzing Tower of Babel is an immense computer system; one that is capable enough to pass the billions of intercepted communications through a filter, and drain away and immediately discard the 99.9 percent of the traffic that is of no interest, and then collect and distribute to intelligence analysts the cleaned remainder that is of interest. Each earth station in the Echelon network has its own computers that enables this real-time sifting of the millions of intercepted messages, real-time, searching on keywords identified by the various participating intelligence agencies to be of interest. This keyword search system is referred to as the *Echelon Dictionaries*. The system operates as a single distributed global network, allowing the stations to function individually as servers for the distributed computer processing system; the NSA's massive computers in Fort Meade, Maryland, however, inhales it all.

*   *   *

With their first morning coffees in front of them, signals intelligence analysts around the world begin their day by logging onto the network. They enter their password to access the Echelon Dictionary system. A screen comes up, displaying the different categories of raw communications-intercepts available for analysis that day. The raw message intercepts are categorized by a four-digit code, for example: *4478* for all Korean diplomatic traffic intercepts in the South Pacific. The analyst types in the four-digit code of interest, and a search result comes back indicating the number of raw-intercepts in that category.

The analyst then begins his or her day's work, reading through electronic reams of communications raw-intercepts. If the intercept is noteworthy, the analyst selects it out of the Echelon Dictionary system in order to translate it in its entirety or to prepare a "gist," a summary. When the gist is finished, it is saved to the intelligence database.

This is no ordinary database, though. NSA's computers can store five *trillion* pages of text. To visualize the immensity of this, imagine a stack of paper stretching 150 miles high, poking well into the ionosphere.

The participating intelligence agencies in the United States, United Kingdom, Australia, Canada, and New Zealand submit lists of keywords. Each intelligence agency has its own four-digit categories of research subjects of interest. The keywords can include names of individuals, ships, government offices, e-mail addresses, or known telex and telephone numbers, all of which are to be targeted. Each agency has its own lexicographer, or dictionary manager, who is solely responsible for deleting keywords because no interesting messages are being generated by the keyword, or who may add Boolean logic to the search parameters, such as the logical operators ". . . AND . . . BUT NOT . . ." to narrow the search in order to reduce the number of irrelevant intercepts.

*   *   *

Raytheon's Strategic Systems Division has developed a very powerful "adaptive, pattern-recognition" software product, named *SilentRunner*. This data-analytic software is aptly named, as one of its uses allows for passive surveillance of *all* computer traffic on a corporation's private network. When up and running, SilentRunner is literally undetectable, even by the corporation's network systems administrator. This forensic software can be utilized in more complex forensic investigations faced by forensic specialists investigating corporate-fraud, such as the theft of intellectual property. Kris Haworth refers to the SilentRunner adaptive-pattern recognition software as a "Sniffer on Steroids."

She once told me of a conversation she'd had with the president of Raytheon's Strategic Systems Division. This executive related to Kris why and how one portion of the software had been invented. "Some unnamed U.S. government agency [I love this part], needed to capture all cell phone traffic everywhere and keep it, forever."

"But," she continued. "How do you go and try to figure out what happened? For example, how can you trace an arms deal between two parties?"

What she was asserting was that keyword searches are not likely to work in this type of investigative environment. Terrorists, for example, are likely to be very circumspect in their communications. Al Qaeda operators, for example, communicate using code words. Shadi Abdullah, a 26-year-old al Qaeda operative now cooperating with German law enforcement authorities, has provided investigators with a list of many of al Qaeda's specific code words. His testimony in a recent trial proceeding in Hamburg, Germany, against another suspected terrorist, is quite illuminating. According to transcripts of dozens of hours of German police interrogation of Abdullah, a "mute" stood as al Qaeda's codeword for a gun with a silencer, whereas, a "toy" referred to the gun itself; "Seven Seas" was used to refer to a forged visa used by al Qaeda operatives to gain entry into EU member countries (seven in this specific code word referred to the seven original EU member countries); al Qaeda's code word for Russian-made hand grenades was "Russian apples"; and a "little girl" was the code word used to refer to a forged driver's license. With these disclosures, the code words used by al Qaeda operatives in the future are likely to change.

With this in mind, a computer-based search engine, one that is able to power through the use of such code words, and is able to discern the underlying topic of any communication employing these kinds of code words, would be invaluable to counterterrorism investigators.

Kris Haworth continued with her description of the necessary under-pinnings of such a topic-based computerized search engine—a search engine possessing the ability to search on the basis of content, or the topic, of a communication—a search engine that would make the notion of a classic keyword search seem archaic. "To do that kind of a search, that kind of search engine would need to have some sort of context analysis," she said. "And *they* [this unnamed U.S. government agency] came up with a way of doing that. And that's the same logic that applies to SilentRunner."

Lest some of the more conservative of our readers become concerned that I am spilling government secrets here, try the following exercise. Log on to the following site: http://www.nsa.gov/releases /first_royalties_nsa_employees_02122001.html.

Incredible as it may seem, NSA, our super secret intelligence agency, has its very own Web site. On it, you will see an amazing press release. The title of the press release is:

NSA Employees Receive First-Ever Royalty Checks

The press release recounts how the NSA's Director, General Michael Hayden, presented:

> . . . the first-ever royalty checks to two NSA employees for their invention of software source code that NSA licensed to Raytheon Company, which then developed a commercial product [SilentRunner]that it has sold to other Department of Defense agencies and commercial entities . . .

This seemed to me to be a curious thing. NSA was licensing technology to the private sector. The last portion of the press release was the most astonishing part.

> The SilentRunner product has also been sold back to NSA for use in the Information Assurance Directorate and the Army Intelligence Branch . . .

I love America. There is no country in the world like it.

*   *   *

The hunt for Osama bin Laden and the members of his al Qaeda cell has many parallels to the story of the killing of Pablo Escobar. During the 1980s, Pablo Escobar was responsible for the assassination of many public figures in Colombia. In 1989, a bomb planted on an Avianca air-liner blew up mid-flight, killing 100 people, including two Americans. The target of the bomb was the leading candidate in Colombia's up-coming presidential election. Paradoxically, the presence of this politi-cian on this flight had made other travelers frantic with concern about their personal safety; the candidate, as a result, de-planed before the plane took off.

The downing of Pan Am Flight 103 over Lockerbie, Scotland, the year before, heightened concerns worldwide about the safety and integrity of air travel. During this time frame, members of Escobar's organization were arrested in Florida for attempting to smuggle 120 Stinger antiair-craft missiles out of the United States. This, together with the downing of the Avianca airliner, catapulted Escobar to the rank of "Public Enemy Number One in the World." He had become a threat to public aviation worldwide.

The manhunt that ensued forged a unique partnership between the U.S. and Colombian governments. During the 16-month manhunt, the FBI, CIA, NSA, DEA, ATF (Alcohol, Tobacco and Firearms) and el-ements of the U.S. military assisted in planning the operation. The most sophisticated tactical surveillance technology in the world was brought to bear.

Escobar had successfully evaded capture for years because of infor-mants within the Colombian military. In one case, Colombian Special Forces stormed a safe house, only to find Escobar's breakfast on the table, still warm. The U.S. Special Forces determined that a change in tactics was required. Since Escobar himself could not be found, his organization was targeted instead. The very foundation underlying Escobar's organi-zation was taken apart, brick-by-brick.

The systematic interception of wireless communications from Pablo Escobar's lieutenants and advisors was disseminated to CIA analysts on the ground in Colombia. The analysts methodically identified each and every important player in Escobar's organization and prepared precise organization charts of the Medillín Cartel.

The charting of communications "traffic" was a standard procedure for U.S. military signals-intelligence teams. The frequency of contacts by individuals within any large organization (in concert with other patterns of communications) often revealed the strength of personal as well as po-litical connections within a large organization. The signals-intelligence teams utilized King Air turboprop planes fitted with special gear to elec-tronically triangulate-in on Escobar's wireless communications as the planes circled overhead.

The combination of communications intercept technology and com-puters, together with specialists on the ground in Colombia, flushed Pablo

Escobar, once and for all. Not quite 10 years later, at the inception of PLO's Intifada, the Israeli military would apply the same tactics against Arafat's PLO, only to receive a worldwide storm of protest about the Israeli assassination of over 100 Palestinians. A challenge even came from the Israeli high court.

*   *   *

In the course of my fact checking, I had occasion to review the elements of the Pablo Escobar story with George Vinson, recently retired from the FBI. At the time of our discussion, he was the head of Security for Barclay's Global Investors, but within a matter of weeks, Governor Gray Davis would appoint George to be the Anti-terrorism Czar for the State of California, and he now serves as California's Director of Homeland Security. Over lunch, I described to George the tracking of Pablo Escobar's cellular phone calls from on high in the Beech King Air. I then laid out my central question: how does any government intelligence agency find—in real time—the one communication that is Pablo Escobar talking on his cell phone at that very moment? "The interception of millions of wireless communications would be involved," I said. "They must have found Pablo Escobar's wireless communications using voice-recognition forensics software. Or some kind of pattern-recognition software similar to Raytheon's SilentRunner."

"You're making it way too complicated," George said, in between bites of his sandwich.

"What do you mean?" I asked.

"These kinds of things," he said, "the intelligence community makes certain to allocate funds to pay for informants. Pablo Escobar was probably doing the same thing and had his own informants. Our guys probably just made sure we were always paying them more money."

"What kind of informants?" I asked.

George finished his sandwich. He always took huge bites of whatever sandwich he was eating, and the thing would always seem to disappear in a flash. "In these kinds of investigations," he said, "you always make sure to allocate the greatest amount of funds to people in the telephone company."

"In Colombia?" I asked.

George nodded. "You know," he continued, "you get the identification for the chip, the little chip card in the cell phones. I can't remember what they're called now."

"The SIM card?"

George nodded. He was talking about the little white card in the international cell phones known as a SIM card. These cards were interchangeable. By knowing the exact SIM card in Escobar's cell phone, the intelligence agencies could intercept any call Escobar initiated or received. The intelligence analysts could then track the signal from up in the King Air.

Mark Bowden, in his book, *Killing Pablo,* disclosed that the Special Forces team tracking Pablo Escobar somehow possessed the ability to actually switch-on Escobar's cell phone without his knowledge. As long as there was battery power in Escobar's cell phone, the intelligence analysts could silently activate the phone. Bowden's book, however, never disclosed how it was that the signals-intercept team knew which specific cellular telephone on the ground was to be switched on. Perhaps George was right. News accounts immediately following the events of 9/11 discussed how search teams in New York City's financial district had pinged the cell phones of people who were missing, hoping to locate people trapped in the wreckage of the World Trade Center.

*   *   *

I compared my more complicated theory with George Vinson's. His premise was that with proper human intelligence on the ground, the completion of the operation would be made far simpler. But something about the matter-of-factness of George's response didn't square entirely with what else I had learned.

I recalled my recent interview with the president of Raytheon's Software Division. Several SilentRunner designers were with us in the room that day, and although it was never stated, it was pretty well implied that at least one of them had been with the NSA in an earlier incarnation.

During the course of my daylong interview with these men, I shared the story of the killing of Pablo Escobar, and the role that the signals-intercept intelligence-gathering activities had played. I described to them the use of Echelon, and the use of a Beechcraft King Air, and how the circling of the aircraft high above a signal emanating from the ground allowed it to triangulate-in on Pablo Escobar's cellular phone signal.

Immediately one of the Raytheon software technologists reminded me that a division of Raytheon manufactured the Beech King Air. I thanked him and then ventured to say that it must have been SilentRunner itself, or some derivation of it, that had been used by the NSA to pick out the Medillín Cartel's communications-intercepts from amongst the millions of intercepted electronic communications.

Two things then happened. First, the president of Raytheon's Software Division, who was sitting next to me at the conference table, congratulated me, saying matter-of-factly, "You broke the code." Then the former NSA technologist quietly pointed out, "The result could have been achieved using voice recognition forensic software. The software's been around for a couple of years now." One year after this interview, I learned the code name for the technology to which he'd referred.

Mike Frost, a former communications specialist in Canada's equivalent of our NSA, the Communications Security Establishment (CSE), wrote of his involvement in microwave communications-intercept operations in the 1980s, which had been conducted at Canadian embassies located in various capitals around the world. In the opinion of this communications specialist, one of the most valuable technologies provided by the NSA to the Canadians for these operations was contained in a small "black box, not much bigger than a briefcase, about six inches high." An NSA engineer in Fort Meade, Maryland, had created the innovative technology. The technology was code named *Oratory*.

The small black box contained a miniature keyword-intercept computer. To Frost, the most amazing part of the technology was that Oratory could handle voice communications intercepts, as well as fax or telex. When used in microwave relay intercept operations, any time the Oratory software program recognized a keyword, the call would be recorded digitally on magnetic tape, to be listened to by analysts back at agency headquarters.

I found myself in a logical loop. Did SilentRunner provide the computer forensic answer to this puzzle? Or did some similar computer forensics software developed independently by NSA? Or did NSA use voice-recognition software to identify Pablo Escobar's cellular conversations? Or did a telephone company informant in Colombia provide the U.S. intelligence agencies with the identification of the SIM card in Pablo's cellular phone? Or was it all of these?

And which of the above methods had been utilized by the Israelis in tracking the Palestinian leader assassinated in Ramalah on August 27, 2001?

In his book *Body of Secrets*, published in 2001, James Bamford described a breakthrough in NSA's ability to identify a single intercept (or document), out of millions of intercepts (or documents), through the use of a new software he referred to in his book as *Semantic Forests*. My eyes jumped to those two words. I knew *Semantic Forests*. It was a software algorithm Raytheon licensed from the NSA in developing SilentRunner.

Raytheon, though, was marketing SilentRunner as a tool to enhance corporate network security. The minute I had laid eyes on this adaptive pattern-recognition software, I believed it possessed fantastic capabilities for forensic analysis and investigation.

The NSA apparently did, as well. The roots of this software reach all the way back to the NSA.

CHAPTER TWENTY

The Metaphysical Theory of Being

U p until now, the standard method of electronically searching for a document related to a particular topic has been by performing a *keyword search*. The disadvantage to this method is significant: Relevant documents that do not include the key words will not be retrieved. The use of Boolean logical operators can significantly improve the efficiency of a keyword search.

The notion of Boolean logic goes all the way back to the year 1847, when George Boole invented the notion of using mathematical symbols and operations to represent a logical expression. Typical Boolean statements included in a keyword search algorithm may include logical operators such as AND . . . OR . . . BUT NOT . . .

In his congressional testimony in 2002, FBI Director Robert Mueller explained that the FBI's keyword search capability was so rudimentary that the FBI couldn't perform a keyword search using the words "flight-school," because it is a compound word. Director Mueller's testimony pertained to the FBI's Minneapolis office's August 2001 request for a search warrant to search the laptop computer of Moussaoui, the so-called twentieth hijacker. Moussaoui's flight instructor had told the FBI that Moussaoui had little flying experience, but had arrived with almost $7,000 in cash to pay for flight simulator training for a Boeing 747. One month earlier, an agent in the FBI's Phoenix office had noted that eight Middle Eastern men taking flying lessons at Phoenix area flight schools were showing keen interest in airport construction and security. The Phoenix-based FBI agent forwarded a memo to FBI headquarters requesting further investigation. Both requests were at FBI headquarters; the responsible officials there never put two and two together. As Mueller's testimony indicates, the FBI simply does not possess the computing resources to effectively do their job. The NSA, however, has awesome capabilities.

I obtained from the U.S. Patent Office the NSA patents on two of the algorithms that drive Raytheon's SilentRunner. Reading the patent examiner's report, I could see that the NSA had several fundamental objectives in mind when they developed their software algorithms. First, they wanted their computers to be able to "deduce" the subject of an intercepted communication, and they didn't want their computers to be limited to using only the words contained in the communication itself. For example, they wanted the computer to be able to quickly determine if an intercepted communication was about an arms deal, and they wanted their computers to be able to do this whether or not "arms deal" was specifically mentioned in the intercepted document, or whether or not a specific type of weapon was mentioned in the intercepted communication. In other words, they wanted the computer to be able to "think," and be able to interpret the contextual meaning of a document, just as a human brain would interpret the nuances of a written communication.

NSA accomplished this by first converting an intercepted communication into a text-based document. The source of the intercepted communication could vary. For example, it could be an intercepted conversation that had later been machine-transcribed; or the communication could be an intercepted document that had later been "read" into machine-readable text by way of an optical character reader (OCR); or it could be something as simple as text generated from a news service, such as the Associated Press.

In addition, the NSA wanted the ability to perform this operation on communications it had intercepted, regardless of the language. The NSA provides training for its linguists in at least 95 languages. It is the interpretation of "unconstrained speech," however, that poses the greatest interpretive challenge for a computer. The U.S. patent examiner summarized the problem this way, ". . . much of the information conveyed in speech is never actually spoken . . . utterances frequently are less coherent than written language." After having accomplished the foregoing, the NSA wanted the ability to search its massive database for *any* other documents that concerned the same topic description, and to group such documents for review.

Whew! Not a small request. However, the authors of the NSA patent were able to accomplish all of their objectives. The authors of the patent were linguists, and they used a linguistic approach. Here is how the patented process works.

First, they arranged for the computer to break each word in a given document down to what the NSA linguists referred to as its "tree root-form." A root-form of a word might be the singular noun "truck," or "motor." Next, they arranged for the computer to discard words having no intrinsic meaning, words such as "the" and "an."

Next, the computer used an electronic dictionary to create a "tree structure" attached to each unique word contained in the document. A word's tree structure contains all the words included in its dictionary definition. The computer then allowed for the tree structure to grow exponentially by further attaching all the definitions of the discrete words contained in the definition of the original word. The tree structure for the word "Dog," for example, might include the words *domestic, carnivore, animal, long muzzle, pointed ears, fur coat, fur-covered tail, bark, wolf, fox, dingo, coyote,* and *canine.* The "extended" tree structure would include further descriptors. For example, since the word *animal* is part of the definition of the word *dog,* the extended tree structure for the original word (in this case, *dog*) would also contain the definition of the word *animal.* This would include words such as *mammal, organism, capable of independent movement, responsive sense organs,* and so on.

The computer then numerically scored the words contained in the intercepted document, taking into account word frequency and salience (the seeming importance of a word based on frequency counts and the word's logical connection to other words found in the document, or somewhat deeper in the document's computed "tree" hierarchy for all words in the document).

It's easy to see that the foregoing can result in a massive computing need. No worry. The NSA has an almost unlimited supply of computer storage space. The result is impressive. Using such a system, an intercepted document about a shipment of "cars" might be easily identified to be related to other documents discussing an upcoming arms deal involving rocket-propelled grenades (RPGs). The computer in this case may find the two documents to be contextually related because it noted that the latter document used a simple code—the writer referred to the rocket-propelled grenades as "cars." The computer saw the descriptions of these other items, or saw dates that were common, or other items that allowed it to link the various communications to each other.

The NSA patent also referred to the software searching through the documents in question by using "N-grams," a user-defined length, N, of consecutive keyword characters on which the computer search is based. Imagine a magnifying lens that magnifies a line of text at a time, but that can only accommodate 18 characters of text at a glance. This magnifying lens would in effect be serving as an N-gram viewer, with N being a length of 18 characters. If the reader moved the lens to the right one character at a time, and after each shift, attempted to make sense of the new "chain" of 18 characters magnified by the lens, the procedure would approximate the manner in which the NSA's Semantic Forests software patent operates. The NSA's software has access to dictionaries, encyclopedias, and thesauri of every language spoken in the world; they possess a very powerful interpretive tool.

*   *   *

Let's turn to Raytheon and see how they utilized the NSA patents. Raytheon licensed the two algorithms from the NSA, then built 23 more algorithms to tune the software they were building so that it would have value in the private sector. SilentRunner is configured to operate within the context of a corporate computer network. Configured this way, it will recognize more than 1,400 different IP protocols, including e-mail, Web pages, digital or music files, JPEG or picture documents, Word documents, instant messaging passwords, and more. Raytheon reasoned that corporations would pay big bucks for such an engine, something approximating $100,000 per location, and that the value to a corporation would be for use as a security filter within a complex corporate computer network. The sniffer program would "silently" perform passive surveillance.

John Suit, one of the architects of this software, described the original design intent in building this tool. "The initial use of the technology was to facilitate discovery," he explained. To do that the tool had to be designed so that it became an invisible "participant" in the network. It could not hinder the network; otherwise its use would become discoverable. John Suit described the software, "And so we built a discovery engine, or collector, that will listen to network traffic," he said.

"It collects everything at the packet level," Jeff Waxman, the CEO of SilentRunner, said.

The two executives were sitting with me in a conference room demonstrating the sniffer. John Suit had connected the sniffer to the corporation's network 10 minutes earlier. "I'm listening on the network," he said. "I don't have any *signature*," he announced. "I don't technically exist on the network. We are entirely passive. Meaning there is no signature."

"We don't rely on SNMP (Simple Network Management Protocol)," John Suit continued. "We are actually analyzing the packets themselves as opposed to relying on another device telling us what's out there."

Jeff Waxman sat forward a little. "There are *'three-letter agencies'* that when you tell them something is passive, they don't want to believe that, and they say, 'Oh, we can detect anything.' And at least three (out of three) have failed to—"

"—verify its existence," John Suit said. Both men had a good laugh at the incongruity: a super secret spy agency not being able to detect the software when it was in use on the spy agency's network.

The language being used by the two men described their background. They weren't speaking Farsi, and it definitely wasn't Pashtu. It was more a combination of Sigint (Signals Intelligence) and Network Protocol, interspersed with a sprinkling of Information Technology.

In our first meeting, two years earlier, John Suit had used an unfamiliar word to describe the origin of the software. The word was *ontology*. He used it often, though, always in the context of the reason the software came into existence as a forensic discovery tool.

I knew that elements of this software came from a *"Sigint"* background; Sigint being signals intelligence, the science most valued by intelligence agencies; the science of detecting everything that can be known about one's enemy through the interception and analysis of his communications signals. James Bamford, who has written extensively on the super secret NSA spy agency, describes this spy art form a little differently; he writes, "'Sigint,' to the uninitiated—a polite term for 'reading someone else's mail.'"

*   *   *

By World War I, instead of using cavalry to venture forth to collect information on the deployment and movement of the opposing force, the military began to rely on the interception of radio communications to deduce the same information. Even if your enemy was broadcasting in code, you could infer a significant amount of information about troop deployment and movement merely by the volume of traffic, or by the nature of the traffic, its source, or the type of unit originating the signal. One of the greatest battles in the Pacific in World War II, the Battle of Midway, was the direct result of a signals intercept.

The Japanese Navy's operational code, JN25, included 45,000 five-digit numbers representing words and phrases. Japanese intercepts occasionally referred to a location designated *AF,* and from the context of the intercepted messages, the American Sigint team in Honolulu suspected that AF referred to Midway Island. To test this hypothesis, the American Sigint team sent a message in the clear that Midway's water purification plant had broken down, causing a water shortage. Within 48 hours, a simple Japanese coded radio communication referred to a water shortage on AF. One month later, Japanese Navy coded radio-intercepts from Admiral Yamamoto read as follows:

Employ Method "C" in attacking enemy fleet.

The Occupation force will assign a portion of its force to shell and destroy enemy air bases on AF. The occupation of AF, and AO [the Aleutians] are temporarily postponed.

Admiral Nimitz's staff correctly deduced from this intercepted communication that Midway was the destination of the Nagumo Japanese carrier force. Admiral Nimitz ordered the aircraft carrier *Yorktown,* crippled just weeks before in the Battle of the Coral Sea, back to Pearl Harbor for emergency repairs. Rear Admiral Jack Fletcher brought the badly damaged *Yorktown* into Pearl Harbor on May 27, 1942. Rear Admiral Spruance's Task Force 16 had steamed into Pearl with its two aircraft carriers, *Enterprise* and *Hornet,* only one day ahead of Fletcher. Spruance's carriers immediately put to sea again two days later to meet the Japanese threat. Two days after this, after an around-the-clock repair operation, Fletcher was able to put to sea again with the *Yorktown*. This immediate redeployment of the Spruance and Fletcher Carrier Striking Forces turned the U.S. Sigint intelligence coup into a striking defeat of the Japanese Navy, and became the turning point of the war in the Pacific. By the end of the 1940s, and with the advent of the Cold War, Sigint became the most valuable method available for collecting intelligence about the new enemy.

*   *   *

From my discussions with him, John Suit seemed to possess skills that included communications intercept and traffic analysis, together with an uncanny ability to design network software. Like many software developers, who also have some deep grounding in the arts (college music majors, for example, seem to predominate as software designers), he is an accomplished artist.

He used the word *ontology* when describing the origin of this adaptive pattern-recognition software, and he was fond of saying that the software was about network "discovery." Sometimes he put the two words together in describing SilentRunner's original framework: "The initial framework for discovery is the ontology."

What did that mean? He had me turned around in circles. I didn't have the foggiest idea what that statement was supposed to mean. I considered whether the key in deciphering his meaning lay with obtaining an understanding of the *one* word he used with which I was unfamiliar. So I asked him what he meant by ontology.

"Ontology is a relationship of entities," he replied. "It's creating bindings of—how things work with each other," he said. "That's really what the ontology is."

I didn't have a clue what those sentences meant, or what he was trying to say. Perhaps it was simply indirection on his part.

I gave up trying to fathom his statements. I knew the software was all about intercepting communications, and making sense of what was going on within the discrete world of a communications network, such as a corporate local area network (a LAN).

It was now almost two years after my first meeting with John. Since that time, I had gained a good understanding of the awesome capabilities of the software. I decided to look up the word *ontology*. I was curious. Why this specific word? Always used in terms of the software's discovery and data collection (i.e., communications intercept) capability.

And there it was. In Webster's Encyclopedic Unabridged Dictionary. The word *ontology* has only one meaning. It has to do with metaphysics, and the metaphysical theory of being.

This is what I now believe. To John Suit, this software creation of his—this SilentRunner, a neural-network pattern-recognition tool—possesses the independent ability to reason. To think.

Therefore, it exists.

*   *   *

SilentRunner can identify threats to a corporation's computer network, coming from outside the organization. Threats such as hacker attacks on the network and even attacks successfully thwarted by the network's firewall. John Suit and Jeff Waxman correctly reasoned that SilentRunner could detect threats coming from within an organization, too. Someone attempting to access proprietary intellectual property on the company's network. Someone attempting this kind of access from within the company and lacking the proper authorization to do so.

One of the twenty-five algorithms driving this sniffer software provides for a virtual network diagram. "This shows you how people communicate, as opposed to how they are physically connected to each other," John Suit explained.

This analytical capability betrays the Sigint origin of this software, as well as the background of its author. What John is describing in essence is a communications traffic analysis algorithm. Something a spy agency would value highly.

The traffic analysis algorithm clusters people by their propensity to communicate with each other, while also showing a direct relationship. Imagine being in the Sierra Nevada, on a cloudless and moonless night. The night sky above has thousands upon thousands of stars visible. Some are visibly more tightly clustered, a galaxy forming a unit within the universe, such as the Milky Way, for example. This is how the SilentRunner traffic analysis algorithm works. It will cluster, much like a mini-galaxy, those communications that are related to one another. In this case, by way of visually depicting the nexus of heavy traffic-count.

"And that is very important because this transcends all communication," John Suit described. "This is how people talk to each other. The more that Joe and Lee e-mail each other, the tighter—or the closer—the cluster will be. They may be on opposite ends of the country, just like Joe and I are on opposite sides of the country, but if we're talking on the phone all of the time, and I'm using this to analyze a PBX billing log—we will have a closeness, relative to everyone else he talks to."

This is how John's notion of a virtual network diagram can be used. All of the communications occurring over a network can be visually displayed, and a natural clustering will result, based upon the frequency of communication. Raytheon had a unique experience in demonstrating this aspect of the software. They were demonstrating the software over the lunch hour at a large New York-based securities brokerage firm. The SilentRunner application was loaded so that it could access the brokerage firm's network. It took twenty minutes or so to collect all the traffic occurring during that time on the network. John Suit then initiated the traffic analysis component of the software. His powerful laptop computer projected the results of the clustering diagrams on the large screen set up in the conference room for the demonstration.

A few small clusters could be seen. There was one large cluster of communications, though, all lit up in red. The communications were highly correlated one to another, because the cluster of pinpoint dots on the black screen was very tight and dense.

One of the executives was curious as to the composition of the cluster. "What is it?" he asked.

"Well, let's see," John Suit said. He double-clicked on one of the dots, and the e-mail communication came up for all in the conference room to see. The e-mail had been sent 10 minutes earlier.

The executive nodded. "Let's see another," he said, and John Suit double-clicked on another pinpoint of light in the cluster, one that he selected at random. The second e-mail came up on the screen for everyone to see. This one had been sent 15 minutes earlier.

"Pick-out another one," another executive said, and John complied by double-clicking on another pinpoint in the tightly displayed cluster. The third e-mail came up, this one sent only five minutes earlier.

"Do another," the first executive said, and John double-clicked once more. The fourth e-mail came up on the screen.

The four e-mails were all discussing the Ally McBeal television episode that had aired the night before. It was lunch hour in New York, and this represented a cluster of communications occurring real-time within the organization. The sniffer had captured 20,000 e-mails, and this cluster represented a series of communications about an Ally McBeal episode.

It also represented reality.

The Ally McBeal example is a simple, though real, demonstration of the traffic analysis clustering capability of the software. I recognized the adaptability of this generalized application for forensics analysis, and the potential hidden benefit for the corporate world. Here are some examples.

The forensics team that works with me demonstrated this tool to an international pharmaceutical company that had just acquired another large pharmaceutical company. The demonstration was being done by teleconference, with participants located in various locations in the United States, and we were using PlaceWare, which allows the teleconference participants to log onto a specific Web site and connect their computers so that they could view the results as we demonstrated what the software could do. When the executives participating in the call heard our description of the clustering analysis that can be done on the basis of communications traffic, and on the basis of topic of communication, they immediately saw an application for it pertaining to their recent corporate merger.

The newly merged pharmaceutical corporation was concerned about achieving the economies of scale that the worldwide merger promised. They were also interested in eliminating duplication of effort. "What if," they theorized, "we could use this tool to see if there are research teams, in both of our houses, who are now at work on commercializing the same product?"

The application these executives perceived was very particular to their industry. It was also very particular to the circumstances they were experiencing. They could use the traffic analysis algorithm in conjunction with the Semantic Forests algorithm to find any communications or documents on the network that corresponded to a particular molecule under study. If there were teams working on the same thing at the same time in this newly merged behemoth, the search algorithms could unearth it, and the corporation could react accordingly.

The process of bringing a new drug to market and receiving FDA approval is a very burdensome and document intensive exercise. Could such a sniffer be used to identify documents and communications within the organization that should be included in the application submittal to the FDA?

You bet'cha. And would this approach significantly reduce the manpower needed to comply with the FDA submission and compliance process? Possibly.

Another possible use for the Semantic Forests algorithms and traffic analysis is in the corporate world. This time, the software was used to investigate the theft of intellectual property. During a demonstration at a large corporation, one of the executives mentioned that the company had received a tip that an individual within the organization was surreptitiously selling the corporation's trade secrets to a competitor. Although the alleged perpetrator was unknown, the company was able to identify the specific division that they believed was involved.

"This narrowed the possibilities down to 25,000 people," John Suit explained. John obtained several documents related to the technology at issue. He loaded these exemplars into the software's content analysis engine. In effect, what he was doing was placing the documents in front of the sniffer, and then asking the sniffer to then go out and see what other similar related content was being accessed on the network, real-time. Imagine placing a scented rag in front of a bloodhound, and then releasing the dog to search for similar scented rags hidden earlier on your property; this is what John was asking the software to do.

An e-mail was immediately discovered in which an individual was found to be sending exactly that kind of information to a competitor in Asia. The information being sent was clearly proprietary.

Another application currently being explored by the SEC is the use of the powerful topical search capabilities of this software (and its "link-analysis" algorithms) to ferret out corporate insider trading. The sniffer possesses the ability to identify all internal communications within a window of time regarding an important piece of insider information. The traffic analysis portion of the software could then perform "link analysis" to any telephone calls proximate in time to the dissemination of the insider information. The software's link analysis algorithms could also connect the dots to the execution of stock trades.

The forensics team that works with me in our lab in San Francisco has successfully used the software to ferret out e-mails in a system. To explore this possibility, I had devised a simple experiment. Tomas Castrejon and Manish Khera, the two computer forensics investigators on my staff who were the most familiar with this software, were asked to run the experiment and document the results. Instead of finding e-mails using the classic keyword search method, this time I wanted to see whether we could employ SilentRunner's ability to mathematically solve for the content of a communication, its topic, to find the documents we were interested in finding. After having the SilentRunner software "sniff" a document or two in question, we would then unleash the pattern-recognition software, bloodhound-like, to find all other communications that were related in topic to the e-mail in question. Our experiment was successful. We now possess the ability to search through millions of documents using keyword search *and* topic analysis search. But as I had sat down with Manish and Tomas to review the results of this experiment, a realization had slowly crept into my subconsciousness. No matter where I directed the conversation, the first thing they wanted to review was the exciting results of tests they had performed using SilentRunner to discover "steganography." The two yahoos had cooked up an unauthorized test. The results of their work are fascinating, and may be of use in the fight against terrorism by intelligence gathering agencies.

"Steganography," the use of secret communications by way of hidden writing, derives from the Greek words, *steganos,* meaning "covered," and the word, *graphein,* which means "to write." The first recorded use of steganography can be found in Herodotus. In fact, there are multiple references to the use of steganography in Herodotus's *The Histories.*

The year was 480 B.C. and Demaratus, an exile living in Persia, observed the preparations of the army of Xerxes, and learned of Xerxes's plan to invade Greece. Demaratus developed a plan to pass this information on to Sparta. "The way they received the news was remarkable," Herodotus wrote.

Demaratus, to achieve his purpose and obtain secrecy so that his message would not be discovered by troops guarding the roads, scraped the wax covering off a pair of wooden tablets. Demaratus wrote of Xerxes's preparations directly on the wood surface, and then recovered the tablets with wax so that the writing could not be discerned. What followed changed the course of history.

Xerxes marched into northern Greece at the head of 200,000 men and his 700 warships. At the narrow pass at Thermopylae, Xerxes waited patiently for four days for the miniscule Greek force there to come to their senses and abandon their posts in light of the insurmountable odds. Exasperated at last, Xerxes attacked the Spartans manning the defenses. For three crucial days, Leonidas and his 300 Spartans held off the Persians to the last man. Xerxes was finally able to move south, to Athens, which he burned. The Athenians, though, had been given the time to prepare their navy and put to sea. The next day, the two fleets engaged off Salamis. The victory of the Athenian fleet was decisive, and Xerxes fled to Persia, leaving his ground troops to fight their way back the best they could. Persia would never invade Greece again.

Herodotus tells of another ancient use of steganography. Histiaeus, in need of sending a message from the Persian court, resolved upon an ingenious method. He shaved the head of his favorite slave, and then tattooed on the man's head his message to his son-in-law, the ruler of Miletus, encouraging a revolt against the Persians. After waiting an appropriate amount of time for his slave's hair to grow in, Histiaeus then sent the man off on his dangerous journey. When the slave arrived in Miletus, he shaved his head so that Histiaeus's son-in-law could read the secret message. Today, steganography is hidden electronically.

Fast-forward 2,481 years. On February 5, 2001, Jack Kelley of *United States TODAY* broke the story that Osama bin Laden and members of his al Qaeda cell were using steganography, embedding messages in pictures posted on popular Web sites. The revelations came about as a result of the start of a trial in New York the day earlier, in which four members of al Qaeda were being prosecuted for the bombings of two U.S. embassies in East Africa. Unidentified intelligence experts disclosed to Kelley that the steganographic methods the terrorists used were similar to the use of "dead drops" by cold war spies decades earlier, in which an agent would deposit a secret communication in a secure location in a public place, such as a park, to be retrieved at some later date by the intended recipient. The intelligence community had proof that al Qaeda terrorists were inserting instructions, maps, and photographs of intended terrorist targets within the body of other images posted on Web sites.

During World War II, the Germans developed perhaps the first method of physically embedding a secret message within a document. German agents in Latin America used a photographic process to shrink a page of text to the size of a dot less than a millimeter in diameter. They then selected an innocuous normal sized message, and then pasted the "microdot" atop a period at the end of a sentence within the body of text in the innocuous message. The intended recipient then reversed the process so that the secret message could be read. An informant, however, had tipped-off the FBI to be on the lookout for a tiny gleam reflected from the dot of microfilm on the surface of the letter. From that time forward, American intelligence agencies were able to read intercepted microdot messages.

Sixty years later, in October 2001, Alex Debat, a former French Defense Ministry Official, confirmed that one man arrested in connection with the failed plot to bomb the American Embassy in Paris had in his possession a codebook for reading disguised messages. French officials also reported that the terrorists were instructed to make all of their communications by way of messages embedded in pictures posted as "dead drops" on the Internet. Reports published in February 2001 revealed that the use of encryption had become so fundamental to al Qaeda's method of operation that encryption techniques were being taught at training camps in Afghanistan. The prospect of discovering stego-images posted on the Internet presents a significant challenge in the battle against terrorism. There are currently an estimated 2 billion Web sites, containing over 28 billion digital images.

This is one reason Tomas and Manish were excited to report to me in my office that day. They had figured a way to use the SilentRunner forensic tool to find evidence of steganography embedded in digital images.

*   *   *

The first academic conference on digital watermarking and steganography was held in 1996. By 1999, over four hundred technical abstracts on the subject of steganography and digital watermarking could be found on the Internet. Much of the research has centered on the placement of hidden copyright notices, referred to as digital watermarking, or the notion of digital fingerprinting, the insertion of hidden serial numbers or other characteristics to allow an object to be distinguished from other similar objects. Both technologies have commercial application by enabling copyright protection of protected works. The insertion of stego-messages into MP3 (digital) music files is achieved in a similar fashion.

Businesses can be affected by steganography as well. Employees or other individuals involved in the theft of intellectual property could transmit the sensitive information via e-mail of a message or document that otherwise might appear innocuous. The communication could contain a significant amount of proprietary material hidden within a digital image or even an MP3 digital music file. To understand how steganography works in the digital age, it is helpful to understand how computers represent images and sounds.

How does a computer paint an image for us to see on the screen? It merely presents the digital image as an array of "pixels," or dots. Each pixel is generated as a result of a digital instruction, the results of which are the different light intensities that appear to us as colors on the screen. Many computer images are coded using an eight-bit string, such as:

"1-1-0-0-0-1-1-0,"

where each bit can contain either a "1" or a "0."

Using this kind of eight-bit instruction convention, 256 different shades of colors can be represented in an image. This is because each instruction "bit" contains one of two possibilities. Since there are eight places for an instruction (i.e., eight bits), this is equivalent to 2^8 possible color outcomes (i.e., $2 \times 2 \times 2 \times 2 \times 2 \times 2 \times 2 \times 2$). The computer "paints" these 256 different possible color shades from combinations of only three primary colors: red, yellow, and blue.

How can text, such as a secret message, be inserted in a digital image? Steganography can be embedded in those areas of the image that will draw the least amount of attention (e.g., those areas of an image where there might be naturally less prominent differentiations in color shading). One method of stego-insertion is called "least significant bit insertion." In this technique, data being inserted is slotted into that "position" within a byte that causes the least amount of color shading change for the affected pixel. For example, if the stego-insertion results in the color "cadmium yellow," instead of the "Mexican Yellow" there originally, the human eye will not discern this miniscule change to the overall image.

How is the insertion of a stego-message digitally represented? The letter "A" (as a stego-insertion example) can be hidden in three pixels using the "least significant bit" insertion method. Each of the letter A's eight bits of binary designation would be inserted in the least most significant "places" that, when changed, will cause the least amount of change to the light intensity of the pixel. The stego-insertion of the letter "A" in our example changed the pixel only slightly, from "Mexican Yellow" to "cadmium yellow."

Another steganography program allows for hiding a message even within a text file. In the typical page of computer-generated text, 80 columns are provided for use. Most writing, however, does not use all 80 columns. For example, if a paragraph ends midway across the page, a considerable number of columns of white space will be unused. One steganography program fills in all these unused spaces with elements of the message to be hidden from view. Other steganography programs allow the user to hide messages in MP3 music and sound files. The information is hidden within the MP3 bit stream during the compression process.

*   *   *

How had Tomas and Manish been able to use a forensics tool such as SilentRunner to detect steganography embedded in digital pictures? They selected and downloaded, at random, 12 JPEG images off the Internet. Some of the randomly selected images were of scenery; others were of people. Digital images saved as Joint Photographic Experts Group (JPEG) are compressed files that save significant amounts of storage space. The compression method is very efficient and provides for a high-quality image, but only a close approximation of the original digital image. Since JPEG images are efficient, they are the predominant images found posted on Web sites because they are easily transmitted.

Manish and Tomas then downloaded three common steganography tools: Hide In Picture, Image Hide, and S-Tools. They then inserted a text message into each of the twelve images using the three different stego-tools.

I asked them what they had embedded.

"The lyrics to American Pie, was one," Manish responded.

The answer caught me by surprise. The song had been recorded before either of the two men had been born. "You mean, 'Bye, Bye, Miss American Pie—drove my Chevy to the levee, but the levee—'"

"The one and the same," Tomas said.

I found out that the lyrics could be downloaded off the Internet for free, but I am not sure about the legality of it. They then typed the lyrics into Notepad, a text-writing tool (also referred to as a text editor), which doesn't involve all the formatting overhead of a typical word processor.

"So you put in the whole song?" I asked. "The whole text? Including the repeat, the refrain?"

"Yes, absolutely," Tomas said. "The whole kit and caboodle. Everything."

They also embedded encrypted versions of the lyrics into one series of pictures, as well as stego-embedding other randomly selected text into other pictures to avoid bias. They then ran their tests.

"At that point, we failed our first couple of tests," Manish explained. I asked what he meant by that.

"When we threw all these images into SilentRunner," he said, "it began clustering around the actual content of the image. That wasn't useful for us, obviously."

Manish was describing the neural-network pattern-recognition software's amazing ability to group together, or cluster, those images that were somehow related to one another. The software first examined the image files at a binary level and then, using a link analysis facility, grouped those images containing a depiction of a horse with other photos of horses. Similarly, the neural network program clustered the digital images of humans, no matter whether they were profile images, straight headshots, or full body shots. The digital images of the landscapes were clustered together off to one side of the screen.

One forensic user, Jim Wilson, a former employee of Raytheon, described exercising the software, just to see what it would do. He downloaded multiple images of actresses, Jennifer Lopez, for example; or Sandra Bullock, Meg Ryan, Madonna, and Julia Roberts. Again, some of the images were profiles only; others were headshots and other full body images in different poses. After the pattern-recognition software analyzed all of the JPEG images at a binary level, Jim had the software cluster the images. He told me that all the Jennifer Lopez's were clustered together in the upper right corner of the screen, below them were all of the images of Madonna, no matter whether the image was a full body shot or just a headshot. Clustered together on the right side of the screen were all the different photos of Sandra Bullock. The software had intelligently placed together the images of the actresses.

Wilson also told me that he had done the same test for a bunch of MP3 digitized music files. It took the whole weekend for the software to analyze all the music files because digitized music is so data intensive. When he came into work the next Monday, he wasn't sure what to expect, other than to be thankful that the machine he was using hadn't crashed. The clustering amazed him. The classical, pop, and jazz selections were in separate clusters, each comprised of several songs.

In their little unauthorized experiment, however, Tomas and Manish didn't want the pattern-recognition software to naturally cluster the digital images by content of the picture. They wanted the software to detect and separate the digital images containing embedded steganography from those images that didn't. To do this, Manish performed an ingenious test. He normalized all the images so they looked somewhat similar.

"How do you do that?" I asked.

"By running mathematical calculations on the images," Manish said.

Tomas sat forward. He could see that I wasn't following this at all. "What we had to do," he explained, "was find a way to make all the pictures look the same so that SilentRunner could then focus on the underlying content."

"Right. I understand that part," I said. "What did you do mathematically to an image to make it similar to another image?"

Tomas gave it another shot. "Mathematically," he said, "we looked at it and said, 'calculate a picture based on the values.'"

I still wasn't getting it, but I wasn't ready to give up yet. "So tell me this," I said. "You have two pictures. One is of a dog, and another is Marilyn Monroe. How do you mathematically make them similar?"

"Fractals," Tomas said.

"They're complex mathematical expressions that can be run on almost anything," Tomas explained. "And when they're run, they create some kind of crazy image, like a very wild looking image that's very deep. If you look at the image, there actually is no start and no finish to it. Like an inkblot. That's what it looks like."

He seemed satisfied with his answer. It showed on his face. "So can you show me a fractal?" I asked. "If you have a dog, can you show me the fractal of the dog?"

"I'd be happy to send you one if you'd like to see it," Manish said.

I wanted to see it, sure. But I wanted it explained to me, too. "Don't send it to me," I said. "Bring it up next time," I said. They both were on the 33rd floor, and my office is on the 34th floor. "That way you can show me the algorithm that you apply. Is it a simple algorithm?" I asked, revealing my ignorance, but neither of them seemed to notice the blunder.

"The Mandelbrot set?" he asked. "In the fractal world?"

I didn't even know there was a "fractal world." I nodded. It seemed the only thing to do. I hadn't the faintest idea what these two guys were talking about.

"There are different sets of mathematical calculations you can run," Manish explained. "And one of the more common ones is Mandelbrot."

"Then get me the Mandelbrot," I said, not having the faintest idea of what it was I was asking for.

I later learned that Mandelbrot, way back in 1975, coined the name fractal from the Latin *fractus,* the verb form of which means, "to break."

I graduated from college in 1975. Somehow, I missed all the excitement about Mandelbrot and fractals. I'm not complaining, but it doesn't seem fair that both Manish and Tomas knew about Mandelbrot sets and fractals, *and* the lyrics to "Bye, Bye Miss American Pie."

I learned. Fractals are geometric shapes that are fractured, or fragmented—and this process repeats, or "iterates," over and over again, until the fracturing process yields infinity. Put another way, a fractal is any pattern that, when enlarged, reveals greater and greater detail, or complexity.

Imagine sitting in an airplane that is flying 35,000 feet above the earth. As you look through the passenger window, you see the coastline of Massachusetts. The coastline itself is a fractal image—a pattern that reveals greater complexity as it is enlarged. As the plane descends, more coastline detail is revealed for you, almost as if you are zooming in for a closer look. At an elevation of 10,000 feet, more coastline detail emerges. As the plane approaches 1,000 feet of elevation, yet more detail surfaces. After the plane lands, if you drive back out to the coast, and then walk a segment of the same coastline, you are able to see even more detail. If you stoop to examine the shoreline at your feet, even more; and if you pull out a magnifying glass, yet more is discernable.

Fractals are formed by making ever-smaller versions of the larger picture; this self-similarity also leads to infinity. Fractals describe many objects in our world, such as clouds, mountains, rivers, and blood vessels. Some (not me) would say that fractals describe reality. Computers have revolutionized this area of mathematics, allowing mathematicians to "see" the shapes and forms their equations take on in the physical world. Before the advent of the computer, they could only attempt to visualize them.

Computers can be used to create fractal images by spinning an equation through a "positive feedback loop." In the case of Manish's experiment, he put his series of digital images through an equation that changed the images slightly—each pixel is recomputed, the coordinates are inserted into one end of the mathematical function, and are changed slightly when they come out the other end. This is iterated by the computer, repeatedly. A popular fractal generator, *Fractint*, is available as freeware on the Internet.

*   *   *

Even after learning everything I could about fractals, one thing still bothered me. I headed back to meet with Tomas and Manish.

"How does what you did make a dog similar to Marilyn Monroe?" I asked. This question had really been bugging me, and I just had to get it out.

Tomas decided to take the first crack at answering. "By their complexness," he began.

Anytime you have to start an answer with, "By their complexness," it is not a good thing.

Tomas plowed on. "A very complex mathematical expression created this type of image, that has no ending, or beginning," he said. "The way the calculation is done, all the images kind of come out looking kind of like the same. There are slight differences, but they were so slight that SilentRunner couldn't pick up on the subtle differences—but those that contained the stego-text would kinda pop out when it went into looking at the under layer stuff."

"Now hold on for a second," I said. Tomas's description jogged my memory. Maybe there was an analogy here. "There's an artist," I said, "that painted a picture a couple hundred years ago, having these images that kind of rotate into a vortex. And the point of view has you looking into this thing, and you see it kind of swirling around and you realize that this vortex has no beginning or end."

I later asked around about the picture I recalled. My wife, Patti, told me the artist was Escher. In retrospect, I don't think the painting had anything to do with fractals. I didn't have any idea what I was talking about.

"That's kind of an example of a fractal, a fractal image," Manish said. He was referring to the Escher painting I had mentioned earlier. But since I couldn't remember the name of the artist when I was talking with Manish and Tomas, or the name of the painting, Manish couldn't have had any idea what I was talking about (since I didn't, to begin with). But he respected me. He wasn't going to tell me that I didn't know what I was talking about.

"Right," I said. "The painting actually goes on into infinity in a sense."

Manish and Tomas nodded. I didn't detect any rolling of their eyes.

"And so," I said, "SilentRunner will detect that all these digital images you were experimenting with, which all look like they're going on into infinity."

"Right," Manish said. "It can't differentiate them based on the image alone now. But what it could do is look at a lower level and it found commonality amongst those digital images that had stego-text embedded inside. So it was able to differentiate the fractalized images into two camps, those containing stego-messages, and those that were free of any steganography."

Manish and Tomas employed fractalization to find the steganography using this sophisticated "neural-network pattern-recognition" software. They used it as a forensic tool. Once the sniffer engine told them that a digital image contained steganography, they could use common tools to extract the stego-messages from within the image.

*   *   *

With experimentation and a little bit of human ingenuity, Manish and Tomas took a sophisticated tool, and on a hunch, proved that it could be used for forensic analysis in a manner never dreamt of by its designers, or by the NSA linguists and software engineers who first conceived of building it. But that's what humans do. They learn from others what is possible to learn, and they invent.

Notes

Preface

Page viii   "The 'shrill voice of professional piety . . .'" Alistair Cooke, "The Prime Minister Was the Patient," *Wall Street Journal* (November 13, 2002).

Chapter One: "Just Move Away from Your Computer Please"

Page 1   "Morgan Fay's chief financial . . ." Morgan Fay is a fictionalized name for a publicly traded corporation. Avalon Partners is the fictionalized name of the actual management partnership established to invest in Morgan Fay. Avalon is the fictional island to which the injured Arthur was removed in Sir Thomas Malory's tale, the *Morte d'Arthur*.

Page 1   "'Excuse me?' . . ." Robin Malory and Cindy Shalott, the Chief Executive Officer and Chief Financial Officer, respectively, of Morgan Fay, are fictionalized names of the two executives of Morgan Fay. At the time of this writing, Cindy Shalott and Robin Malory are serving out their respective prison sentences.

Page 1   "'I'd appreciate it . . .'" Interview with Leland Altschuler.

Page 2   "'I've got the computer . . .'" Interview with Michael P. Murphy.

Chapter Two: "It's Gonna be a 'Raid'"

Page 10   "In Kris Haworth's world, . . ." Interview with Kris Haworth.

Page 11   " 'You need to get in there . . .'" Interview with Michael P. Murphy.

Page 12   ". . . Cindy Shalott, Morgan Fay's CFO, . . .'" Interview with Leland Altschuler.

Page 13   "One of them would call . . ." William Boni and Gerald Kovacich, *I-Way Robbery: Crime on the Internet* (Boston: Butterworth-Heinemann, 1999), pp. 111–113.

Page 13   ". . . they called it social engineering . . ." Richard Power, *Tangled Web: Tales of Digital Crime from the Shadows of Cyberspace* (Indianapolis, IN: Que, 2000), p. 300.

Page 14   "If Kris ended up . . ." Kevin Mandia and Chris Prosise, *Incident Response: Investigating Computer Crime* (Berkeley, CA: Osborne/ McGraw-Hill, 2001), pp. 92–94, 158–159.

Page 14   "The memo would be . . ." Eoghan Casey, *Digital Evidence and Computer Crime* (London: Academic Press, 2000), p. 58.

Page 17   "Peter Gutmann, regarded . . ." Peter Gutmann is a professor of computer science at the University of Auckland in New Zealand.

Page 18   "An imaged hard drive . . ." P. Gutmann, "Secure Deletion of Data from Magnetic and Solid-State Memory," *Sixth USENIX Security Symposium Proceedings, San Jose, California, July 24, 1996, pp. 77-90 of the Proceedings.* John Patsakis, president and general counsel of Guidance Software, the maker of *EnCase,* the premier forensic imaging tool used by computer forensic specialists, agrees. "It is possible to take a disk apart and use an electron microscope to read information from the individual magnetic spots on the surface of a disk that may have been intentionally erased." John Markoff, "Data Very Hard to Hide from Computer Sleuths," *Wall Street Journal* (January 14, 2002).

Page 18   "However, the DOD's national security . . ." Matt Villano, "Hard-Drive Magic: Making Data Disappear Forever," *New York Times* (May 2, 2002).

Page 19   "The second category, . . ." Matt Villano, "Hard-Drive Magic: Making Data Disappear Forever," *New York Times* (May 2, 2002).

Page 19   "Here comes a forensic . . ." Eoghan Casey, Eoghan Casey, *Digital Evidence and Computer Crime* (London: Academic Press, 2000), pp. 44–46.

Page 20   "Newspapers throughout the . . ." Jaxon Van Derbeken, "Dramatic Start to Mauling Trial," *San Francisco Chronicle* (February 20, 2002).

CHAPTER THREE: "A DOG'S JUST RUN PAST"

Page 21   "'The barking started,' . . ." Testimony of Esther Birkmaier, *Reporters Redacted Transcript of Proceedings in The People of the State of California v. Marjorie Knoller and Robert Noel* (vol. 1, March 9, 2001), pp. 12–31.

Page 22   "In fact, just outside . . ." Michael Pena, Matthew Taylor, and Jaxon Van Derbeken, "Powerful Dogs Maul Woman, Kill Her," *San Francisco Chronicle* (January 27, 2001).

Page 22   "Esther Birkmaier found herself . . ." Testimony of Esther Birkmaier, *Reporters Redacted Transcript of Proceedings in The People of the State of California v. Marjorie Knoller and Robert Noel* (vol. 1, March 9, 2001), pp. 12–31.

Page 23   "'There's a woman screaming . . .'" Michael Pena, Matthew Taylor and Jaxon Van Derbeken, "Powerful Dogs Maul Woman, Kill Her," *San Francisco Chronicle* (January 27, 2001).

Page 23   ". . . surveying the horrific scene. . . ." Michael Pena, Matthew Taylor and Jaxon Van Derbeken, "Powerful Dogs Maul Woman," *San Francisco Chronicle* (January 27, 2001).

Page 24   ". . . marking Whipple's attempt . . ." *Reporters Redacted Transcript of Proceedings in The People of the State of California v. Marjorie Knoller and Robert Noel* (vol. 1, March 9, 2001), p. 49.

Page 24   "'No matter what I did,' . . ." Jaxon Van Derbeken, "Prison Gang Duo Linked to Dog That Killed Woman," *San Francisco Chronicle* (January 30, 2001).

Page 24   "'We're a little puzzled . . .'" Jaxon Van Derbeken, "S. F. Lawyers Adopt Con Who Bred Killer Dog," *San Francisco Chronicle* (January 31, 2001).

Page 25   "'The disclosure of that . . .'" Robert Noel, Letter to San Francisco District Attorney Terrence Hallinan, January 31, 2001.

Page 25   "'The dogs have lawyers,' . . ." Phillip Matier, Andrew Ross, "Tale of Vicious Dog Takes Bizarre New Twist," *San Francisco Chronicle* (January 31, 2001).

Page 25   "'I would not think . . .'" Marianne Costantinou, Pamela Podger, and Peter Hartlaub, "Dog Case Gets Weirder: Killer Pet's Owner Lashes D. A.," *San Francisco Chronicle* (February 2, 2001).

Page 26   "As the grand jury . . ." Pamela J. Podger, Jim Herron Zamora, and Jaxon Van Derbeken, "Legal Struggle Begins For Couple in Dog Attack," *San Francisco Chronicle* (March 29, 2001).

Page 26   "Authorities learned of . . ." Phillip Matier and Andrew Ross, "Contract Reportedly Out on Life of Dog Case Prosecutor," *San Francisco Chronicle* (November 21, 2001). Two weeks later, at a black-tie ceremony at the home of millionaires Anne and Gordon Getty, Guilfoyle married San Francisco Supervisor Gavin Newsome.

Page 26   ". . . the press reported . . ." Jaxon Van Derbeken, "Joint Trial for Couple in Dog-Mauling Case: S. F. Judge Okay's Sex-with-Dogs Evidence—If It's Relevant," *San Francisco Chronicle* (January 16, 2002).

Page 26   "During the grand jury proceedings, the prosecutors . . ." Jaxon Van Derbeken, "S. F. Grand Jury Questions Attorney in Dog Case," *San Francisco Chronicle* (March 23, 2001).

Page 27   "'Are you concerned . . ." Testimony of Robert Noel, *Reporters Redacted Transcript of Proceedings in The People of the State of California v. Marjorie Knoller and Robert Noel* (vol 3, March 23, 2001), p. 674.

Page 27   "The veterinarian also . . ." Jaxon Van Derbeken, "Vet Gave Warning About Killer Dog: Bane Was Unsafe to Handle, He Testifies," *San Francisco Chronicle* (February 21, 2002).

Page 28   "These platters are all . . ." Lee Gomes, "An Ode to Disk Drives: Big, Often Barely Legal and Very Symbolic," *Wall Street Journal* (July 22, 2002).

Page 28   "... the computer's operating system ..." Peter Stephenson, *Investigating Computer-Related Crime* (Boca Raton, FL: CRC Press, 2000), p. 99–100.

Page 31   "... the alleged perpetrator ..." Interview with Lee Teitsworth.

CHAPTER FOUR: SHE'D DELETED A HELLUVA LOT OF E-MAIL

Page 32   "The computer forensic specialists ..." From an interview with Kris Haworth.

Page 34   "The computer's operating system ..." Eoghan Casey, *Digital Evidence and Computer Crime* (London: Academic Press, 2000), p. 63.

Page 34   "Think of the swap file ..." Peter Stephenson, *Investigating Computer-Related Crime* (Boca Raton, FL: CRC Press, 2000), p. 101.

Page 34   "There are other spaces ..." Peter Stephenson, *Investigating Computer-Related Crime* (Boca Raton, FL: CRC Press, 2000), p. 102.

Page 35   "Even if she had, ..." Norbert Zaenglein, *Disk Detective: Secrets You Must Know to Recover Information from a Computer* (Boulder, CO: Paladin Press, 1998), pp. 24–27.

Page 35   "... 10 billion electronic messages ..." Katie Hafner, "E-Mail, 30 Years Later: Billions Served Daily," *New York Times* (December 6, 2001).

Page 35   "In 1990, ..." Eric Arnum, ed., *Messaging Online,* as reported by Katie Hafner. See "E-Mail, 30 Years Later: Billions Served Daily," *New York Times* (December 6, 2001).

Page 35   "'A computer hard drive is sort ...'" Maria Godoy, "CyberSleuths Seek Truth About Enron," *Tech Live: TechTV* (February 11, 2002).

CHAPTER FIVE: "YOU NEED TO GET OVER THERE"

Page 37   "This time Murphy ..." Interview with Michael P. Murphy.

Page 37   "Altschuler had no notion ..." Interview with Leland Altschuler.

Page 39   "As Altschuler and Bergman ..." Interview with Emmett Bergman.

Page 41   "People were assembling ..." Interview with Lisa Liao.

Page 41   "They had almost ... " Interview with Shelly Connor.

CHAPTER SIX: "YOU'RE NOTHING BUT A GOON IN A SUIT"

Page 43   "Lee Altschuler's team now found ..." Interview with Leland Altschuler.

Page 44   "Emmett Bergman recalls things ..." Interview with Emmett Bergman.

Page 46   "Shelly had called ahead . . ." Interview with Shelly Connor.

Page 47   "Murphy would need . . ." Interview with Tony Rosen.

Page 52   "He dialed Shalott at home, . . ." Interview with Michael P. Murphy.

CHAPTER SEVEN: "OH, AND BY THE WAY"

Page 55   "'Initially it was the trade . . .'" From an interview with Jacobus Sadie.

Page 55   "The auditors at PricewaterhouseCoopers . . ." Interview with Michael P. Murphy.

Page 56   "Kris Haworth would use . . ." From an interview with Kris Haworth.

Page 56   ". . . she would use the sniffer . . ." From an interview with Kris Haworth. *Dtsearch* and NTI's DS2 perform a similar physical level search," Kevin Mandia and Chris Prosise, *Incident Response: Investigating Computer Crime* (Berkeley, CA: Osborne/McGraw-Hill, 2001), p. 267.

Page 56   "The client-provided search . . ." Kevin Mandia and Chris Prosise, *Incident Response: Investigating Computer Crime* (Berkeley, CA: Osborne/McGraw-Hill, 2001), p. 268.

Page 57   ". . . he has to read all . . ." From an interview with Stephen Hibbard.

Page 57   "The wheelbarrow loads . . ." From an interview with Alex Jarvis.

Page 59   "Consider FBI Director Mueller's . . ." David Johnston and Neil A. Lewis, "Whistle-Blower Recounts Faults Inside the FBI" *New York Times* (June 7, 2002).

Page 59   ". . . *Moro Bay,* for example . . ." Moro Bay is a fictional issue codeword I have created for purposes of maintaining confidentiality.

Page 61   "It will try all . . . " Jennifer Lee, "And the Password Is . . . Waterloo," *New York Times* (December 27, 2001).

Page 62   "Stephenson, when undertaking . . ." Peter Stephenson, *Investigating Computer-Related Crime* (Boca Raton, FL: CRC Press, 2000), pp. 159–160. Peter Stephenson, an experienced information security specialist, utilizes the WordCrack application tool. To break into WordPerfect files, Stephenson uses either Decrypt or WPCrack. At the operating system level, he will use Glide to crack Windows95 passwords; and when in DOS-based systems, he uses either Cracker Jack or PCUPC. For Novell network operating systems, he will try NetCrack; for NT networks, IOphtCrack. For files encrypted and compressed with PKZip, Stephenson resorts to Zipcrack.

Page 62   "'It is amazing,' . . . " Peter Stephenson, *Investigating Computer-Related Crime* (Boca Raton, FL: CRC Press, 2000), pp. 160–161.

Page 63   "Matt Larson, a computer forensics . . ." From an interview with Matt Larson.

Page 63   " . . . Nortek circumvents the BIOS-level . . ." "Notebook/Laptop Password Solutions," *Nortek Computers Ltd.* (August 20, 2002), available: www.nortek.on.ca.

Page 64   "He had arranged . . ." From an interview with Tomas Castrejon.

Page 65   ". . . describes the Lucifer encryption . . ." Simon Singh, *The Code Book* (New York: Random House, 1999), pp. 248–250. Another excellent source describing DES encryption is David Kahn, *The Code-Breakers, The Story of Secret Writing* (New York: Scribner, 1967/1996), pp. 979–983.

CHAPTER EIGHT: MAFIOSI HAVE RIGHTS, TOO, DON'T'CHA KNOW?

Page 67   "'Little Nicky' Scarfo's father . . ." Declan McCullagh, "FBI Hacks Alleged Mobster," *Wired News* (December 6, 2000), available: www.wired.com/news.

Page 67   "The elder Scarfo . . ." George Anastasia, "Scarfo's High-Tech Case Ends with Plea," *Philadelphia Inquirer* (March 1, 2002).

Page 68   ". . . and computer spreadsheets detailing . . ." Ronald D. Wigler, *Brief of the United States in Opposition to Defendant Scarfo's Pretrial Motions, United States of America v. Nicodemo S. Scarfo, and Frank Paolercio,* United States District Court, District of New Jersey, July 17, 2001, p. 4.

Page 68   "'I knew PGP . . .'" John Schwartz, "Organized Crime Case Raises Privacy Issues," *New York Times* (July 30, 2000).

Page 68   "The FBI was forced . . . " Ronald D. Wigler, Sealed Application, *In the Matter of the Application of the United States of America for an Order Authorizing the Surreptitious Entry Into the Premises of Merchant Services of Essex County, Located at 149 Little Street, Belleville, New Jersey, for the Purpose of Conducting a Search for Evidence of Violations of Title 18, U.S.C. §§ 371, 892–894, 1955 and 1962,* United States District Court of New Jersey, June 8, 1999.

Page 68   ". . . because 'Little Nicky' had bragged . . ." Leo A. Dawson Jr., Affidavit in Support of Application, *In the Matter of the Application of the United States of America for an Order Authorizing the Surreptitious Entry Into the Premises of Merchant Services of Essex County, Located at 149 Little Street, Belleville, New Jersey, for the Purpose of Conducting a Search for Evidence of Violations of Title 18, U.S.C. §§ 371, 892–894, 1955 and 1962,* United States District Court of New Jersey, May 8, 1999. pp. 16–17.

Page 68   "WHEREFORE, IT IS . . ." Hon. G. Donald Haneke, Order, *In the Matter of the Application of the United States of America for an Order Authorizing the Surreptitious Entry Into the Premises of Merchant Services of Essex County, Located at 149 Little Street, Belleville, New Jersey, for the Purpose of Conducting a Search for Evidence of Violations of Title 18,*

U.S.C. §§ 371, 892–894, 1955 and 1962, United States District Court of New Jersey, May 8, 1999, pp. 4–5.

Page 69   "The FACTOR files yielded . . ." Ronald D. Wigler, *Brief of the United States in Opposition to Defendant Scarfo's Pretrial Motions, United States of America v. Nicodemo S. Scarfo, and Frank Paolercio,* United States District Court, District of New Jersey, July 17, 2001, p. 8.

Page 70   "Nicky Scarfo's attorneys demanded . . . " Vincent C. Scoca and Norris F. Gelman, *Motion for Discovery Pursuant to Rule 16 of the Federal Rules of Criminal Procedure, United States of America v. Nicodemo S. Scarfo,* United States District Court, District of New Jersey, June 21, 2000.

Page 70   "More importantly, they alleged . . ." A pen register is a mechanical device that records the numbers dialed on a telephone by monitoring the electrical impulses caused when the dial on the telephone is released. It does not overhear oral communications and does not indicate whether calls are actually completed. The Justice Department argued in Scarfo that the key logger system used against Scarfo was akin to a pen register in that ". . . it monitored each computer character or symbol as inputted from the keyboard." Ronald D. Wigler, *Brief of the United States in Opposition to Defendant Scarfo's Pretrial Motions, United States of America v. Nicodemo S. Scarfo, and Frank Paolercio,* United States District Court, District of New Jersey, July 17, 2001, p. 41.

Page 70   ". . . the FBI's pen register. . ." Vincent C. Scoca and Norris E. Gelman, *Motion to Suppress Evidence Seized by the Government Through the Use of a Keystroke Recorder, United States of America v. Nicodemo S. Scarfo,* United States District Court, District of New Jersey, June 2001, p. 2.

Page 70   "Scarfo's attorneys were alleging . . ." Ronald D. Wigler, *Brief of the United States in Opposition to Defendant Scarfo's Pretrial Motions, United States of America v. Nicodemo S. Scarfo, and Frank Paolercio,* United States District Court, District of New Jersey, July 17, 2001, p3. The Fourth Amendment to the U. S. Constitutions reads as follows: "The right of the people to be secure in their persons, houses, papers, and effects, against unreasonable searches and seizures, shall not be violated, and no Warrants shall issue, but upon probable cause, supported by Oath or affirmation, and particularly describing the place to be searched, and the persons or things to be seized." The Government's reply brief summarizes well the thinking of the framers of our Constitution: ". . . The Fourth Amendment's requirement of particularity (in a warrant) 'arises out of a hostility to the Crown's practice of issuing "general warrants" taken to authorized the wholesale rummaging through a person's property in search of contraband or evidence.' Such writs, or general warrants, were open-ended, unfocused, and were issued without probable cause before a magistrate and without particularity."

Page 70   ". . . he wanted more information . . ." Declan McCullagh, "How Far Can FBI Spying Go?" *Wired News* (July 31, 2001), available: www.wired.com/news.

Page 70   "The *New York Times'* headline . . ." John Schwartz, "Organized Crime Case Raises Privacy Issues," *New York Times* (July 30, 2001).

Page 70   ". . . Judge Politan expressed his concern . . ." Nicholas H. Politan, U.S.D.J., Re: Criminal Action No. 00–404 (NHP), *United States v. Nicodemo S. Scarfo, et al.,* United States District Court, District of New Jersey, August 7, 2001, p. 5.

Page 71   "The Justice Department's response . . ." Ronald D. Wigler, *Government's Request for Modification of August 7, 2001 Order Pursuant to §4 of the Classified Information Procedures Act and Rule 16(d) of the Federal Rules of Criminal Procedure, United States of America v. Nicodemo S. Scarfo, el al.,* United States District Court, District of New Jersey, August 23, 2001, p. 5.

Page 71   "Judge Politan wryly observed. . ." Nicholas H. Politan, District Judge, Re: *Criminal Action No. 00–404 (NHP), United States v. Nicodemo S. Scarfo, et al.,* United States District Court, District of New Jersey, December 26, 2001, p. 2.

Page 71   "He ordered the record . . ." Nicholas H. Politan, District Judge, Re: *Criminal Action No. 00–404 (NHP), United States v. Nicodemo S. Scarfo, et al.,* United States District Court, District of New Jersey, December 26, 2001, p. 5.

Page 72   "Supervisory Special Agent Murch's . . ." Randall S. Murch, Affidavit, *United States of America v. Nicodemo S. Scarfo, and Frank Paolercio,* United States District Court, District of New Jersey, October 4, 2001, pp. 6–7.

Page 72   "Shortly afterward, Scarfo's attorneys . . ." George Anastasia, "Scarfo's High-Tech Case Ends With Plea," *Philadelphia Inquirer* (March 1, 2002).

Page 73   "Dave's response was . . ." Interview with Dave Gully.

Page 73   "This virus also installed . . ." David M. Ewalt, "Dangerous New Virus, Same Old Hole," *InformationWeek* (November 22, 2001).

Page 73   "According to their unnamed . . ." Bob Sullivan, "FBI Software Cracks Encryption Wall," *MSNBC* (November 20, 2001).

Page 73   "'We can't discuss it . . .'" "FBI Confirms 'Magic Lantern' Project Exists," *Reuters* (December 12, 2001).

Page 74   "The Associated Press . . ." Carrie Kirby, "Network Associates Mired in Security Debate: FBI Reported to Have Asked Firm for Help," *San Francisco Chronicle* (November 28, 2001).

Page 74   "The technology to install . . ." Robert Lemos, "FBI Snoop Tool Old Hat for Hackers," *CNET News.com,* November 21, 2001.

Page 74   "The University of Nebraska . . ." Bill Hayes, "Virus Alert—W32/BadTrans@MM Internet worm," University of Nebraska at

Lincoln, May 2, 2001, available: www.unl.edu/security/virus_alerts /badtrans.htm.

Page 74 "The FBI's sting, . . ." Allison Linn, "Bogus Company Used to Catch Hackers," *Associated Press* (May 9, 2001).

Chapter Nine: DumbFellas

Page 75 "Prewett also served . . ." Case CROO—550C, *United States of America v. Vassili Gorshkov, Transcript of Proceedings,* United States District Court, Western District of Washington, at Seattle, May 17, 2001.

Page 76 "'A mysterious computer . . .'" John Markoff, "Thief Reveals Credit Card Data When Web Extortion Plot Fails," *New York Times* (January 10, 2000).

Page 76 "'Pay me $100,000, . . .'" Michael Eskenazi, "Is Leaving Home Without It the Least of Your Worries?" *Time* (January 10, 2000).

Page 76 "'I kept wondering, . . .'" "Hijacked Web Site Regroups After Infamous Attack," *Associated Press* (February 29, 2000).

Page 77 "One month later, in January 2000, . . ." Mike Brunker, "E-Business vs. the Perfect Cybercrime: U.S. Authorities Can't Touch Credit Card Fraud from Overseas," *MSNBC* (March 3, 2000).

Page 77 "'I'm not aware . . .'" Mike Brunker, "E-business vs. the Perfect Cybercrime: U.S. Authorities Can't Touch Credit Card Fraud from Overseas," *MSNBC* (March 3, 2000).

Page 77 "A computer in Chelyabinsk, . . ." Mike Brunker, "E-Business vs. the Perfect Cybercrime: U.S. Authorities Can't Touch Credit Card Fraud from Overseas," *MSNBC,* March 3, 2000.

Page 78 "The knowledgeable source . . ." "CD Universe Evidence Compromised," *MSNBC* (June 7, 2000), available: http://zdnet.com.com /2100-11-502482.html?lgacy=zdnn.

Page 78 "In December 2000, . . ." Paul A. Greenberg, "FBI Probes Credit Card Info Hack," *News Factor Network* (December 13, 2000), available: www.EcommerceTimes.com.

Page 78 "Credit-card industry sources . . ." Robert Lemos and Ben Charny, "Egghead Scrambles to Gauge Damage," *ZDNN* (December 22, 2000).

Page 79 "The hacker would use . . ." Interview with Tom Arnold, Chief Technology Officer of CyberSource, an Internet merchant services credit card processing firm. The reference to a "one-time use cipher pad refers to a method of encoding messages to escape detection. During World War I, major Joseph Mauborgne, head of cryptographic research for the U.S. Army, devised a code system employing the use of a randomly generated pass phrase. The pass phrase was used to encode, and decode a message. This system involved the compilation of a thick pad consisting of hundreds of sheets of paper. Each sheet of paper would contain a single randomly generated password. There would be two copies of the code pad, one for the receiver, and one for the sender. Once the message was encoded, sent, received and decoded, both sender and receiver would destroy the page on the code pad used to encode the message. The next time a message needed to be exchanged, the next sheet of paper on the code pad would be next up, providing both sender and receiver with the randomly generated pass phrase that should then be used. See Simon Singh, *The Code Book: The Evolution of Secrecy from Mary Queen of Scots to Quantum Cryptography* (New York: Doubleday, 1990) p. 120.

Page 79   "Investigation into Egghead.com . . ." Jeff Sheahan, Press Release "Details of Alleged 3.7 million Credit Card Number Theft," January 8, 2001, available: www.emergency.com/2000/cc-stolen.htm.

Page 79   ". . . while Dillinger preferred . . ." James M. Flammang, *100 Years of the American Auto* (Lincolnwood, Illinois: Publications International, 2002) p. 159.

Page 82   "Patterson e-mailed Ivanov . . ." Testimony of Michael Prewett, Case CROO—550C, *United States of America v. Vassili Gorshkov, Transcript of Proceedings,* United States District Court, Western District of Washington, at Seattle, May 17, 2001, p. 22.

Page 86   "It took the U.S. Department . . ." Case CR00–550C, "Transcript of Proceedings Before The Honorable John C. Coughenour, United States District Judge," *United States of America v. Vassili Gorshkov,* United States District Court, Western District of Washington at Seattle, p. 5.

Page 87   "In May 2001, . . ." Michelle Delio, "Stung Russian Hacker Guilty," *Wired News* (October 17, 2001).

Page 87   "On May 7, 2001, . . ." Press Release, "Russian National Arrested and Indicted for Penetrating U.S. Corporate Computer Networks, Stealing Credit Card Numbers, and Extorting the Companies by Threatening to Damage Their Computers," *U.S. Department of Justice, United States Attorney, District of Connecticut,* May 7, 2001.

Page 87   "On June 20, 2001, . . ." Press Release, "Russian Computer Hacker Indicted in California for Breaking into Computer Systems and Extorting Victim Companies," *U.S. Department of Justice, United States Attorney, Central District of California,* June 20, 2001.

Page 87   "On August 16, 2001, . . ." Press Release, "Russian National Indicted on Computer Intrusion Charges," *U.S. Department of Justice, Eastern District of California,* August 16, 2001.

Page 87   "On October 10, 2001, . . ." Press Release, "Russian Computer Hacker Convicted by Jury," *U. S. Department of Justice, United States Attorney, Western District of Washington,* October, 10, 2001.

Page 87   "News accounts have reported . . ." Kevin Coughlin and Robert Rudolph, "Mob Case Is Raising Cyber-Fear," *Star Ledger* (July 30, 2001).

Page 88   "Two scientists, . . ." Joe Loughry and David A. Umphress, "Information Leakage from Optical Emanations," *ACM Transactions on Information and System Security,* vol. 5, no. 3, August 2002, pp. 262–289.

Page 88   "He has demonstrated . . ." Marcus G. Kuhn, "Optical Time-Domain Eavesdropping Risks of CRT Displays," *Proceedings 2002 IEEE Symposium on Security and Privacy,* May 12–15, 2002, Berkeley, California, pp. 3–18.

Page 88   "'A telescope could be . . .'" Will Knight, "Monitor's Flicker Reveals Data on Screen," *New Scientist* (April 28, 2002).

Page 89   "The flashing optical . . ." Markus G. Kuhn and Ross J. Anderson, "Soft Tempest: Hidden Data Transmission Using Electromagnetic Emanations" *Information Hiding, Springer-Verlag Gerlin Heidelberg,* 1993, p. 139; and Joe Loughry and David A. Umphress, "Information Leakage from Optical Emanations," *ACM Transactions on Information and System Security,* vol. 5, no. 3, August 2002, p. 283.

CHAPTER TEN: EVEN A TICK CAN SWELL ONLY SO FAR

Page 90   "What he saw is disturbing . . ." Interview with Alex Jarvis.

Page 91   "According to archaeologist . . ." Denise Schmandt-Besserat, *Before Writing: from Counting to Cuneiform* (Austin, Texas: University of Texas Press, 1992), p. 168. Also, for an amazing read on the same subject with regard to pre-Flood civilizations, see: Ian Wilson, *The Biblical Flood as a Real Event and How It Changed the Course of Civilization* (New York: St. Martin's Press, 2001), pp. 94—102.

Page 91   The first generally accepted . . ." Franz-Josef Arlinghaus, "Art.: Bookkeeping, Double-entry Bookkeeping," as found in Christopher Kleinhenz, editor, *Medieval Italy: An Encyclopedia* (New York: Garland, 2002), available also at: http://www.franzarlinghaus.de/Bookkeeping.html. p. 4(of 7). Also see, Michael Scorgie, "Untapped Sources for Accountants" as found in *Genizah Fragments— The Newsletter of Cambridge University's Taylor-Schechter Genizah Research Unit at Cambridge University Library* No. 29, April 1995. http://www.lib.cam.ac.uk/Taylor-Schecter/GF/GF29.html.

Page 92   "Put simply, Enron . . ." Rebecca Smith and Kathryn Kranhold, "Enron Knew Foreign Portfolio Had Lost Value," *Wall Street Journal* (May 6, 2002).

Page 94   ". . . 'the proliferation of special-purpose . . .' " James Covert, "Retailers May Face Heightened Scrutiny Over Use of 'Special-Purpose Entities,' *Dow Jones Newswires* (March 29, 2002).

Page 94   "You call this loan . . ." Paul Zielbauer, "More Connecticut Records About Enron Deal Emerge, *New York Times* (March 22, 2002).

Page 95   "Enron bet on deregulation . . ." Rebecca Smith, "How Enron's Plan to Market Electricity Nationwide Fizzled," *Wall Street Journal* (March 25, 2002).

Page 95   "California almost imploded. . . ." Mark Martin, "'Proof' of Energy Scam; State Officials Point to New Evidence Power Firms Sought to Rip Off California," *San Francisco Chronicle* (March 3, 2003).

Page 96   "California's 'Big-Four' . . ." Steven E. Ambrose, *Nothing Like It in the World* (New York: Simon & Schuster, 2000), p. 19. See also: Matthew Josephson, *The Robber Barons* (New York: Harcourt, Brace and Jovanovich, 1934).

Page 96   "California's Public Utilities Commissioner, . . ." Richard W. Stevenson, "Enron Trading Gave Prices Artificial Lift, Panel Is Told," *New York Times* (April 12, 2002).

Page 96   "The report prepared . . ." Richard A. Oppel Jr., "Report Voices Suspicions on Energy Crisis: California Pricing May Have Been Manipulated," *New York Times* (August 14, 2002).

Page 96   "Prosecutors have now empanelled . . ." Peter Elkind and Bethany McLean, "The Feds Close In on Enron," *Fortune* (September 2, 2002).

Page 97   "That's why somewhere . . ." B. Mark Smith, *Toward Rational Exuberance: The Evolution of the Modern Stock Market* (New York: Farrar, Straus and Giroux, 2001) pp. 17 to 19. Daniel Drew, in his years as a cattle drover, hit upon the idea of plying his scrawny 'critters' with salt, then depriving them of water as he drove them down the length of Manhattan. Drew instructed his drovers to 'let them critters drink their fill' before the cattle were inspected by potential buyers. The Fulton Street butchers paid top dollar for the bloated animals, a price that included thousands of pounds of water. When Drew later hung his shingle on Wall Street, he secretly sold stock, in quantities far in excess of the amount justified by the assets of the companies he controlled. He was accused of 'watering' the stock of these companies, and the term 'watered stock' stuck in the Wall Street lexicon.

Page 97   "Shirley Hudler, the Enron manager . . ." Marie Brenner, "The Enron Wars," *Vanity Fair* (April 2002), p. 184.

Page 98   "Things get weird, . . ." Complaint, *JPMorganChase Bank, for and on behalf of Mahonia Limited and Mahonia Natural Gas Limited, Plaintiff, against Liberty Mutual Insurance Company, et al., Defendants,* Supreme Court of The State of New York, filed December 11, 2001, New York County Clerk's Office.

Page 99   "'I wish we could . . .'" Sherron S. Watkins, "Anonymous Letter to Kenneth Lay," *Enron Corporation* (August 14, 2002).

Page 99 "He grew visibly frustrated . . ." John R. Emshwiller and Katherine Kranhold, "A Year Later, Enron Ex-CEO Skilling Is Awaiting His Fate," *Wall Street Journal* (August 14, 2002).

Page 99 "Executives who articulated disagreement . . ." John R. Emshwiller and Katherine Kranhold, "A Year Later, Enron Ex-CEO Skilling Is Awaiting His Fate," *Wall Street Journal* (August 14, 2002).

Page 99 "Fastow's response was telling, . . ." Anita Raghavan, Kathryn Kranhold, and Alexie Barrionuevo, "How Enron Bosses Created a Culture of Pushing Limits: Fastow and Others Challenged Staff, Badgered Bankers; Porsches, Ferraris Were Big," *Wall Street Journal* (August 26, 2002).

Page 100 "She was concerned . . ." Testimony of Sherron S. Watkins before the House Energy and Commerce Subcommittee, February 14, 2002.

CHAPTER ELEVEN: "BAD TUNA"

Page 102 "When Jaco Sadie and I . . ." Interview with Jacobus Sadie, Alex Jarvis, and Michael P. Murphy.

CHAPTER TWELVE: "101 WAYS TO COOK THE BOOKS"

Page 108 "At seven o'clock . . ." Jerry Markon and Jared Sandberg, "Ex-WorldCom Officials Are Indicted," *Wall Street Journal* (August 2, 2002).

Page 108 "The next morning, . . ." Kurt Eichenwald, "2 Ex-Officials at WorldCom Are Charged in Huge Fraud," *New York Times* (August 2, 2002), and Elizabeth Douglass, Josh Meyer, and Thomas S. Mulligan, "2 Former WorldCom Execs Arrested, Will Face Fraud Charges," *Los Angeles Times* (August 2, 2002).

Page 108 "FBI agent, Paul Higgins, . . ." Sealed Complaint, *United States of America v. Scott D. Sullivan and David F. Myers,* Southern District of New York, July 31, 2002, p. 5.

Page 108 "The *New York Times* likened . . ." Kurt Eichenwald, "2 Ex-Officials at WorldCom are Charged in Huge Fraud," *New York Times* (August 2, 2002).

Page 108 "WorldCom, however, had . . ." Scott D. Sullivan, "Exhibit 4—Untitled June 24, 2001 Memo," *WorldCom: Revised Statement Pursuant to Section 21(a)(1) of the Securities Exchange Act of 1934,* July 8, 2002.

Page 109 "In this meeting, . . ." Cynthia Cooper, "Cap Ex," *WorldCom Internal Audit Correspondence,* June 12, 2002; and Sealed Complaint, *United States of America v. Scott D. Sullivan and David F. Myers,* United States District Court for the Southern District of New York, July 31, 2002, p. 14.

Page 109   "As a result, WorldCom was . . ." Complaint, *Securities and Exchange Commission v. WorldCom, Inc.,* United States District Court for the Southern District of New York, June 26, 2002.

Page 109   "As reported by U.S. Deputy Attorney . . ." Kurt Eichenwald, "2 Ex-Officials at WorldCom are Charged in Huge Fraud," *New York Times* (August 2, 2002).

Page 109   "In an e-mail sent . . ." Deborah Solomon, Jared Sandberg, and Laurie P. Cohen, "U.S. Prosecutors Plan to Indict Two Former WorldCom Officials," *Wall Street Journal* (July 25, 2002).

Page 110   "WorldCom's controller responded . . ." Sealed Complaint, *United States of America v. Scott D. Sullivan and David F. Myers,* Southern District of New York, July 31, 2002, p. 15.

Page 110   "During the course of this meeting, . . ." Sealed Complaint, *United States of America v. Scott D. Sullivan and David F. Myers,* Southern District of New York, July 31, 2002, p. 15.

Page 110   "Pressure was being brought . . ." Michael H. Salisbury, "Revised Statement Pursuant to Section 21(a)(1) of the Securities Exchange Act of 1934," *WorldCom* (July 8, 2002), p. 2.

Page 110   "Scott Sullivan, WorldCom's then-CFO, . . ." Cynthia Cooper, "Cap Ex," *WorldCom Internal Audit Correspondence,* June 12, 2002, p. 1; and Sealed Complaint, *United States of America v. Scott D. Sullivan and David F. Myers,* Southern District of New York, July 31, 2002, p. 14.

Page 111   "Her correspondence also indicated . . ." Cynthia Cooper, "Cap Ex," *WorldCom Internal Audit Correspondence,* June 12, 2002.

Page 111   "KPMG replaced Andersen . . ." Michael H. Salsbury, "Sworn Statement Pursuant to Section 21(a)(1) of the Securities Exchange Act of 1934," *WorldCom* (June 30, 2002), p. 1.

Page 111   "After Cynthia Cooper's revelations . . ." Interview with Kerry Francis.

Page 111   "We were not . . ." Geoffrey Colvin, "Wonder Women of Whistle-blowing," *Fortune* (August 12, 2002), p. 56.

Page 111   "The forensic accountants determined . . ." Interview with Jacobus Sadie.

Page 116   "WorldCom's fraud was not . . ." Jared Sandberg and Susan Pulliam, "WorldCom's Revision Might Double," *Wall Street Journal* (August 8, 2002).

Page 117   "'The boost from postacquisition . . .'" Kurt Eichenwald, "For WorldCom, Acquisitions Were Behind Its Rise and Fall," *New York Times* (August 8, 2002).

Page 117   ". . . it had now become . . ." Kurt Eichenwald, "For WorldCom, Acquisitions Were Behind Its Rise and Fall," *New York Times* (August 8, 2002).

Page 117   "At Morgan Fay, . . ." Interview with Jacobus Sadie.

Page 118   "'We called it house-of-cards . . .'" Marie Brenner, "The Enron Wars," *Vanity Fair* (April 2002), p. 195.

Page 118   "In response to a question . . ." Marie Brenner, "The Enron Wars," *Vanity Fair* (April 2002), p. 195.

Page 118   "'We were told constantly, . . .'" Marie Brenner, "The Enron Wars," *Vanity Fair* (April 2002), p. 198.

Page 118   "What a straightforward expedient! . . ." Interview with Jacobus Sadie.

Page 120   "This time, Myers went . . ." Yochi J. Drazen, "WorldCom Official Tried to Quash Employee's Accounting Concerns," *Wall Street Journal* (August 27, 2002).

Page 121   "The federal indictment . . ." Indictment, *United States of America v. Robin S. Malory and Cindy Shalott,* United States District Court, Southern District of New York.

Page 122   "A record 257 . . ." Ram Charan and Jerry Useem, "Why Companies Fail," *Fortune Magazine* (May 27, 2002), p. 50.

Page 122   "'We are investigating more . . .'" Susan Pulliam, "SEC Broadens Accounting Inquiries, Opening a Record Number of Cases," *Wall Street Journal* (May 2002).

Page 122   "Woodruff-Sawyer projects . . ." *Projected Cumulative Outstanding Cash Settlement Values* (San Francisco: Woodruff-Sawyer, 2001).

Page 123   "'Has your CEO ever . . .'" *BusinessWeek Annual CFO Conference,* June 1998.

Page 123   "He said that the workers . . ." Interview with Dan Wetzel.

CHAPTER THIRTEEN: "THE CIDER HOUSE RULES"

Page 124   "Tony had been in Minneapolis . . ." Interview with Tony Rosen.

Page 125   "Supposedly the pulp was . . ." James Bamford, *Body of Secrets: Anatomy of the Ultra-Secret National Security Agency* (New York: Doubleday, 2001), p. 518.

Page 128   "Lonnie Martin, the chief executive . . ." Rebecca Blumenstein, "As It Deepens, Telecom Bust Is Taking a Heavy Human Toll," *Wall Street Journal* (August 19, 2002).

Page 129   "Suddenly, in mid-2001, . . ." Rebecca Blumenstein, "As It Deepens, Telecom Bust Is Taking a Heavy Human Toll," *Wall Street Journal* (August 19, 2002).

Page 129   "An estimated $2 trillion . . ." Gretchen Morgenson, "Bullish Analyst of Tech Stocks Quits Salomon," *New York Times* (August 16, 2002).

Page 129   "Scott Sullivan, the chief financial . . ." Cynthia Cooper, "Cap Ex," *WorldCom Internal Audit Correspondence,* June 12, 2002; see also: Michael H. Salisbury, "Revised Statement Pursuant to Section

21(a)(1) of the Securities Exchange Act of 1934," *WorldCom* (July 8, 2002), p. 3.

Page 130   "They explained that the instructors . . ." Interview with former high-ranking FBI agents.

Page 130   "This phenomenon is confirmed . . ." Press Release and Data Summary, "2002 Report Card on the Ethics of American Youth," *Josephson Institute of Ethics* 2002, available at: http://www.josephsoninstitute .org/Survey2002/survey2002-pressrelease.htm.

Page 131   "Then, the special agents . . ." Philip Shennon, "FBI Denial of Search Warrant for Suspect's Belongings Is at Center of Inquiries," *New York Times* (June 7, 2002).

Page 131   "When the FBI later . . ." Indictment, *United States of America v. Zacarias Moussaoui. Indictment,* United States District Court, Southern District of New York.

Page 131   "The seven federal judges on the secret Foreign Intelligence Surveillance Court. . ." David Johnston, Neil A. Lewis, and Don Van Natta Jr., "FBI Inaction Blurred Picture Before Sept. 11: Agency Was Cautious With Data," *New York Times* (May 27, 2002).

Page 132   "'Losses were never allowed . . .'" Marie Brenner, "The Enron Wars," *Vanity Fair* (April 2002), p. 195.

Page 132   "'We have to be able . . .' Fastow had barked,'" Marie Brenner, "The Enron Wars," *Vanity Fair* (April 2002), p. 195.

Page 133   "One of Tony's responsibilities . . ." Interview with Tony Rosen.

Page 133   "Mike Murphy, the forensics . . ." Interview with Michael P. Murphy.

Page 133   "'We were in constant communication. . . .'" Interview with Ken Avery.

CHAPTER FOURTEEN: "YEAH, 'NFW.'"

Page 138   "'Cindy went to the penitentiary . . .'" Interview with Ken Avery.

Page 141   "Shortly thereafter, Carl Bass . . ." Tom Hamburger, Richard B. Schmitt and John R. Wilke, "Auditor Who Questioned Accounting for Enron Speaks to Investigators," *Wall Street Journal* (April 1, 2002).

Page 141   ". . . 'We could always bully . . .'" Marie Brenner, "The Enron Wars," *Vanity Fair* (April 2002), p. 184.

Page 141   "One Florida circuit court judge . . ." Jason Hoppin, "Florida Judge Compares Milberg to Squeegee Boy," *The Recorder* (April 16, 2002).

Page 142   "'When do you need me? . . .'" Interview with Michael P. Murphy.

Page 142   "'That's why it's so cool . . .'" Interview with Bill Leimbach.

Page 143   "'This is going to be . . .'" Julie Creswell, "Banks on the Hot Seat," *Fortune* (September 2, 2002), pp. 79–80.

Page 143   "The kickback money was . . ." Kurt Eichenwald, "A Method Becomes Clearer In a Methodical Investigation," *New York Times* (August 22, 2002).

Page 144   "The very next day, . . ." Carrie Johnson, "Judge Freezes Assets of Former Enron CFO, Kin: Total Could Reach $20 Million," *Washington Post* (August 24, 2002).

Page 146   "After completing the interviews . . ." Interview with Michael. P. Murphy.

CHAPTER FIFTEEN: DUMBFELLAS GO CORPORATE

Page 148   "Early in the month of June 2002, . . ." Riva D. Atlas, "Big Board Issues Its Ideas on Corporate Governance," *New York Times* (June 7, 2002).

Page 148   "Almost simultaneously, . . ." Randall Smith and Susanne Craig, "Is CEOs' Petition for Change Sincere?" *Wall Street Journal* (June 7, 2002).

Page 148   "Congress's investigative arm, . . ." Carolyn Lochhead, "Federal Energy Regulators Inept, U.S. Report Says," *San Francisco Chronicle* (June 13, 2002).

Page 148   "A systems access limitation . . ." Interview with Gene Morse, who provided a first hand analysis of the investigative steps undertaken by WorldCom's forensic accountants.

Page 149   "Essbase, a sophisticated data mining . . ." *Hyperion Essbase,* available: www.hyperion.com/products/bi_platform/platform_services/hyperion_essbase.cfm.

Page 149   ". . . 'instructed on a quarterly . . .'" Devlin Barrett, "Myers Enters Guilty Plea in WorldCom Fraud Case," *Associated Press* (September 27, 2002).

Page 150   "In response to another . . ." Patricia Hurtado, "Ex-WorldCom Exec Pleads Guilty," *Newsday* (October 7, 2002).

Page 150   "In late 1999, . . ." Interview with Gene Morse.

Page 152   "Sullivan caught her by dialing . . ." Susan Pulliam and Deborah Solomon, "How Three Unlikely Sleuths Discovered Fraud at WorldCom," *Wall Street Journal* (October 30, 2002).

Page 158   "By this time, . . ." "Cap Ex—Telephone Call from Corner Office, Bldg 4, Floor 3," *WorldCom Internal Audit Correspondence,* June 12, 2002.

Page 158   "The evening of June 25, 2002, . . ." Simon Romero and Alex Berenson, "WorldCom Says It Hid Expenses, Inflating Cash Flow $3.8 Billion: Telecommunications Company's Future in Doubt," *New York Times* (June 26, 2002).

Page 159   "'Paul J. Higgins, being duly sworn, . . .'" Sealed Complaint, *United States of America v. Scott D. Sullivan and David F. Myers, Defendants,*

United States District Court, Southern District of New York, July 31, 2002.

CHAPTER SIXTEEN: THE LEXICOGRAPHER AND THE DORMANT ACCOUNTS

Page 160   "The fact that the Swiss banks . . ." Paul A. Volcker, Chairman, Independent Committee of Eminent Persons, "Report on Dormant Accounts of Victims of Nazi Persecution in Swiss Banks," *Report of the Independent Committee of Eminent Persons,* December 1999, p. 2.

Page 161   "The forensic accountants signing . . ." Paul A. Volcker, "Report on Dormant Accounts of Victims of Nazi Persecution in Swiss Banks," *Report of the Independent Committee of Eminent Persons,* December 1999, p. 1.

Page 161   "Their challenge was . . ." Interview with Frank Piantidosi.

Page 161   "'Without the computer, . . .'" Interview with Frank Hydoski.

Page 161   "By the time the analysis undertaken . . ." Interview with Mary Jane Schirber. Arthur Andersen, Coopers & Lybrand, Deloitte & Touche, KPMG, and Price Waterhouse were the five international audit and accounting firms selected by the Independent Committee to carry out the forensic accounting investigation. See Appendix U to the *Report of the Independent Committee of Eminent Persons,* which lists the actual firms as follows: Andersen Worldwide SC; Arthur Andersen/ London, England; Arthur Andersen AG/Zurich, Switzerland; Coopers & Lybrand/London, England (a legacy firm of Pricewaterhouse-Coopers); Coopers & Lybrand AG/Zurich, Switzerland (a legacy firm of PricewaterhouseCoopers); Coopers & Lybrand International (a legacy firm of PricewaterhouseCoopers); Deloitte & Touche/London, England; Deloitte & Touche Experta/Zurich, Switzerland; Deloitte Touche Tohmatsu; KPMG/London, England; KPMG Fides Peat AG/Zurich, Switzerland; KPMG International; Price Waterhouse; Price Waterhouse/London, England (a legacy firm of Pricewater-houseCoopers); Price Waterhouse AG/Zurich, Switzerland (a legacy firm of PricewaterhouseCoopers); PricewaterhouseCoopers (world-wide) (a legacy firm of PricewaterhouseCoopers); Pricewaterhouse-Coopers/London, England; PricewaterhouseCoopers AG/Zurich, Switzerland. Paul A. Volcker, "Report on Dormant Accounts of Victims of Nazi Persecution in Swiss Banks," *Report of the Independent Committee of Eminent Persons,* December 1999, p. A-212.

Page 161   "At its very peak, . . ." Paul A. Volcker, Chairman, Independent Committee of Eminent Persons, "Report on Dormant Accounts of Victims of Nazi Persecution in Swiss Banks," *Report of the Independent Committee of Eminent Persons,* December 1999, p. 4.

Page 162   With the taking of *Lebensraum, . . ."* Ian Kershaw, *Hitler 1936—1945: Nemesis* (New York: Norton, 2000), p. 21.

Page 162   "After 1936, . . ." See Ian Kershaw, *Hitler 1936—1945: Nemesis* (New York: Norton, 2000).

Page 162   "The introduction of a new law . . ." Paul A. Volcker, Appendix II, "Timetable of the Introduction of Exchange Controls in Europe, *Report of the Independent Committee of Eminent Persons,* December 1999, p. A-201.

Page 167   "The book narrated . . ." Simon Winchester, *The Professor and the Madman: A Tale of Murder, Insanity, and the Making of the Oxford English Dictionary* (New York: Harper Collins, 1998), pp. 31, 129,182, 217, and 220.

Page 169   "The investigators attempted to obtain . . ." Paul A. Volcker, Glossary, *Report of the Independent Committee of Eminent Persons,* December 1999, p. A-214.

Page 170   "This provided the investigators . . ." Paul A. Volcker, Glossary, *Report of the Independent Committee of Eminent Persons,* December 1999, p. A-214, p. A-214.

Page 171   "Not surprisingly, the investigators' research revealed that the banks in Poland began experiencing steep declines in savings deposits during this same time period, and this, after steady year-to-year increases having been experienced," B. Helen Junz, "Report on the Pre-War Wealth Position of the Jewish Population in Nazi-Occupied Countries, Germany, and Austria," Appendix S, *Report of the Independent Committee of Eminent Persons,* December 1999, p. A-192.

Page 172   ". . . they loaded into the lexicographer's tables . . ." Paul A. Volcker, "Annex 6: Potential Intermediary Accounts and Looted Assets," *Report of the Independent Committee of Eminent Persons,* December 1999, pp. 101–105.

Page 172   "The forensic accountants were able . . ." Paul A. Volcker, "Annex 6 Potential Intermediary Accounts and Looted Assets, *Report of the Independent Committee of Eminent Persons,* December 1999, p. 103.

Page 172   "The forensic accountants also linked . . ." Paul A. Volcker, "Annex 6 Potential Intermediary Accounts and Looted Assets, *Report of the Independent Committee of Eminent Persons,* December 1999, p. 103.

Page 172   "Sadly, the forensic accountants identified . . ." Paul A. Volcker, *Report of the Independent Committee of Eminent Persons,* December 1999, p. 16. See also: Annex 6, "Potential Intermediary Accounts and Looted Assets," pp. 103 to 104.

Page 173   "When the final matching process . . ." Paul A. Volcker, "Annex 6: Potential Intermediary Accounts and Looted Assets," *Report of the Independent Committee of Eminent Persons,* December 1999, p. 103.

Page 174   "On March 14, 1938, . . ." Ian Kershaw, *Hitler 1936—1945: Nemesis* (New York: Norton, 2000), p. 79.

Page 181   ". . . other countries had laws . . ." Paul A. Volcker, "Annex 9: Swiss Law on the Treatment of Dormant Accounts: A comparison to European and U.S. Law," *Report of the Independent Committee of Eminent Persons,* December 1999, p. 123.

Page 181   "The lexicographer's database matching . . ." Paul A. Volcker, "Annex 4: Identification of Accounts Probably or Possibly Related to Victims of Nazi Persecution," *Report of the Independent Committee of Eminent Persons,* December 1999, p. 62.

Page 182   "The forensic accountants found that there . . ." Paul A. Volcker, "Annex 4: Identification of Accounts Probably or Possibly Related to Victims of Nazi Persecution," *Report of the Independent Committee of Eminent Persons,* December 1999, pp. 57–58.

Page 182   "Thirty-four million continental Europeans . . ." Paul A. Volcker, "Annex 4: Identification of Accounts Probably or Possibly Related to Victims of Nazi Persecution," *Report of the Independent Committee of Eminent Persons,* December 1999, p. 74.

Page 182   "'The death of an individual . . .'" Josef Stalin, as reported in the *San Francisco Chronicle* (September 29, 2002).

Page 182   "Of 3,300,000 Polish Jews, . . ." Helen B. Junz, "Report on the Pre-War Wealth Position of the Jewish Population in Nazi-Occupied Countries, Germany, and Austria," Paul A. Volcker, Appendix S, *Report of the Independent Committee of Eminent Persons,* December 1999, p. A-192.

CHAPTER SEVENTEEN: "I'M SO GLAD YOU'RE HERE"

Page 183   "He used computerized . . ." Interview with Jim Littley.

Page 183   "In the year 2002, . . ." Interview with Gene Morse.

Page 184   "As a student, . . ." Interview with Mark J. Nigrini.

Page 185   "The odds against . . ." Mark J. Nigrini, *Digital Analysis Using Benford's Law* (Vancouver, British Columbia: Global Audit, 2000), p. 58.

Page 185   "A sophisticated data mining . . ." Interview with Tom Aleman.

Page 186   "He became a forensic accountant . . ." Interview with John O'Connor.

Page 188   "This individual was prosecuted . . ." Allison D. Burroughs, "Felony Information Received for Filing," *United States of America v. Larry M. Swanson,* United States District Court, District of Massachusetts, October 31, 2000.

Page 189   "O'Connor's recollection was . . ." L. Kim Tan, "Exec Charged in Scam," *Boston Herald* (December 23, 1999).

Page 189   "'Larry Swanson somehow convinced this young woman . . .'" Interview with John O'Connor. See also: J. M. Lawrence, "'Secret Agent' Sorry for Scheme," *Boston Herald* (October 10, 2001).

Page 189 "He told her the disks . . ." L. Kim Tan, "Exec Charged in Scam," *Boston Herald* (December 23, 1999).

Page 191 ". . . '$588,000 in checks . . .'" L. Kim Tan, "Exec Charged in Scam," *Boston Herald* (December 23, 1999).

CHAPTER EIGHTEEN: "MORE VALUABLE THAN HEROIN"

Page 193 "The Santa Clara county investigators . . ." Jon Swartz, "Avant Moves to Dismiss DA in Suit: Fight with Rival Cadence Heats Up," *San Francisco Chronicle* (June 10, 1997).

Page 193 "In 1994, . . ." Carol Emert, "Avant Settles Theft Case with Plea: Firm Pays Fine, 5 People Going to Jail," *San Francisco Chronicle* (May 23, 2001).

Page 193 "In December 2001, . . ." *Office of the National Counterintelligence Executive, News & Developments*, p. 5, available: www.ncix.gov/news/2001/sep01.html#article6.

Page 194 "'Hiring a worker who brings . . .'" "Job Hopper Flies the Coop," *News & Developments, Office of the National Counterintelligence Executive*, p. 5, available: www.ncix.gov/news/2001/sep01.html.

Page 194 "'Certain business information . . .'" Loretta Principe, "Spy vs. Spy," *Network World*, March 30, 1998, available: www.nfusion.com/careers/0330man.html.

Page 194 "In a survey undertaken . . ." Douglas Pasternak, with Gordon Witkin, "The Lure of the Steal," *U.S. News & World Report* (May 6, 1996).

Page 194 "Few had referred these incidents . . ." "Annual Report to Congress on Foreign Economic collection and Industrial Espionage," *National Counterintelligence Center (NACIC)*, July 1995, p. 9, available: www.fas.org/spg/othergov/indust.html.

Page 194 "The same report . . ." Douglas Pasternak, with Gordon Witkin, "The Lure of the Steal," *U.S. News & World Report* (May 6, 1996).

Page 194 "The U.S. intelligence community . . ." "Annual Report to Congress on Foreign Economic Collection and Industrial Espionage," *National Counterintelligence Center (NAICIC)*, p. 1, available: www.ncix.gov/nacic/reports/fy98.htm.

Page 195 "In fact, France . . ." Peter Schweizer, "The Growth of Economic Espionage: America is Target Number One, *Foreign Affairs,* January/February 1996, p. 11–12; as attached to the "Legislative History—Economic Espionage Act of 1996" *Congressional Record—Senate,* October 2, 1996.

Page 195 "Douglas Pasternack, . . ." Douglas Pasternak with Gordon Witkin, "The Lure of the Steal," *U.S. News & World Report* (May 6, 1996), as attached to the "Legislative History—Economic Espionage Act of 1996" *Congressional Record—Senate,* October 2, 1996.

Page 195 In a Senate hearing in 1996, . . ." Senator Kohl, "Appendix O: Legislative History—Economic Espionage Act of 1996" *Congressional Record—Senate,* October 2, 1996, p. 7.

Page 195 "'. . . mounting evidence that many . . .'" Senator Specter, "Legislative History—Economic Espionage Act of 1996" *Congressional Record—Senate,* October 2, 1996.

Page 195 "The American Society . . ." Melissa Eberhart, "Confidential Data Leaves with Job-Hopping Employees," available: www.goodstaf .com/employers/articles/confidential.html. See also: Juan Carlos Perez, "Insiders, Not Hackers, Biggest Information Theft Risk," *InfoWorld* (September 30, 2002), available: http://staging.infoworld .com/articles/hn/xml/02/09/30/020930hninsiders.xml. The ASIS annual survey is now undertaken in conjunction with PricewaterhouseCoopers and the U.S. Chamber of Commerce.

Page 195 "The corporations estimated . . ." Kevin Poulsen, "Show Me the Money," *Tech TV* (April 17, 1998), available: www.techtv.com/cybercrime/print/0,23102,20000191,00.html.

Page 196 "'It is a great pity . . .'" Lionel Ashcroft, "Mission San Rafael," *Marin County Historical Society,* 1997, available at: http://www .marinhistory.org/articles/mission.htm.

Page 196 "A moving truck . . ." Interview with Kris Haworth.

Page 196 "After that, maybe she could . . ." Pegasys Semiconductor and Baldur Technologies are fictitious representations of actual corporations, as is Larry Hooper, the Director of Security at Pegasys Semiconductor.

Page 199 "In fact, almost everything . . ." Interviews with Matt Larson and Laurel Sutcliffe.

Page 202 "He also estimated . . ." Louis J. Freeh, "Threats to U.S. National Security," *Senate Select Committee on Intelligence,* January 28, 1998, available: www.fas.org/irp/congress/1998_hr/s980128f.htm.

Page 203 David Sikorski, another member . . ." Interview with David Sikorski.

Page 203 "Who could have guessed . . ." Available at: www.drdwg.com.

CHAPTER NINETEEN: HUNTING THE WORLD'S GREATEST OUTLAW

Page 207 "Our National Security Agency . . ." James Bamford, *Body of Secrets: Anatomy of the Ultra-Secret National Security Agency* (New York: Doubleday, 2001), p. 410.

Page 207 "Sometime in 2000, . . ." James Risen, "Chilling Tale of bin Laden's Rise to Power," *New York Times* (October 14, 2001).

Page 207   "On August 27, 2001, . . ." Neil A. Lewis and David Johnston, "Jubilant Calls on Sept. 11 Led to FBI Arrests," *New York Times* (October 28, 2001).

Page 208   "Other writings in the late 1990s, . . ." Steve Wright, *An Appraisal of Technologies of Political Control* (Luxembourg: European Parliament: Scientific and Technologies Options Assessment, 1998).

Page 208   "These documents describe . . ." Nicky Hager, *Secret Power: New Zealand's Role in the International Spy Network* (Nelson, New Zealand: Potton, 1996), p. 29.

Page 208   "Positioned in geostationary orbits . . ." *Itelsat,* available: www.intelsat.com/satellites/satellites_coveragemaps.asp.

Page 208   "One of the more recent . . ." James Bamford, *Body of Secrets: Anatomy of the Ultra-Secret National Security Agency* (New York: Doubleday, 2001), p. 407.

Page 208   "The first is located . . ." Nicky Hager, *Secret Power: New Zealand's Role in the International Spy Network* (Nelson, New Zealand: Potton, 1996), p. 30.

Page 209   "They enter their password . . ." Nicky Hager, *Secret Power: New Zealand's Role in the International Spy Network* (Nelson, New Zealand: Potton, 1996), p. 29.

Page 209   "NSA's computers can store . . ." James Bamford, *Body of Secrets: Anatomy of the Ultra-Secret National Security Agency* (New York: Doubleday, 2001), p. 427.

Page 209   "Each agency has its own . . ." Nicky Hager, *Secret Power: New Zealand's Role in the International Spy Network* (Nelson, New Zealand: Potton, 1996), p. 49.

Page 210   "When up and running, . . ." Interview with John Suit.

Page 210   "She once told me . . ." Interview with Kris Haworth.

Page 210   "According to transcripts . . ." Desmond Butler and Don Van Natta Jr., "Al Qaeda Informant Helps Investigators Trace Group's Trail," *New York Times,* February 17, 2003.

Page 212   "The manhunt that ensued . . ." Mark Bowden, *Killing Pablo: The Hunt for the World's Greatest Outlaw* (New York: Atlantic Monthly Press, 2001). The story of the killing of Pablo Escobar is taken primarily from Bowden's text, as well as from an oral summary provided by Bowden.

Page 213   "Not quite 10 years . . ." Tarik Kafala, "Israel's 'Assassination Policy'" *BBC News* (August 1, 2001), available: http://news.bbc.co.uk /1/hi/world/middle_east/1258187.htm. Also see: Alan Phillips, "PLO Founder Killed by Israeli Missile Attack, *The Telegraph* (August 28, 2001), available: www.telegraph.co.uk/news/main .jhtml?xml=/news/2001/08/28/wmid28.xml. See also: Steve Niva, "Sharon's Master Plan Dangerous to All Sides, *Common Dreams News Center* (October 13, 2002), available: www.commondreams.org

/views02/0402–09.htm. Also see: Robert Fisk, "Death by Remote Control As Hit Squads Return," *Fontenelles* (April 13, 2001), available: http://home.mindspring.com/~fontenelles/fisk12.htm.

Page 215   "The technology was code named, . . ." Mike Frost and Michael Gratton, *Spyworld: Inside the Canadian and American Intelligence Establishments* (Toronto, Ontario: Doubleday-Canada, 1994), pp. 152–153.

CHAPTER TWENTY: THE METAPHYSICAL THEORY OF BEING

Page 216   "The notion of Boolean . . ." Wayne Amsbury and Srirama Channavajjala, patent examiners, *United States Patent: 5,937,422,* available: http://patft.uspto.gov., p. 7.

Page 216   "Director Mueller's testimony . . ." David Johnston and Neil A. Lewis, "Whistle-Blower Recounts Faults Inside the FBI," *New York Times* (June 7, 2002).

Page 216   "Moussaoui's flight instructor . . ." Jim Yardley, "FBI Didn't Pursue Information on Terror Suspect, Papers Show," *New York Times* (May 24, 2002).

Page 216   "One month earlier, . . ." Erik Lichtblau and Josh Meyer, "FBI Agent's Memo Said to be Detailed," *Los Angeles Times* (May 23, 2002).

Page 217   ". . . 'much of the information conveyed . . .'" Wayne Amsbury and Srirama Channavajjala, Erik Lichtblau, and Josh Meyer, "FBI Agent's Memo Said to be Detailed," *Los Angeles Times* (May 23, 2002), p. 7.

Page 218   "Next, the computer used . . ." Gregory Henderson, Patrick Schone, and Thomas Crystal, "Text Retrieval via Semantic Forests," *The Seventh Text Retrieval Conference (TREC–7),* 1999, p. 1.

Page 218   "The NSA patent . . ." Channavajjala, Gregory Henderson, Patrick Schone, and Thomas Crystal, "Text Retrieval via Semantic Forests," *The Seventh Text Retrieval Conference (TREC–7),* 1999, p. 7.

Page 219   "The NSA's software . . ." James Bamford, *Body of Secrets: Anatomy of the Ultra-Secret National Security Agency* (New York: Doubleday, 2001), pp. 616–617. The NSA provides training for its linguists in at least 95 languages.

Page 219   "John Suit, one of the architects. . ." Interview with John Suit.

Page 219   "Jeff Waxman sat . . ." Interview with Jeff Waxman.

Page 220   ". . . 'Sigint,' to the uninitiated . . .'" James Bamford, *Body of Secrets: Anatomy of the Ultra-Secret National Security Agency* (New York: Doubleday, 2001), p. 8.

Page 220   "The Japanese Navy's . . ." Gordon Prange, *Miracle at Midway* (New York: McGraw-Hill, 1982), p. 19.

Page 220   ". . . the American Sigint team in Honolulu . . ." Gordon Prange, *Miracle at Midway* (New York: McGraw-Hill, 1982), p. 45.

Page 221 "Employ Method 'C' . . ." *The Japanese Story of the Battle of Midway* (Translated), OPNAVP32–1002, (Washington, DC: U.S. Office of Naval Intelligence, 1947), p. 24.

Page 221 "Rear Admiral Jack Fletcher . . ." Gordon Prange, *Miracle at Midway* (New York: McGraw Hill, 1982) p. 385.

Page 225 "But as I had sat down . . ." Interview with Tomas Castrejon and Manish Khera.

Page 226 ". . . derives from the Greek words, . . ." Simon Singh, *The Code Book: The Evolution of Secrecy from Mary Queen of Scots to Quantum Cryptography* (New York: Doubleday, 1999), p. 5.

Page 226 "The first recorded use . . ." Herodotus, trans. George Rawlinson, *The Histories,* (New York: Everymans Library/Alfred A. Knopf, 1910/1997), pp. 592–608.

Page 226 "Xerxes marched into . . ." Ellis Knox, "The Persian Wars, History of Western Civilization," *Boise State University,* available: http://history.boisestate.edu/westciv/persian/14.htm.

Page 226 ". . . his al Qaeda cell . . ." Jack Kelley, "Terrorist Instructions Hidden Online," *USA Today* (February 5, 2001).

Page 227 "During World War II, . . ." Simon Singh, *The Code Book* (New York: Random House, 1999), p. 6–7.

Page 227 "Sixty years later, . . ." "Fitting Together the Puzzle of Osama bin Laden's Network as Arrests Reach 150," *Associated Press* (October 5, 2001); and Ryan Mulcahy, "Steganography Seen as Possible Terrorist Tool," *CIO.com* (October 30, 2001), available: http://64.28.79.79/online; and Gina Kolata, "Veiled Messages of Terror May Lurk in Cyberspace," *New York Times* (October 30, 2001).

Page 227 "There are currently . . ." Jack Kelley, "Terror Groups Hide Behind Web Encryption," *USA Today* (February 5, 2001).

Page 228 "The first academic conference on digital watermarking and steganography was held in 1996," Fabien A. P. Petitcolas, "Digital Watermarking & Steganography," *The Information Hiding Homepage,* 1997–2001, available: www.cl.cam.ac.uk/~fapp2/steganography.

Page 228 "By 1999, . . ." Ross J. Anderson and Fabien A. P. Petitcolas, "Information Hiding: An Annotated Bibliography," *Computer Laboratory, University of Cambridge,* 1999, available: www.cl.cam.ac.uk/~fapp2/steganography/bibliography.

Page 228 "The insertion of stego-messages . . ." Owen Gibson, "Hidden Web Codes Could Be Linked to bin Laden," *Guardian* (October 10, 2001), available: http://media.guardian.co.uk.

Page 228 "Employees or other individuals . . ." Declan McCullagh, "Secret Messages Come in .Wavs," *Wired News* (February 20, 2001), available: www.wired.com/news.

Page 228 "Since there are eight places . . ." Ben Richter, "The Security of Electronic Data and Intellectual Property," paper presented at

SANS Cyber Defense Initiative West Track, San Francisco, February 7, 2002, p. 6.

Page 228 "One method of stego-insertion . . ." Neil F. Johnson and Sushil Jajodia, "Exploring Steganography: Seeing the Unseen," *IEEE Computer Magazine* (February, 1998), pp. 26–34. See also: Neil F. Johnson and Sushil Jajodia, "Exploring Steganography: Seeing the Unseen," *IEEE Computer Magazine* (February, 1998), pp. 28–29. Gina Kolata describes the method as well, in: "Veiled Messages of Terror May Lurk in Cyberspace," *New York Times* (October 30, 2001).

Page 229 "Another steganography program . . ." Andy Jones and Gerald L. Kovacich, "What InfoSec Professionals Should Know about Information Warfare Tactics by Terrorists," *Secure e-Business* (March, 2002), available: www.shockwavewriters.com/Articles /GLK/whatinfosecprosshouldknow.htm.

Page 229 "Digital images saved . . ." Neil F. Johnson and Sushil Jajodia, "Exploring Steganography: Seeing the Unseen," *IEEE Computer Magazine* (February, 1998), pp. 26–27.

Page 230 "One forensic user, . . ." Interview with Jim Wilson.

Page 231 "I later learned that Mandelbrot, . . ." Benoit Mandelbrot, *The Fractal Geometry of Nature* (New York: Freeman, 1982), p. 4.

Page 232 "Put another way, . . ." *Fractals: The Organization of Chaos,* available: http://www2.gvsu.edu/~housedt/Fractal.html.

Page 232 "Computers can be used . . ." Alan Beck, "What Is a Fractal?" *Fractal Gallery,* available: http://www.glyphs.com/art/fractals/what_is.html.

Page 232 ". . . the coordinates are inserted . . . " Adam Lerer, "Creating Fractals: The Basics," *World of Fractals,* available: http://www.angelfire .com/art2/fractals/lesson1.htm.

Page 232 "A popular fractal generator, . . ." Primary authors: B. Tyler, T. Wegner, J. Osuch, W. Loewer, M. Peterson, and Pieter Branderhorsti, "Fractint," *Math Archives* (The Stone Soup Group, 1990), available: http://archives.math.utk.edu/software/msdos/complex.variables /fractint/.html.

INDEX